AUSTRO-MARXISM

AUSTRO-MARXISM

Texts translated and edited by
TOM BOTTOMORE AND PATRICK GOODE

with an Introduction by
TOM BOTTOMORE

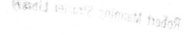

1978

CLARENDON PRESS · OXFORD

Oxford University Press, Walton Street, Oxford OX2 6DP

OXFORD LONDON GLASGOW NEW YORK
TORONTO MELBOURNE WELLINGTON CAPE TOWN
IBADAN NAIROBI DAR ES SALAAM LUSAKA
KUALA LUMPUR SINGAPORE JAKARTA HONG KONG TOKYO
DELHI BOMBAY CALCUTTA MADRAS KARACHI

English translation of Karl Renner's *The Institutions of Private Law and their Social Functions* © *Routledge and Kegan Paul Ltd. 1949*

English translation of all other excerpts in this volume and Selection © *Tom Bottomore and Patrick Goode 1978*

Introduction © *Tom Bottomore 1978*

British Library Cataloguing in Publication Data

Austro-Marxism.
  1. Communism—Addresses, essays, lectures
  I. Bottomore, Thomas Burton   II. Goode,
  Patrick
  335.4'08   HX15   77-30292
  ISBN 0-19-827229-4
  ISBN 0-19-827230-8   Pbk.

Printed in Great Britain by
Cox & Wyman Ltd.,
London, Fakenham and Reading

Preface & Acknowledgements

The texts translated in this volume are intended to provide an introduction to the work of an important and influential group of Marxist thinkers whose writings are still little known in the English-speaking world and are greatly neglected elsewhere. With the exception of Karl Renner's study of law the major books of the Austro-Marxists have not been published in English, and there has been no comprehensive account of their work as a whole. My introduction to the present volume will, I hope, remedy this deficiency in some degree by presenting a brief account of the context and scope of their achievements, both intellectual and political.

The initial translations were made by Patrick Goode, and they were then revised by both editors. Patrick Goode also contributed most of the editorial footnotes and compiled the bibliography. In editing the translated texts we excluded some passages, and occasional footnotes, which referred to current events and policies, or quoted writings, that would be of relatively little interest to the present-day reader. These omissions in the text are indicated by a three-point ellipses (. . .). Editorial footnotes are distinguished from those of the authors by the sign [Eds.].

I am grateful to a number of people for access to material used in my introduction, and for comments on early versions of it. In particular, I should like to thank Professor Ernst Herlitzka, Director of the Verein für Geschichte der Arbeiterbewegung (Vienna) and Dr. Hans Schroth, Librarian of the Verein, for giving me access to material in their archives and permitting me to quote from it. Professor Marie Jahoda and Dr. Peter Milford were kind enough to comment on some parts of the introduction and I have benefited from their suggestions, as well as from those that were made by Patrick Goode.

I would also like to express my gratitude to the University of Sussex for grants from the Arts Research Fund which enabled me to visit Vienna on two occasions.

Copyright permission for the publication of these translations has been given by Dr. Peter Milford for the excerpts from Rudolf Hilferding's writings, and by Dr. Franz Hentschel, Director of the Verlagsanstalt 'Vorwärts' AG (Vienna) for the other texts. In one case, the extract from *The Institutions of Private Law and Their Social Functions* by Karl Renner, trans. A. Schwarzchild, Routledge & Kegan Paul Ltd., London, 1976. Reprinted by permission of the Publishers.

Tom Bottomore

Contents

Introduction

1. What is Austro-Marxism?

The term 'Austro-Marxism' was apparently coined by an American socialist, Louis Boudin, a few years before the First World War,[1] to describe a group of young Marxist thinkers in Vienna—the most prominent among them being Max Adler, Otto Bauer, Rudolf Hilferding, and Karl Renner—who were also active in the Austrian socialist movement. Through their books, their journals, and their political activities, they had a considerable influence upon European socialism in the first two decades of the twentieth century, as critics of 'revisionism' in German Social Democracy and exponents of a form of Marxism which could claim to be a rigorous and undogmatic science of society while retaining its revolutionary character. Later, after the rise of Bolshevism, they occupied a position, both intellectually and politically, between the increasingly reformist Social Democratic parties and the newly established Communist parties; a position that was symbolized by Friedrich Adler's role in the creation of the short-lived 'Second-and-a-half' International.[2] But in the postwar period, after

---

[1] See the article by Otto Bauer, pp. 45–8 below. Boudin published, in 1907, a book entitled *The Theoretical System of Karl Marx* (reprinted 1967) in which he defended Marx's theory against the criticisms formulated by Böhm-Bawerk, Bernstein, and others. His book was translated into German, and it became more widely known in Europe than in the U.S.A., where it attracted little attention. A few years later Boudin met some of the Austro-Marxists in Europe, and it was presumably at this time that he began to refer to them by this name. After the First World War, with the decline of the American Socialist party, Boudin ceased to be active in party politics, but he continued to write on Marxism and socialism, and he maintained his association with the Austro-Marxists. Much later indeed, after the Second World War, he corresponded quite extensively with Friedrich Adler about a book he hoped to complete on the development of Marxism during the past century; and in one letter (28 February 1951) he refers nostalgically to '... what I still believe to have been our Golden Age, the unforgettable period of the first decade of this century'. In the same letter he mentions Otto Bauer's article and his own coinage of the term 'Austro-Marxism'.

[2] See Julius Braunthal, *History of the International*, vol. ii (1967), pp. 230–6, 264–5. This nickname was bestowed upon it by representatives of the Third International. It was formed at a conference in Vienna in February 1921 as the Inter-

the defeat and dismemberment of the Habsburg Empire, the influence of Austro-Marxism in the European socialist movement declined, and although it remained a powerful force in Austria until 1934 its particular contribution to international Marxist thought was overshadowed by new intellectual and political trends, and gradually came to be largely forgotten.

This oblivion is quite undeserved, for the Austro-Marxists made a notable contribution to the development of Marxist social science, and their analyses of the changes in twentieth-century capitalism, as well as their studies of Marxism as a method of social inquiry, retain much of their value today. The first important fact to be noted about their work is that it was the product of a distinctive 'school' of thought. Most other eminent Marxist thinkers of this century either contributed an individual reinterpretation of Marxism, in the manner of Sorel, Gramsci, or Lukács, or formulated mainly the doctrines of new political movements, as did Lenin, Trotsky, and Mao Tse-Tung. But the Austro-Marxists elaborated, so to speak, a scientific programme, a systematic framework of ideas within which intellectual inquiry—and more particularly, social research—could be carried on in a co-ordinated way by a group of thinkers.

From this aspect their work is broadly comparable with that of the school which developed around the Frankfurt Institute of Social Research;[3] but the concerns of the two schools were very different, and they might be said indeed to represent two extreme and contradictory forms of Marxist thought. In the early years of the Frankfurt Institute some of its associates had a strong interest in sociological, psychological, and historical research, encouraged by the first Director of the Institute, Carl Grünberg (who himself had close relations with the Austro-Marxists);[4] but when he was succeeded by Max Horkheimer the main emphasis came to be

---

[3] See Martin Jay, *The Dialectical Imagination: The Frankfurt Institute of Social Research, 1923–1950* (1973).
[4] See below, pp. 9–10.

national Working Union of Socialist Parties with the aim, in Friedrich Adler's words, of trying 'to organize the International of the future', and dissolved again, after failing to establish co-operation with the Third International, in May 1923 when a congress of Socialist parties decided to create the Labour and Socialist International.

placed increasingly upon a more philosophical type of social analysis. The principal thinkers of the Frankfurt School became distinguished eventually by their preoccupation with metaphysical and aesthetic questions, by their critical attitude to modern science and the modern forms of positivism and empiricism, and by their revival of a broadly Hegelian style of Marxist thought. The Austro-Marxists, on the other hand, were mainly interested in the development of Marxism as an empirical social science—in effect, as sociology. Their philosophical concerns, as is particularly evident from Max Adler's writings, centred upon problems in the theory of knowledge and the philosophy of science; influenced above all by neo-Kantianism and by the ideas of Ernest Mach they showed a close affinity, in their general outlook and preoccupations, with the new positivist doctrines which later assumed a distinctive form in the Vienna Circle.

There is another important difference between the two schools, connected with their divergent intellectual orientations, which concerns their relationship to political life. The members of the Frankfurt Institute were not, for the most part, deeply involved in political activity, and they were inclined in fact to emphasize their political detachment.[5] For this reason among others Karl Korsch, who had been closely associated with the creation of the Institute but was much more active in politics than were most of its members, soon ceased to be involved in its work. The leading Austro-Marxists, on the other hand, grew up in the socialist student movement at the University of Vienna, and they were all subsequently engaged, with whatever differences of style and degree, in the practical politics of the Austrian Social Democratic Party. Their monthly journal *Der Kampf*, in which much of their writing appeared, was a party journal, and they also contributed frequently to the party's daily newspaper, the *Arbeiter-Zeitung*. As a result of this involvement there is to be found in much of their work a practical and realistic reflection upon the relation between social theory and political action (and more narrowly upon the role of intellectuals in political movements); expressed particularly in their studies of Marxist education and socialist culture, of nationalities and

[5] Jay, op. cit., p. 14.

nationalist movements, of the economic development of capitalism, imperialism, and the changing class structure, and of
new elements in the labour movement such as the postwar
revolutionary movements and the workers' councils.
Together with these differences between the two schools
there was one important similarity. The Austro-Marxists,
like the members of the Frankfurt Institute, wanted to engage
in controversy with the exponents of new social and philosophical doctrines, to assimilate what seemed useable in the
modern social sciences, and to extend Marxist thought in new
directions. Hence they examined critically the ideas of neo-
Kantian philosophy (especially in their bearing upon the
methodology of the social sciences), the Austrian marginalist
economic theory, and the theories of nationalism; and they
attempted to bring within the scope of Marxist theory such
fields of study as law,[6] psychology,[7] and cultural history.[8]
Somewhat later, in the 1920s and the early 1930s, there was

[6] See especially the major work by Karl Renner, published in an English translation, with an introduction by Otto Kahn-Freund, under the title *The Institutions of
Private Law and Their Social Functions* (1949). An excerpt from this book, expounding Renner's general conception of a Marxist theory of law, will be found on pp.
267–76 below.
[7] The Austro-Marxists were interested in both social psychology and psycho-
analysis, although they devoted comparatively little attention to the latter. However,
Alfred Adler worked for some years in the educational administration of the
Socialist town council of Vienna and he contributed a number of articles to the early
issues of *Der Kampf* on school reform and new methods of teaching. On the relation
of Austro-Marxism to social psychology Paul Lazarsfeld has made some interesting
observations in his autobiographical essay 'An Episode in the History of Social
Research: A Memoir' (in *The Intellectual Migration: Europe and America 1930–
1960*, ed. Donald Fleming and Bernard Mailyn, 1969, pp. 270–337). Lazarsfeld's
own early work was influenced by his participation in the Socialist Student movement and his contact with Austro-Marxism; he notes that his study of the occupational choices of young people (published in *Jugend und Beruf*, 1931) emphasized
the importance of social stratification and 'urged separate attention to the problems
of working class youth', while the articles he contributed to *Der Kampf* at this time
had 'a visible Marxist tinge'. Lazarsfeld also recounts how he came to undertake
the well-known survey of Marienthal: 'For reasons I cannot remember, I was interested in doing a leisure-time study, and I discussed it with a leader of the Socialist
Party, Otto Bauer. He considered it silly to study leisure problems at a time of severe
unemployment, and it was he who suggested the new topic ... .' The study was
published as *Die Arbeitslosen von Marienthal*, by Marie Jahoda, Paul F. Lazarsfeld,
and Hans Zeisel (1932), and an English translation has recently appeared.
[8] *Der Kampf* published several articles by W. Hausenstein on the social history
of art (one of which is translated below, pp. 276–85); but also many contributions
on the history of education, and of libraries and museums, particularly by Robert
Danneberg, and on general literary and cultural movements.

a tenuous link between Austro-Marxism and the Vienna Circle, mainly through Otto Neurath, who was broadly in sympathy, both politically and intellectually, with the Austro-Marxists and contributed regularly to *Der Kampf*. Two of his early contributions[9] analysed his experience with the workers' councils and the Central Planning Office in Bavaria in 1919, but later he wrote mainly on philosophical subjects from a Marxist standpoint;[10] and in his monograph *Empirische Soziologie*[11] he argued forcefully that Marxism was the most complete of all the attempts to create what he called a 'strictly scientific unmetaphysical physicalist sociology',[12] which conformed closely, in his view, with the methodological conceptions of logical empiricism. Most of the members of the Vienna Circle, however, showed little interest in Marxism,[13] and there is no indication that they had any close relationship with the Austro-Marxists, or in particular with the leading philosophical representative of Austro-Marxism, Max Adler.[14]

The Austro-Marxist school had an active existence for a third of a century, from the founding of the *Marx-Studien*[15] in 1904 by Max Adler and Rudolf Hilferding to the suppression of the Austrian Social Democratic Party and the dispersion of its leading members in 1934.[16] During this time

[9] *Der Kampf*, xiii (1920), pp. 136–41, 224–7.

[10] See, for example, his review of Carnap's *Logische Aufbau der Welt* in *Der Kampf*, xxi (1928), pp. 624–6, and of Mannheim's *Ideologie und Utopie* in *Der Kampf*, xxiii (1930), pp. 227–32.

[11] English translation, 'Empirical Sociology: The Scientific Content of History and Political Economy', in Otto Neurath, *Empiricism and Sociology*, edited by Marie Neurath and Robert S. Cohen (1973), pp. 319–421.

[12] Ibid., p. 349.

[13] Moritz Schlick, in his essay 'L'École de Vienne et la philosophie traditionelle', was strongly critical of Neurath's radicalism, but Carnap seems to have been more favourably disposed, and is reported as having said that Neurath's political views in the 1920s and 1930s were also his own. See Marie Neurath and Robert S. Cohen, op. cit., p. xiii. See also Carnap's intellectual autobiography in P. A. Schilpp (ed.), *The Philosophy of Rudolf Carnap* (1963), pp. 23–4.

[14] Though it is difficult to establish in detail what were Max Adler's relations with other thinkers, since shortly after his death in 1937 his family, in fear of the Nazis, destroyed all the papers and correspondence in their possession.

[15] See Bibliography.

[16] But its influence has persisted, in a more limited way, until the present time, and a part of the Austrian socialist movement might still be regarded as 'Austro-Marxist'. Renner, in a preface to two essays written a few years before his death in 1950, expressed the hope that this work would 'stimulate the younger generation of socialists to develop further, through their own research and teaching, the school of Austro-Marxism'. Karl Renner, *Wandlungen der Modernen Gesellschaft* (1953), p. 13.

Austro-Marxism passed through several distinct phases. Its 'golden age', in terms of the formation of a distinctive style of Marxist thought and research, was undoubtedly the period up to 1914, when Adler, Bauer, Hilferding, and Renner were publishing their major works. The First World War brought about a political division within the Austro-Marxist group between those who opposed the war and adopted a more revolutionary position, and those who supported it (with whatever qualifications); and this division persisted after the war, although it did not lead to a schism as happened in many other European labour movements after the Russian Revolution and the founding of the Third International. The Austro-Marxists continued to write in the same journals and to belong to the same party, and as Otto Bauer pointed out, one of the strengths of postwar Austro-Marxism was that it succeeded in maintaining the unity of the working-class movement.[17] None the less, there was now a greater diversity of views, and a certain decline in the distinctiveness of Austro-Marxism as a coherent intellectual movement.[18]

More significant for the fate of Austro-Marxism, however, were the postwar changes in the situation of the Austrian socialist movement. From having been one of the major movements in European socialism, in the multi-national Habsburg Empire, prominent in the councils of the Second International, and occupying an important place in relation to the German labour movement, its activities now became more confined within the boundaries of a small, economically weak country. Thus its influence upon events, as appeared in the

[17] See his essay below, pp. 45–8.

[18] Many years later Karl Renner, who belonged to the more reformist wing of Austro-Marxism, made a number of critical comments on some of his former comrades in a correspondence with Jacques Freundlich. Thus he writes '. . . I have been re-reading Otto Bauer's writings of the interwar period and found to my horror that they contain many false analyses and extremely misleading predictions. . . . His mind does not live with things, but in the midst of the images of things. . . . When I consider his work as a whole I find that it did not make any real innovations . . . such as Hilferding, for example, achieved in his *Finance Capital*' (letter of 22 November 1946). But as we have seen (n. 16, p. 5 above), Renner still attached importance to developing the ideas of Austro-Marxism as a whole. In the postwar period Hilferding also ceased to be so closely associated with the Austro-Marxist group as he became more deeply involved in the activities of the German Social Democratic Party and then, in 1933, went into exile, first in Denmark and subsequently in Switzerland and France.

course of the revolutionary movements in Central and Eastern Europe immediately after the war, and at the same time its intellectual influence, were considerably reduced. Furthermore, the Austro-Marxists found themselves in an awkward position between the Second and Third Internationals; they were Marxists, and to a large extent revolutionary Marxists, who did not associate easily with the increasingly reformist socialist parties of Western Europe, but at the same time they were highly critical of Bolshevik theory and practice.[19] As in the case of other Marxists who separated themselves from the newly established Communist parties and the Third International, their work became largely submerged in the efficiently organized flood of 'official Marxist' writing. For their part the Austro-Marxists themselves consistently ignored the work of those Marxist thinkers who were associated with the Third International;[20] and they showed a tendency to withdraw within the boundaries of their own particular domain, as they were able to do more successfully than some other individual Marxist thinkers because they were also the leaders of a socialist party which was by no means ineffectual in bringing about important social changes in their own country.[21]

This partial eclipse of Austro-Marxism in the 1920s and 1930s, and its almost total eclipse later on, does not mean that it can be regarded as a purely ephemeral and negligible tendency in Marxist thought. On the contrary, I think it can be argued that this was one of the most thorough, consistent, and intelligent attempts yet made to develop Marxism as an empirical social science, and that the neglect it has suffered is less the consequence of a considered intellectual judgement than the product of a collocation of unfavourable historical events. In the following pages I shall give a brief description of the

[19] This accounts for the active participation of several leading Austro-Marxists in the 'Second-and-a-half International'. See n. 2, p. 1 above.

[20] For example, neither Lukács's *History and Class Consciousness*, nor Korsch's *Marxism and Philosophy* (both published in 1923), was reviewed in *Der Kampf*, and so far as I can discover none of the Austro-Marxists ever referred to either of them. Lukács, who lived in Vienna from 1919 to 1929, seems to have had no contact with the Austro-Marxists, although he was familiar with their writings and referred to them briefly, in a highly critical way, in some of the essays in *History and Class Consciousness*. His criticism was directed mainly against their conception of a 'scientific' analysis of society in the manner of 'objective and exact sciences'.

[21] See below, pp. 38–9.

milieu in which the Austro-Marxist school developed, and the principal influences upon it, before going on to examine the contribution which it made to Marxist theory and research, and to the practice of the socialist movement.

2. Origins and Development

The emergence and development of Austro-Marxism resulted on one side from economic and political changes in the Habsburg Empire, and on the other side from a remarkable flowering of intellectual life in the capital, Vienna. During the period from 1848 to the end of the nineteenth century, and especially during the 1890s, the Empire was rapidly transformed from an agricultural to an industrial state, in which a quarter of the employed population (and in some regions almost a half) was engaged in industry. The total population increased from less than thirty million to fifty million, and the population of Vienna rose from little more than half a million in 1864 to 1,675,000 in 1900, and more than two million in 1914. This process of industrialization and urbanization was accompanied by the growth of new political movements: the Christian Social movement, a variety of nationalist movements, and the labour movement.[22]

The effective beginnings of the Austrian labour movement are to be found in the revolution of 1848, when several workers' associations and newspapers were established, but it was another twenty years before a significant Social Democratic movement emerged from the Vienna Workers' Educational Society.[23] This was soon suppressed, its leaders were put on trial for high treason in 1870, and most of the working-class organizations, including the trade unions, were dissolved. Thereafter, the Austrian labour movement was rent by internal dissension, and it was again crippled by government repression and the declaration of a state of emergency in 1883. Only in 1889, at the 'unity' conference held in Hainfeld,[24] did

[22] See Otto Bauer's essay below, pp. 48–52.

[23] Even so, this was one of the first in Europe. Julius Braunthal, History of the International, i. 116, writes that '... during the period of the First International the elements of Socialist parties on a national scale existed only in Germany and Austria'.

[24] The conference took place from 30 December 1888 to 1 January 1889. For the statement of principles, drafted by Viktor Adler and revised by Karl Kautsky, which was adopted at Hainfeld, see Ernst Winkler, Die österreichische Sozialdemokratie im Spiegel ihrer Programme (1971), pp. 26–30.

Viktor Adler succeed in reconciling the various factions and establishing a united Social Democratic Labour Party.

From that time the different sections of the labour movement—the consumer co-operatives, the trade unions, and the Social Democratic Party—grew rapidly and began to exert a strong influence upon political and intellectual life. Renner, in his autobiography, notes the tremendous impact of the first May Day demonstration of the Viennese workers in 1890, when 200,000 people assembled in the Prater, and expresses the feeling of young people at that time that 'something new had appeared on the historical stage, and held prodigious events in store for our generation'.[25] During the next few years student groups began to be formed, and the first of them, 'Der Heilige Leopold' (deriving its name from the inn where the early meetings were held), to which Renner, and a little later Max Adler and Hilferding, belonged, joined with another group, 'Veritas', made up of young university teachers, to create in 1895 a larger and more public association, the 'Freie Vereinigung Sozialistischer Studenten und Akademiker', under the chairmanship of Max Adler. It was here that the leading Austro-Marxist thinkers formed their relationships with each other, and began to work out their own distinctive ideas. As Renner later observed, the 'Freie Vereinigung' was '... for three decades the intellectual and social meeting place of all the socialist students in the University of Vienna ... [but] it had the character of a scientific seminar rather than a social club'.[26]

In the 1890s, however, the Austrian socialist movement was still intellectually dependent, to a large extent, upon German Marxism, especially in the person of Karl Kautsky, who had a particularly close association with Vienna and with Viktor Adler.[27] But already there was emerging a more independent outlook. The principal direct influence came from Carl Grünberg,[28] who was for many years the only

[25] Karl Renner, *An der Wende zweier Zeiten* (1946), p. 203.

[26] Ibid., p. 279.

[27] Karl Kautsky (1854–1938) was born in Prague, and lived in Vienna from 1863 to 1880, where he was active in the socialist movement.

[28] Carl Grünberg (1861–1940) studied at the University of Vienna, and was lecturer, then professor, of political economy in Vienna from 1894 to 1924, teaching mainly in the fields of economic history, agrarian questions, and the history of

'professorial Marxist' in Europe besides Antonio Labriola, and who has been called the 'father of Austro-Marxism'.[29] Almost all the most prominent Austro-Marxists were students of Grünberg: Renner, Hilferding, Max Adler, and somewhat later Gustav Eckstein, Bauer, and Friedrich Adler. What they acquired from him, it seems clear, was a conception of Marxism as a social science which should be developed in a rigorous and systematic way through historical and sociological investigations. In his inaugural lecture[30] at the opening of the Frankfurt Institute of Social Research Grünberg summed up his view as being that '... the materialist conception of history neither is, nor aims to be, a philosophical system ... its object is not abstractions, but the given concrete world in its process of development and change'. And his pupil Max Adler, whom Grünberg cited as having made in a very precise fashion the necessary distinction between 'historical materialism' as a systematic, empirical, historical discipline, and 'philosophical materialism' as a metaphysical doctrine, introduced the *Festschrift* for Grünberg's seventieth birthday with a reference to him as 'the master of *real historical observation* of social life'.[31]

It was not only as a university teacher that Grünberg helped to form the particular outlook of the Austro-Marxists. He was also active in the development of workers' education, which became a special preoccupation of Austrian Social Democracy; and together with Ludo Hartmann[32] and others he founded the *Sozialwissenschaftlicher Bildungsverein* (Association for Social Science Education) which provided a forum for the discussion of current problems, among them the

---

[29] See Günther Nenning, 'Biographie C. Grunberg', in *Indexband zu Archiv für die Geschichte des Sozialismus und der Arbeiterbewegung* (1973), pp. 126–8.

[30] Carl Grünberg, *Festrede* (1924).

[31] *Festschrift für Carl Grünberg zum 70 Geburtstag* (1932), p. 1.

[32] Ludo Hartmann (1865–1924) was a historian who taught at the University of Vienna, an active member of the Social Democratic Party, and the prime mover in the attempts to develop 'University Extension' teaching.

---

socialism. In 1910 he founded the journal for which he is chiefly remembered, the *Archiv für die Geschichte des Sozialismus und der Arbeiterbewegung*, and in 1924 he moved from Vienna to Frankfurt as the first Director of the newly established Institute of Social Research; but he was obliged to retire in 1928 after a stroke which incapacitated him for the rest of his life.

nationalities problem which became an important issue toward the end of the century.[33]

There were other important intellectual currents in Vienna at the end of the nineteenth century which contributed to shaping the ideas of Austro-Marxism. One of these was the positivism of Ernst Mach,[34] whose teaching and writings had their effect subsequently not only upon the Austro-Marxists, but also upon the philosophers of the Vienna Circle. Max Adler wrote later that he could see in Marx's work '... only a form of natural science positivism, more or less in the manner of Ernst Mach ...'.[35] At the same time Max Adler, in particular, was strongly influenced by the neo-Kantian revival in German philosophy; and a considerable part of his writing was devoted to presenting philosophical Marxism as a Kantian 'critique', and to analysing the relation between Kant and Marx from the point of view of the theory of knowledge.[36]

Other movements of thought provoked a reorientation of Marxism by posing new problems and theories for analysis and debate. One of these, as I have already mentioned, was the rapid growth of nationalist movements and doctrines in the last decade of the nineteenth century, and their influence in academic circles. Both Renner and Bauer attempted, in this situation, to develop an aspect of Marxist theory that had received little attention hitherto; namely, the analysis of the phenomenon of nations and nationalism, and their relation to the development of the economy and social classes.

A second, equally significant movement, was the emergence

---

[33] One of the particular interests of the Association was to bring university students, many of whom were passionately involved in the various nationalist movements, into contact with the working-class movement, and thus lead them to examine in a more informed and critical way both national and social problems.

[34] Ernst Mach (1838–1916), after being professor of mathematics in Graz and of physics in Prague, was appointed to the chair of history and theory of the inductive sciences at the University of Vienna in 1895.

[35] Max Adler, *Marxistische Probleme* (1913), p. 62. See also his long essay 'Mach und Marx. Ein Beitrag zur Kritik des modernen Positivismus', *Archiv für Sozialwissenschaft und Sozialpolitik*, xxxiii (1911), 348–400. Friedrich Adler also wrote a study of Mach's philosophical views, in much the same spirit, *Ernst Machs Überwindung des mechanischen Materialismus* (1918).

[36] See especially, Max Adler, *Kant und der Marxismus* (1925), which brought together essays on Kant published from 1904 onwards. See also the discussion on pp. 15–17 below.

of the Austrian marginal utility school of economics.[37] Not only did the Austrian school formulate a theoretical system that was quite incompatible with Marxist economics, but two of its members, Menger and Böhm-Bawerk, were particularly hostile to socialism, and the latter published in 1896 a major criticism of Marxist economic theory[38] which had some influence upon the views of the revisionists among the German Marxists. In Vienna Böhm-Bawerk's book gave rise to a lively controversy, and elicited the first critical writings of the Austro-Marxists in the field of economics.[39]

By the end of the nineteenth century some of the major concerns and ideas of Austro-Marxism had evidently been formulated, but the school did not yet exist. Its creation occupied the first decade of the twentieth century, and the initial impetus seems to have been provided by the revisionist controversy in Germany. At the party conference of 1901 changes in the Hainfeld programme were discussed, and although Viktor Adler claimed that no concessions had been made to Bernstein's ideas, they were debated, and they seem to have had some influence upon the text of the programme; for example, references to the 'increasing pauperization' of the working class were eliminated. From this time, the Austrian S.D.P. took a more or less 'centrist' position between Kautsky's 'orthodoxy' and Bernstein's 'revisionism', just as later on it adopted a similar position between the predominant tendencies of the Second and Third Internationals. Austro-Marxism was both the intellectual expression of this political outlook, and one of the forces which helped to shape it. Against Bernstein the Austro-Marxists wanted to uphold the revolutionary character of Marxism, and to defend the general validity of Marx's historical method and his analysis of capital-

---

[37] Its leading members were Carl Menger (1840–1921), Eugen Böhm-Bawerk (1851–1914), and Friedrich von Wieser (1851–1926), all of whom taught at the University of Vienna.

[38] E. Böhm-Bawerk, *Zum Abschluss des Marxschen Systems* (1896), translated as *Karl Marx and the Close of his System* (1898), and reprinted, ed. Paul Sweezy, together with Hilferding's rejoinder (1949).

[39] See especially, Rudolf Hilferding 'Böhm-Bawerks Marx-Kritik', *Marx-Studien* (1904), and Gustav Eckstein, 'Der vierfache Würzel des Satzes vom unzureichenden Grunde der Grenznutztheorie', *Neue Zeit*, xx (1901–2), 810–16.

ism. On the other hand, they were critical of Kautsky's somewhat dogmatic and unsophisticated materialism and determinism; they wanted to take account of new conceptions in
epistemology and the philosophy of science, and to engage in
empirical investigations of new social phenomena (and to this
extent, at least, were more sympathetic to Bernstein's
endeavours).

This outlook might well have remained no more than a
vague intellectual tendency in European Marxism had it not
been for the accident that a number of talented thinkers happened to come together in the University of Vienna, and the
socialist clubs, and in the course of their association, in the
particular circumstances of that time and place, worked out
systematically a distinctive version of the Marxist theory of
society. The first public indication of the emergence of a new
school of thought was the foundation, in 1904, of the *Marx-
Studien*, edited by Max Adler and Rudolf Hilferding, in which
all the major early works of the Austro-Marxists were first
published. The elaboration of a particular style of Marxist
thought, revealed in the *Marx-Studien*, was confirmed by the
founding, in 1907, of a new theoretical journal, *Der Kampf*,[40]
edited by Otto Bauer, Adolf Braun, and Karl Renner, which
soon came to rival Kautsky's *Die Neue Zeit* as the leading
European Marxist review.

The first decade and a half of the twentieth century was
undoubtedly the most brilliant intellectual period in the history of Austro-Marxism. It was also the time when the leading
members of the school were most closely associated with each
other, not only in the *Marx-Studien* and *Der Kampf*, in the
Association for Social Science Education, and in a new
society, 'Zukunft', which was founded in 1903 by Max Adler,
Hilferding, and Renner as a workers' school in Vienna, but
also through their regular meetings at the Café Central. As
Nenning has remarked, '. . . in the Vienna of that period the
move to a new café was a clear indication that a new era was
beginning',[41] and the Café Central became, from the middle
of the decade, the meeting place of the Austro-Marxists. It

---

[40] See the editorial statement in the first issue, pp. 52–6 below; and for further
details of the journal see the Bibliography.

[41] G. Nenning, 'Biographie C. Grünberg', p. 104.

was there, for instance, that Trotsky made their acquaintance while he was living in Vienna from 1907 to 1914.[42] This intellectual upsurge was stimulated by the increasing success of the socialist movement in Austria, for after its long campaign for the extension of the suffrage the S.D.P. found itself, as a result of the 1907 elections, the largest single party in Parliament, with eighty-seven deputies. The Austro-Marxists could thenceforth address themselves to a mass movement that was active in every sphere of economic, political, and cultural life.

But as Otto Bauer subsequently wrote, 'war and revolution dissolved the Austro-Marxist school';[43] it lost some of its coherence, and also its dynamism, as a distinct intellectual orientation, while as a political doctrine it became more clearly divided between right wing and left wing tendencies. Some of the members of the school formed new intellectual and political attachments; Hilferding, in particular, settled in Germany and was an active participant in the German socialist movement, became a member of the U.S.P.D.[44] and editor of its journal *Freiheit*, subsequently edited *Die Gesellschaft*, was Minister of Finance in two governments of the Weimar Republic, and seems not to have maintained very close relations with the Austro-Marxist group, while Max Adler became an editor of *Der Klassenkampf* (to which he was also a frequent contributor), a journal of the left wing of German Social Democracy, published from 1927 to 1931. But in spite of this 'dissolution' of the school the Austrian S.D.P. remained a

---

[42] He recounted these meetings, and described the leading Austro-Marxists in unflattering terms from the political standpoint of a Russian revolutionary, in his autobiography: 'It was Hilferding who first introduced me to his friends in Vienna, Otto Bauer, Max Adler, and Karl Renner. They were well-educated people whose knowledge of various subjects was superior to mine. I listened with intense and, one might almost say, respectful interest to their conversation in the "Central" Café. But very soon I grew puzzled. These people were not revolutionaries.' *My Life* (1930), p. 213.

[43] See p. 46 below.

[44] The Unabhängige Sozialdemokratische Partei Deutschlands (Independent Social Democratic Party of Germany) was constituted at a conference at Gotha in 1917 by a variety of groups in opposition to the majority of the German S.D.P. over its attitude to the war. The U.S.P.D. brought together very diverse elements, from Kautsky on the right to Rosa Luxemburg on the left, and formed a third grouping in the fragmented German socialist movement. For a brief account see Julius Braunthal, *History of the International*, ii. 59–61, 123–4, 221–3.

united party, and most of the Austro-Marxist thinkers managed to sustain among themselves a degree of intellectual agreement and co-operation. It will be necessary later on to consider how their ideas developed in the changed social and political conditions of the postwar world, but first we must look at the works in which their particular form of Marxist theory was originally expressed.

3. Theoretical Foundations

The specific concerns and ideas of the Austro-Marxists are revealed very plainly by four major studies which appeared in the early issues of the *Marx-Studien*: by Max Adler on the philosophy of science;[45] by Otto Bauer on nationality and nationalism;[46] by Rudolf Hilferding on the recent development of capitalism;[47] and by Karl Renner on the social functions of law.[48] Adler's philosophical writings were evidently of fundamental importance in creating the distinctive outlook of the school. He set himself the task of formulating, in a rigorous manner, the theoretical and methodological principles of Marxism as a social science, and provided a framework for social analysis which was generally accepted by his fellow thinkers.

The important influences upon Adler's thought from outside Marxism itself were the neo-Kantian revival which imparted a new direction to German philosophical thinking in the latter part of the nineteenth century,[49] and the positivism of Ernst Mach which was itself related to neo-Kantianism.[50] What he absorbed from neo-Kantian philosophy was not an ethical theory with which to supplement Marxism, as was being attempted by some German thinkers,[51] but the idea of a critique of knowledge applied to the foundations of a science

---

[45] *Kausalität und Teleologie im Streite um die Wissenschaft* (1904).
[46] *Die Nationalitätenfrage und die Sozialdemokratie* (1907).
[47] *Das Finanzkapital* (1910).
[48] *Die Soziale Funktion der Rechtsinstitute* (1904).
[49] The revival was signalled and stimulated by two notable studies of Kant: Kuno Fischer, *Kants Leben und die Grundlage seiner Lehre* (1860); and Otto Liebmann, *Kant und die Epigonen* (1865).
[50] See H. Stuart Hughes, *Consciousness and Society* (1958), pp. 107–8.
[51] See especially, Karl Vorländer, *Kant und der Sozialismus* (1900); and for a critical rejection of this approach Adler's essay translated below, pp. 63–5.

of society.[52] The question he posed—how is society possible?
—was the same as that which Simmel formulated;[53] it asked
what categorical principles and *a priori* concepts are necessary
in order to comprehend, and to explain in terms of empirical
regularities, the phenomena of social life. And he went on to
suggest that just as Kant's question concerning nature as an
object of thought followed the emergence of Newtonian
physics, so the similar question about society followed the
construction of Marx's social theory.

According to Adler, Marx had been able to construct his
theory of society by introducing the fundamental concept of
'socialized humanity', sketched briefly in the *Theses on Feuerbach*, which made possible for the first time an investigation
of the causal regularities in social life, and a rapprochement
between the natural sciences and the social sciences which
would eventually allow them to be brought together in 'a
single scientific conceptual scheme'.[54] This concept of 'socialized humanity' or 'social association' Adler regards, in neo-
Kantian fashion, as being 'transcendentally given as a category
of knowledge'.[55] It is a concept furnished by reason, not derived from experience, which is a precondition of an empirical
science.

Throughout Adler's presentation of Marxism the main
emphasis is upon its character as an empirical science which,
like all empirical sciences, attempts to establish causal connections among the phenomena in its field. This strongly
empiricist cast of Adler's philosophy of science undoubtedly
owed a good deal to the influence of Mach's positivism,[56]
although it was encouraged too by the teaching of Carl Grün-

---

[52] What interested him chiefly was epistemological neo-Kantianism, of which the
best known version was that of the Marburg school originated by Hermann Cohen;
but as will be seen Adler's position was more empiricist than that taken by the
Marburg philosophers.

[53] Georg Simmel, 'How is Society Possible?', translated in Kurt Wolff (ed.),
Georg Simmel, 1858–1918 (1959). Adler wrote a short study of Simmel, *Georg
Simmels Bedeutung für die Geistesgeschichte* (1919), in which he considered some of
these affinities.

[54] See below, p. 60.

[55] See below, pp. 65–6.

[56] On Mach, see especially Leszek Kolakowski, *Positivist Philosophy* (1972), pp.
141–53; and Allen Janik and Stephen Toulmin, *Wittgenstein's Vienna* (1973),
pp. 132–45.

berg;[57] and in this respect it contrasted sharply with other developments in neo-Kantian philosophy in Vienna, which led to a preoccupation with the construction of formal models that were taken to be independent of all experience. One philosopher of science who emphasized this kind of model-building was Heinrich Hertz, whose views have been described as 'falling into place alongside the other attempts to define the scope, conditions of validity, and boundaries, of different media, symbolisms, modes of expression and/or languages, which were a dominant feature of Viennese intellectual and cultural debate from 1890 on'.[58]

Among such attempts there were two which had a particular importance in the history of social thought and as objects of criticism by the Austro-Marxists. The first is to be found in the work of the economists of the Austrian marginalist school, and especially of Carl Menger, its founder. Menger was primarily interested in questions of method, and he formulated a conception of economics as a 'science of human action', not based upon or corrigible by empirical observation, but constructed in the form of a rational model, from a direct understanding of the elements of human action. Economic theory ('pure theory') in this sense formulates what Menger called 'exact' laws, as distinct from 'empirical' laws to which he assigns a subordinate place, although the exact relation between the two kinds of law is not very clearly set forth.[59] Menger's doctrine led to the interpretation of economic phenomena in terms of the subjective evaluations of individuals, not as they might be empirically observed and investigated in their social context, but as 'typical', rationally constructed evaluations assumed to be universally valid; and this subjective, individualistic character of the doctrine was criticized by Hilferding, who contrasted its presuppositions with those of Marxism in his reply to Böhm-Bawerk's study of Marx's economic theory.[60]

The second example of such construction of rational models

---

[57] See above, pp. 9–10.
[58] Janik and Toulmin, op. cit., pp. 139–41, 146.
[59] See the discussion by T. W. Hutchison in J. Hicks and W. Weber (eds.), *Carl Menger and the Austrian School of Economics* (1973), pp. 15–37.
[60] See below, pp. 84–91.

is Kelsen's 'pure theory of law',[61] in which law—as a body of
norms—is treated as an independent, closed system, the
analysis of which is confined to showing the logical interrelation of the various normative elements, and does not need
or depend upon any inquiry into either the ethical basis of law
(natural law doctrine) or its social context (sociology of law).
Adler, in *Die Staatsauffassung des Marxismus* (1922), analysed
in some detail the differences between a sociological (i.e.
Marxist) theory and a formal (or 'pure') theory of law, and
devoted one chapter of his book to a particular criticism of
Kelsen's views.[62]

It was Karl Renner, however, in his study of the social functions of legal institutions,[63] who presented most fully the
Austro-Marxist alternative to Kelsen's type of legal theory.
Renner, it is true, took as his starting point the conception of
law as a system of norms which could be analysed and interpreted in its own right, but he then proceeded to extend his
inquiry in a sociological direction by investigating how the
same legal norms could change their functions in response to
changes in society, and particularly changes in its economic
structure. He described the subject matter of his study as
being 'the mutual relations between law and economics', and
although he did not deal with all aspects of this problem (and
excluded from this particular study, for example, the specific
question of how a legal norm develops from its economic
background) he formulated in the concluding section of the
book a number of sociological questions—how is the law
determined by economics, how are changes in the functions
of law related to changes in the legal norms themselves, and
what are the fundamental causes of these changes?—which
he considered to be the most important that modern jurisprudence had to confront.

In this book, and in many of his other writings, Renner
quite clearly attributes an active role to law in conserving or

---

[61] Hans Kelsen, *Hauptprobleme der Staatsrechtslehre* (1911).

[62] Adler's book was in part a response to a later work by Kelsen, *Sozialismus und
Staat: Eine Untersuchung der Politischen Theorie des Marxismus* (1920).

[63] Renner, *Soziale Funktion*. See the excerpt on pp. 267–76 below, and also the
discussion by Otto Kahn-Freund in his introduction to the English translation of
Renner's book.

modifying existing social relations and does not regard law as a mere reflection of economic conditions. He cites, as being consonant with this view, some of Marx's comments on law in the Introduction to the *Grundrisse*;[64] and it is evident that his whole conception corresponded with a general Austro-Marxist interpretation of the relation between 'base' and 'superstructure' which was systematically expounded, as part of a comprehensive analysis of Marx's concepts and method, by Max Adler.[65]

The greater part of Max Adler's work was devoted to this clarification and vindication of the theoretical foundations of Marxism, in opposition to a variety of alternative theoretical schemes and philosophies of science. In its negative, critical aspect his thought can be regarded, as Peter Heintel suggests,[66] as being directed against three main intellectual tendencies: first, against a 'superficial positivism' which conceives the constitution of a social science as a simple matter of empirical observation of self-evident psychological interactions among individuals; second, against the formalism of neo-Kantianism which concentrates attention upon the validity of abstract models divorced from any empirical investigation; and third, against various uncritical forms of social teleology which were presented as alternatives to a causal social science.[67]

In its positive aspect Adler's methodological analysis, as I have already suggested, was intended to establish the character of Marxism as a sociological theory; that is, as a set of causal statements, open to empirical testing, and dealing with a specific object, 'socialized humanity'. On one side this conception provides an alternative to those holistic views which treat society as a complex of meanings that can somehow be comprehended in its totality through an act of intuition or *Verstehen*.[68] On the other side it enables Adler to establish in

[64] Renner, *Soziale Funktion*. English trans., pp. 56–7.

[65] See the excerpt from Adler's discussion of 'ideology as appearance', pp. 253–61 below.

[66] Peter Heintel, *System und Ideologie. Der Austromarxismus im Spiegel der Philosophie Max Adlers* (1967), pp. 15–17.

[67] Adler summed up his methodological views in his last major work, *Das Rätsel der Gesellschaft* (1936), from which these critical observations have been taken.

[68] His criticism of such views is clearly formulated in the essay on Othmar Spann, pp. 69–76 below.

a different way the distinctive reality of the 'social' (of 'social facts' in the language of another, cognate conception) by his assertion that social association is a transcendental condition of experience in exactly the same sense as are space, time, and categories in Kant's theory of knowledge. On these grounds he is able to exclude, as methodologically unsound, all the individualistic, psychologistic theories of social life; one version of which is to be found in the works of the Austrian marginalist economists.

Two particular features of Adler's methodological views deserve to be noticed here. First, while asserting that '... Marxism does not aim to be anything but the science of the laws of social life and its causal development',[69] he insists upon the fact that there are diverse types of causality and that the form which the causal relation takes in social life is not 'mechanical causality', but one that is mediated by human consciousness.[70] All the phenomena of social life, including those of the economic sphere, are *mental*, not material, phenomena,[71] and the relations of causality among them are, in some sense, relations between individual human minds. We might say, therefore, that Adler's conception of social causality involves treating motives as causes; in a context, however, in which motives are analysed not as individual psychological phenomena but as forces that are at work in 'socialized humanity' and thus have their effect as 'social forces'.

The second important feature in Adler's methodology is his analysis of the relation between causality and teleology. As we have seen, he rejected teleological social doctrines and insisted upon the idea of causality as the essential basis of any science, including a social science; but at the same time he recognized that practical social life is purposive, goal-oriented, and guided by valuations. His attempts to reconcile these two aspects took diverse forms. In his early work on causality and teleology (1904) he seems to argue that it is a matter of different perspectives; a science of society has to be concerned

---

[69] See below, p. 64.

[70] See below, pp. 72–3.

[71] This argument is developed particularly in the chapter on ideology in *Lehrbuch der materialistischen Geschichtsauffassung*, see below, pp. 253–61.

strictly with the causal determination of phenomena in its field, but science reveals only one aspect of life, whereas 'the complete reality of our being' is to be found in man's practical, conative activity. 'The teleological relation, which could not have any significance in constituting the domain of scientific knowledge, becomes a practical act in the consciousness of the real individual ... in so far as he develops science for his own ends, in order to shape the world in his own image.'[72] In a later work, *Der soziologische Sinn der Lehre von Karl Marx* (1914), Adler tries to establish a direct relation between causality and teleology: 'The causal mechanism of history is transformed directly, by the scientific illumination of it, into a teleology, without suffering thereby any breach in its causally determined character. It is simply that the scientific knowledge of a particular social situation now enters as a cause into this causal mechanism.'[73] Later still, in his *Lehrbuch der materialistischen Geschichtsauffassung* (1930–2), he returns to an analysis of the nature of motives as causes, but also devotes greater attention to the complexity of social causation and to the difficulties we confront in trying to establish precise causal links in complicated social situations.

The end result of Adler's ever-renewed attack upon the problem of the relation between causality and teleology, science and values, determinism and human freedom, may not now be seen as entirely convincing or successful; but this was certainly one of the most profound and persistent efforts by a Marxist thinker (or for that matter, by any philosopher of the social sciences) to deal with these difficult questions. What his methodological writings display—and in this respect his work is comparable with that of Max Weber—is a consistent, painstaking attempt to provide the ground for a genuinely empirical social science, capable of development and correction, while acknowledging the distinctive significance of meaning and values in practical social action.

Adler's general conception of Marxism as a sociological theory was broadly shared by the other Austro-Marxist

[72] See below, p. 77.
[73] op. cit., p. 25.

thinkers, whatever reservations they may have had about the strength of his commitment to a Kantian theory of knowledge,[74] and it constituted the framework of ideas which largely directed and inspired the work of the whole school. In this sense, sociology in Austria could be mainly identified with Austro-Marxism, not only in its substantive form, but also as the principal source of criticism of the diverse counter-sociological influences in Austrian thought and culture;[75] and the destruction of Austro-Marxism in 1934 with the suppression of the socialist movement put an end, at least temporarily, to sociology in Austria and to an important current of sociological thought in a wider context.

4. The Analysis of Modern Capitalist Society

The Austro-Marxists lived through a period of profound changes in their own society, in European capitalism, and in world politics. Some of these changes were already apparent at the end of the nineteenth century, and the interpretation of them was a major element in the revisionist controversy which itself provided an intellectual and political stimulus to the formation of Austro-Marxism. In the course of their studies over more than three decades the Austro-Marxists examined diverse aspects of the changes in twentieth-century capitalist society, but their work can be seen as beginning with Hilferding's analysis of the trends in economic development, comprehensively presented in his book *Finance Capital*, which was unquestionably one of the school's most original contributions to Marxist social theory.[76]

Hilferding's study is concerned with the problems of circulation and of the process of capitalist production as a whole which were discussed by Marx in the second and third volumes of *Capital*, and his intention is to develop Marx's analysis in the light of later economic developments. Thus the

---

[74] See especially the comments of Otto Bauer, p. 52 below, and also in the preface to the second edition of his book on the national question.

[75] See particularly, for an illuminating discussion of this point, John Torrance, 'The Emergence of Sociology in Austria', *European Journal of Sociology*, xvii. 2 (1976).

[76] An English translation of the book is at last due to appear, to be published by Routledge and Kegan Paul. There is a useful general commentary on Hilferding's work as a whole by Wilfried Gottschalch, *Strukturveränderungen der Gesellschaft und politisches Handeln in der Lehre von Rudolf Hilferding* (1962).

five sections of the book are devoted to the theory of money,[77] the growth of joint-stock companies, the restriction of competition by cartels, economic crises, and imperialism. In Hilferding's view there had occurred a structural change in capitalism, the origin of which was the development of the joint-stock company, which separates ownership from the actual direction of production. Marx had commented on the early stage of this process, but Hilferding claims that his own analysis goes beyond that of Marx, who had not treated dividends as a specific economic category and had not dealt with what Hilferding calls the *Gründergewinn* (the founder's profit).[78]

The growth of joint-stock companies is accompanied by an increasing centralization of capital, as a result of which a small number of people acquire effective control over a large number of companies; and a crucial role in this whole process of expansion of joint-stock companies and centralization of economic control is played by the credit system and the banks. There is a merging of banking and industrial capital to produce the phenomenon which Hilferding calls 'finance capital', in which the banks assume a dominant position.[79] At the same time technological progress makes ever larger quantities of capital necessary, the volume of fixed capital increases, the rate of profit tends to fall, and competition becomes too expensive, with the result that there is a movement toward the formation of cartels, trusts, and monopolies which is favoured, or even demanded, by the banks.

The development of cartels in turn creates a new relation of the capitalist class to the state. First, in order to protect, and so far as possible monopolize, the domestic market the cartel favours tariff barriers which require the active intervention of the state in the economy. Second, although Hilferding

---

[77] Hilferding gives up the conception of money as a commodity, and treats it as the 'reflection of the value of the totality of commodities in circulation'.

[78] The 'founder's profit', which arises when a joint-stock company is formed, is the difference between the capital value of the enterprise calculated on the basis of the rate of profit and the value calculated on the basis of the current rate of interest (the rate of profit being assumed to be higher).

[79] The involvement of the banks with industry was particularly close in Austria and this fact undoubtedly coloured Hilferding's analysis. See the recent study by Bernard Michel, *Banques et banquiers en Autriche au début du XXe. siècle* (1976).

emphasizes that cartels cannot prevent economic crises, he argues that there is a trend toward the suppression of competition and the planned organization of production which creates a basis for a future rational organization of the world economy. In this process the state plays an important role, and begins to assume the character of a conscious, rational structuring of society in the interests of all; it establishes the organizational preconditions for socialism. Thus Hilferding concludes—and this is an idea which reappears in the writings of Bauer and Renner—that revolutionary politics does not consist in abolishing the state but in seizing state power in order to bring this rationalization and conscious direction of social life to full fruition. However, there is another aspect of this closer relationship between the nation state and the cartels which has a pre-eminent significance for the present and the immediate future; namely, the emergence of imperialist policies, involving a struggle for world markets and raw materials and the export of capital to non-industrialized countries; and hence an increasingly evident political conflict between the major capitalist states. Hilferding's theory of imperialism, derived from his analysis of finance capitalism, will be examined more fully later, in the context of the general Austro-Marxist view of the growth of nationalism and international rivalries.

It follows from Hilferding's argument about the structural changes in the capitalist economy that while he agrees with Rosa Luxemburg in regarding finance capitalism and imperialism as the final stage of capitalism, he does not conceive its dissolution as resulting from an inevitable economic breakdown. On the contrary, the extension of cartels (tending toward a general cartel) and the intervention of the state in economic life make possible some degree of control of economic crises, and a partially planned development of the economy. The breakdown of capitalism would be a consequence of social and political forces; of a movement led by the working class and its political party, to complete the process of establishing a substantively rational economic system —that 'rational interchange between man and nature' which Marx saw as a characteristic feature of socialism.[80]

[80] There are some noteworthy similarities between Hilferding's ideas on the breakdown of capitalism and those which Schumpeter later expounded, from a

INTRODUCTION

In his later writings Hilferding developed further two of
the ideas formulated in *Finance Capital*. First, he observed a
strengthening of the trend toward central regulation and
organization of the economy, encouraged by the needs of a
war economy, and in an essay of 1915 he coined the expression
'organized capitalism' to describe this new situation, which he
examined further in an essay dealing with the transition to
socialism, published in 1924.[81] By this time he had also concluded that a moderation of the opposition between classes
and between diverse economic interests had improved the
chances of a peaceful transition to socialism. In a still later
work, a comprehensive reappraisal of the materialist conception of history which he began to write during his exile in
Arles (1939–41),[82] Hilferding discussed again the role of the
state, to which he now attributed an even greater influence
upon the course of social development, especially in the
twentieth century when the scale of economic resources and
the advanced level of technology had made possible an un-
precedentedly effective organization of society from above in
what he called the 'total state'. At the same time he now attributed a more fundamental importance to the role of force, as
distinct from economic factors, in the organization and transformation of society.[83]

In much the same way as Hilferding, though with varying
degrees of emphasis, other Austro-Marxist thinkers came to
attach considerable importance to the largely independent
role of the state in organizing and changing the economic
system and the social structure. Such a view is particularly

[81] 'Die Probleme der Zeit', *Die Gesellschaft*, vol. i (1924).
[82] 'Das historische Problem'. Published, with an introduction, by Benedikt
Kautsky, in *Zeitschrift für Politik* (N.S.), i. 4 (1954), 293–324.
[83] It is worth noting here, as a more general feature of this work, that in his preliminary discussion setting out the principles of a Marxist sociology, and dealing
with such methodological questions as the concept of society and the nature of
social causation, Hilferding adheres very closely to the scheme of analysis that Max
Adler formulated. This illustrates well the acceptance of a common method, and the
continuity of ideas in Austro-Marxist thought.

different ideological standpoint, in *Capitalism, Socialism, and Democracy* (1942); and
as we shall see Schumpeter also paid serious attention to the Austro-Marxist theory
of imperialism. It seems likely that Schumpeter's life-long preoccupation with
Marx's social theory, his emphasis upon its sociological character, and his approach
to a number of specific problems, were all influenced by his close acquaintance with
Austro-Marxist thought in his earlier years.

evident in the writings of Karl Renner. In his analysis of legal institutions Renner, as I noted earlier, attributes a positive social influence to law and poses as problematic the interaction between law, i.e. the activity of the state, and economic interests. Later, in a series of articles on 'Problems of Marxism' published in 1916, he argues that capitalist society has been transformed[84] as a result of what he calls 'state penetration of the economy', which is advancing toward 'direct state management of the economy'. This socialization of the economy in a form not foreseen by Marx poses new problems; socialism cannot now be related to a *laissez-faire* economy, but must be seen in relation to an economic order which is already, and to an increasing extent, planned and organized by the state. These conditions, as Renner continues to argue in his subsequent writings, up to the posthumously published *Wandlungen der modernen Gesellschaft* (1953), make necessary a different conception of the transition from capitalism to socialism, which no longer has a primarily destructive sense (destruction of a repressive state apparatus and a *laissez-faire* economy) but involves a more constructive extension of the welfare functions of the state and of the rational organization of the economy under a regime of public ownership; although the transition has still to be accomplished by a working-class party through political struggles.

Similar ideas are to be found in Otto Bauer's writings, even though he adopted a more radical position with respect to the political strategy and tactics of the S.D.P. They are expressed, for example, in his conception of the 'slow revolution', by which he meant the gradual construction of a socialist society after the conquest of political power by a working-class party, through radical reforms in all spheres of social life, involving in many cases the consolidation and gradual extension of reforms already undertaken by the bourgeois state.[85] In a more comprehensive study of the postwar changes in Austrian society, *The Austrian Revolution* (1923), Bauer not only points

---

[84] See below, pp. 91–101. 'Capitalist society, as Marx experienced and described it, no longer exists!'

[85] Otto Bauer, *Der Weg zum Sozialismus* (1919). The social legislation enacted during the first two years of the Republic, and the radical reforms carried out by the Socialist administration of Vienna during the 1920s and the early 1930s, provide practical examples of this process.

out the limits imposed upon the revolutionary movement by the economic weakness of Austria, by the military strength and capacity to intervene of the victorious Allied Powers, and by the political division between the working class and the peasantry (and for these reasons among others he was inflexibly opposed to any attempt to establish a 'dictatorship of the proletariat' on the Russian or Hungarian model), but also advocates strongly that the working class should use the predominant position it acquired with the establishment of the Republic to begin the construction of a socialist society by means of legislation to extend the provision of social welfare, create works councils, regulate conditions of employment, and improve the facilities for the education and training of workers.

The Austro-Marxists' view of the changing role of the state was also affected in some degree by their analysis of the class structure. Hilferding, in *Finance Capital*, discusses briefly the significance of the 'new middle class' of white-collar employees, which he distinguishes from the working class by its social situation rather than its economic position; and in his unfinished study, *Das historische Problem*, he embarks upon a more comprehensive analysis of the class structure in which three major aspects are singled out for attention: first, the complexity of social stratification in modern capitalist society, where numerous social groups and classes exist, each having a particular *interest*; second, the relative autonomy of the state, which has its own interests, especially in modern societies where its activities are multifarious and it employs and directs large numbers of officials; and third, the difficulties of the process whereby *interests* are articulated in *consciousness*. With regard to the last point, Hilferding considers especially the problems that beset the development of a socialist political consciousness in the working class.

This theme is also dominant in Max Adler's long analysis of changes in the working class,[86] published in 1933 after the defeat of the working-class movement in Germany, where he distinguishes five separate strata in the working class which have given rise, in his view, to three different political orientations—that of the labour aristocracy and bureaucracy, that of

[86] See below, pp. 217–48.

the workers who are still employed, and that of the unemployed—leading to extensive and harmful conflicts within
the class. He then discusses the means by which such divisions
and conflicts might be overcome in order to create a general
socialist consciousness, and goes on to consider the problem
of extending this consciousness to the middle strata, who are
now proletarianized as a result of the economic crisis but remain ideologically hostile to the workers, so that a class-
conscious majority can be formed from the various anti-
capitalist interests.

Renner also paid close attention to the growth of the middle
strata, composed of white-collar employees in the public service and private enterprise, but he interpreted the relation
between this 'service class' and the working class in a somewhat different way, especially in the essays written toward the
end of his life and published as *Wandlungen der modernen
Gesellschaft* (1953). Here he argues that the members of the
service class have become effectively 'propertyless', are closer
to the rising working class, and even tend to merge with it at
its boundary. On the other side, the condition of large sections
of the working class has changed with the development of
contracts of employment which give these workers a legal
status resembling that of officials. These developments have
produced a restructuring of social classes which offers new
opportunities for a democratic socialist movement to accomplish a gradual and peaceful transition to socialism.[87]

There was one aspect of the class structure, both in the
Habsburg Empire and in the Republic which followed it, that
had a particular importance; namely, the division between the
industrial working class and the peasantry. The Republic,
especially, was almost equally divided politically between the
working class in Vienna and a few other industrial areas, and
the peasantry in the rest of the country. This situation represented, according to some of the Austro-Marxists, and more
particularly Otto Bauer, an 'equilibrium between class forces'
in which the relative autonomy of the state was enhanced, and
in which its actions might be deflected in one direction or
another by various political forces.

The Austro-Marxist analysis of capitalist society, in the

[87] See below, pp. 249-52.

period from the beginning of the century to the early 1930s, was characterized by the following principal ideas, making due allowance for the differences between individual thinkers to which I have drawn attention. The centralization of the economy through cartels, the involvement of the banks, and state intervention were creating a more organized economy which facilitated the transition to socialism and could indeed be regarded as a stage of development toward a socialist society. The increasing independence of the state, not only in economic matters, but in the provision of welfare services, also represented a movement toward socialism, which could be carried further by a working-class party. The changes in the class structure, and in the situation of various classes, produced on one side a real improvement in the condition of the working class, but at the same time a greater differentiation within the working class, and a growth in the middle strata. Hence, socialist politics had to aim at overcoming these internal divisions, and beyond this, at creating alliances between the working class and sections of the new middle class and of the peasantry, with the object of acquiring the support of a clear majority of the population.

This notion of majority support was crucial in the thought of the Austro-Marxists and in the politics of the S.D.P. It reflected not only the conclusions of their analysis of modern capitalism concerning the real possibility and the overwhelming desirability of a peaceful transition to socialism, but also their profound commitment to democratic socialism, which emerges clearly in their writings on dictatorship and democracy, in Otto Bauer's assessment of the Bolshevik Revolution, and in their attitude to the politics of the Third International.

To some extent this analysis of capitalist society, and the political judgements derived from it, were modified after the early 1930s, as a consequence of the rapid growth of Fascist movements in Europe and the triumph of National Socialism in Germany. Hilferding, in *Das historische Problem*, came to attribute a still greater importance to the independent role of the state and its use of force in shaping society, and introduced into his analysis the concept of the 'total state' as a new phenomenon in modern society. Otto Bauer undertook an analysis

of Fascism[88] according to which it appeared as the violent
reaction of the bourgeoisie to the advance of democratic
socialism, and so brought into question the very possibility of
a democratic and peaceful attainment of power by the working
class. And in *Zwischen zwei Weltkriegen?* (1936) he was led to
a reassessment of the Soviet regime, as constituting after all
some kind of socialist bulwark against the tide of capitalist
reaction. Nevertheless, these analyses of the tendencies in
capitalist society which produced Fascism could not be fully
developed, or situated adequately in their historical context,
by most of the Austro-Marxist thinkers. Only Karl Renner
lived through the Second World War and the destruction of
the National Socialist regime, and in the postwar conditions of
the development of Western capitalism in democratic forms
he was able to resume the analysis of capitalism in terms of
those themes which had figured prominently in Austro-
Marxist thought before the 1930s, and which seemed to
acquire an even greater significance after 1945.

5. *Nationalism and Imperialism*

One of the most important and difficult problems which the
Austrian S.D.P. had to confront was that of the relationship
between the diverse nationalities in the Habsburg Empire, and
the emergence toward the end of the nineteenth century of
more vigorous national movements. Nationalism posed a
challenge to the socialist movement in several respects—by
its potentially divisive effect upon the working class, by its
attraction for large sections of the peasantry among whom the
S.D.P. itself needed to find support in order to gain political
power, by its influence upon considerable numbers of intellectuals and university students, and by its association with
imperialism.

It is not surprising, therefore, that some of the Austro-
Marxist thinkers—especially Karl Renner and Otto Bauer—
should have undertaken studies of the situation of the
nationalities in the Empire, analysed the phenomenon of
nationalism, and attempted to develop a Marxist theory of the
nation. Renner's interest in these questions was aroused
particularly, as he recounts in his autobiography, by his

[88] See below, pp. 167–86.

youthful experience of military service in the multi-national army, and much of his early writing is devoted to the national problem.[89] Two themes predominate in his work: first, the need for a proper constitutional and legal regulation of the position of the various nationalities in the Empire, which would put an end to the political struggles for power embodied in the nationalist movements; and second, more broadly, the idea of the Empire transformed into a 'state of nationalities' (*Nationalitätenstaat*) which could eventually provide a model for the socialist organization of the world as a whole.[90] Thus, in *Das Selbstbestimmungsrecht der Nationen* (1918) he writes that his aim is '. . . to give substance to the legal concept of the nation, first within the narrow framework of the state of nationalities, in order to present an example for the future national order of mankind'.

While Renner focused his attention upon the legal and constitutional aspects, Otto Bauer, in *Die Nationalitätenfrage und die Sozialdemokratie* (1907) attempted more ambitiously to provide a theoretical and historical analysis of the national problem within the framework of a Marxist sociology. This analysis leads him to a conception of the nation as a historical phenomenon—'the nationality of the individual is only one aspect of his determination by the history of society, by the development of the conditions and techniques of labour'[91]— and to reflections upon the place of national communities in a socialist world order.[92]

Renner and Bauer did not differ only in respect of their general approach to the national problem; they also differed, to some extent, in the practical solutions that they proposed.[93]

---

[89] See *Staat und Nation. Zur österreichischen Nationalitätenfrage* (1899), published under the pseudonym Synopticus; also *Der Kampf der österreichischen Nationen um der Staat* (1902). Renner continued to be preoccupied with these problems and wrote many later essays and books on the subject.

[90] The S.D.P. party conference held at Brünn in 1899 passed a resolution on the national problem which incorporated similar ideas; thus it began by stating that 'Austria should be transformed into a democratic federation of nationalities'. See Winkler, *Die österreichische Sozialdemokratie*, pp. 31–2.

[91] See below, p. 109.

[92] See below, pp. 109–17.

[93] There is a useful review of their proposals and a general discussion of the national problem in Robert A. Kann, *The Multinational Empire*, vol. ii (1964), especially pp. 154–78.

Renner's aim was to preserve the multi-national character of the Empire, as something valuable in itself, in a democratic federal state. Bauer emphasized much more strongly the subordination of the national question to the interests of the working class; in commenting upon the Brünn programme he observes that 'a Social Democratic programme concerning nationalities has to start from the position of the working class in society; it has to incorporate the particular national problems of Austria in the great social problem'.[94] Nevertheless, he continued to think in terms of a multi-national federal state until the First World War, when the rising tide of Slav nationalism in particular led him to advocate a policy of national independence and separate national states.

After the First World War, when the dismemberment of the Habsburg Empire by the victorious Allied Powers was an accomplished fact, both Renner and Bauer—accepting this reorganization of Central and Eastern Europe into national states—advocated a union (*Anschluss*) between Austria and Germany, not only on the grounds that Austria by itself was too small and poorly endowed economically to be able to survive, but also on the basis of their conception of the cultural unity of the German speaking people which had always been an important element in their thought. The peace treaties of 1919 precluded an *Anschluss* between Germany and Austria, but the idea lingered on in Austro-Marxist thought, at least up to 1933, when the reference to it was eliminated from the party programme and the need to defend Austrian independence against National Socialist Germany was affirmed.

The commitment of Bauer and Renner, in different periods, to the multi-national state or to the *Anschluss* between Germany and Austria, were influenced on one side by the idea that from the standpoint of a future socialist society it was desirable that the world should be organized in larger economic regions, and that there should be a political order transcending the nation state (and Renner, in particular, thought that the nationality principle had begun to lose some of its importance as a basis for the formation of states). On the other side, they were concerned about the growth of national movements, and of intense nationalist feeling, which

[94] Bauer, *Die Nationalitätenfrage*, p. 528.

they saw as being closely connected, in certain aspects, with the development of modern imperialism.

The Austro-Marxist theory of imperialism was first set out in a comprehensive manner by Rudolf Hilferding in *Finance Capital*.[95] There Hilferding argues that the development of cartels and monopolies leads to a new form of protectionism in which import tariffs serve to eliminate foreign competition in the domestic market. Monopoly prices, however, tend to reduce sales, and in order to maintain and extend large-scale production exports become increasingly important. Furthermore, a new form of expansion appears with the export of capital, which extends the economic region and the scale of production, and by developing production in areas where labour is very cheap helps to maintain a high rate of profit. The extension of the economic region by the cartels thus has a number of objectives: to open up new markets, to obtain raw materials, and to provide fresh opportunities for capital investment. This expansion requires the support and active intervention of the state, in acquiring and maintaining control over the new economic areas, in some cases by means of colonial conquest; and in due course it leads to national expansionist policies and increasing conflict among the leading capitalist states.

Hilferding goes on to discuss the way in which these economic tendencies in modern capitalism, and the expansionist policies to which they give rise, transform nationalism from a doctrine of national independence, cultural autonomy, and self-determination into the idea of world domination. Nationalism becomes the ideology of imperialism. In this part of his analysis Hilferding draws upon the earlier study of the national question by Otto Bauer,[96] who had examined the connection between protectionist policies, territorial expansion, and the new forms of nationalism. Thus, in studying imperialism the Austro-Marxists adopted the same approach as in their other work; they did not deal only with economic factors, nor regard political and ideological struggles as mere 'reflections' of economic forces, but attempted to depict a whole *social* process of development in which economic,

---

[95] See especially Chapters 21, 22, and 25.
[96] Bauer, *Die Nationalitätenfrage*. See especially Chapter 30.

political, and ideological elements were interwoven, however much the economic changes might be seen as preponderant.

Nationalism, from this standpoint, was a potent and partly independent force that facilitated the implementation of imperialist policies; and in Renner's writings of a later period it acquired still greater significance in his conception of 'social imperialism', to which I shall refer again below.

In this respect the Austro-Marxist view differs from that expounded by Lenin in his pamphlet on imperialism,[97] even though Lenin based his own work upon Hilferding's '... very valuable theoretical analysis', as well as upon J. A. Hobson's[98] '... excellent and comprehensive description of the principal economic and political characteristics of imperialism'. Lenin's definition of imperialism in terms of five essential features—monopolies, finance capital, export of capital, formation of international cartels, territorial division of the world—scarcely differs from that of Hilferding,[99] and there is little disagreement either about the conception of imperialism as a distinct stage in the development of capitalism. But Lenin does not give any indication that he would have regarded nationalism as an important contributing factor in the emergence of imperialism, or that in dealing with the political aspects of imperialism (which the censorship obliged him to exclude from his study) he would have done more than show them as consequences of the economic changes.

There are, however, some other differences between the Austro-Marxist and the Leninist conceptions of imperialism which Lenin himself mentions in later sections of his pamphlet. Most important, perhaps, is that while Hilferding and other Austro-Marxists were inclined to emphasize the extent to which finance capitalism and imperialism brought about a centralization, organization, and planning of the economic process which could be regarded as a positive step toward a socialist society, and as facilitating a more or less peaceful transition, Lenin describes the imperialist stage as being one of stagnation and decay, as the period of 'moribund capital-

[97] V. I. Lenin, *Imperialism, the Highest Stage of Capitalism* (1916).

[98] J. A. Hobson, *Imperialism: A Study* (1902).

[99] Although Lenin made critical references to some aspects of Hilferding's work, without entering into any detailed discussion.

ism', and so appears to formulate a version of the 'economic breakdown' theory of capitalism. Another feature of Lenin's study is the attention which he gives to the consequences of imperialism in producing a division in the working-class movement between a reformist (or 'opportunist') and a revolutionary tendency, the latter being held to correspond, in some sense, with the real and vital interests of the working class,[100] and therefore to be promoted by a consciously revolutionary party and revolutionary intellectuals. The Austro-Marxists, as I have indicated in discussing their studies of the development of social classes, attributed a greater significance to the complexity of social stratification in twentieth-century capitalist society, to the difficulties that stand in the way of forming a socialist consciousness among a majority of the population as a precondition for constructing a democratic socialist society, and to the need to preserve the unity of the working class movement as an essential basis for this advance toward a democratic conquest of power.

The most interesting discussion of the Austro-Marxist theory by a social scientist outside the Marxist tradition is to be found in the writings of Joseph Schumpeter. In his early essay on imperialism[101] Schumpeter gives credit to Bauer and Hilferding for having shown the connection between protectionism, the formation of cartels, and imperialism, and he concludes his exposition of their theory by saying: 'Thus we have here, within a social group [the entrepreneurs] that carries great political weight, a strong, undeniable, economic interest in such things as protective tariffs, cartels, monopoly prices, forced exports (dumping), an aggressive economic policy, an aggressive foreign policy generally, and war, including wars of expansion with a typically imperialist character.'[102] But at the same time he argues that there are counter-tendencies within capitalism, and that it is therefore '... a

---

[100] This idea of a 'real' revolutionary class consciousness was later provided with a philosophical justification by Lukács, in his essays in *History and Class Consciousness* (1923).

[101] J. A. Schumpeter, 'Zur Soziologie der Imperialismen' (1919. English trans. 1951). But see also the discussion in E. M. Winslow, *The Pattern of Imperialism* (1948), pp. 158–69.

[102] op. cit., p. 110.

basic fallacy to describe imperialism as a necessary phase of capitalism ...';[103] and he goes on to proffer an alternative explanation of modern imperialism as '... a heritage of the autocratic state, of its structural elements, organizational forms, interest alignments, and human attitudes, the outcome of precapitalist forces which the autocratic state has re-organized ...'.[104] Later, in *Capitalism, Socialism and Demo-cracy* (1942), he makes some more detailed criticisms of cer-tain aspects of the Austro-Marxist theory,[105] and in *Business Cycles* (1939) he refers briefly to Renner's concept of 'social imperialism' as being perhaps nearer the truth than his own original theory, thus intimating his acceptance of the idea of imperialism as the doctrine and practice of a whole people.

This conception would certainly be consonant with the Austro-Marxist emphasis upon nationalism as an element in the development of imperialism, though neither Renner nor any other thinker seems to have elaborated the notion fully. What is clear, however, is that while Hilferding and Bauer, in their early writings on the subject, were chiefly concerned with the imperialism of the period up to the First World War as an outcome of the development of capitalism, they would not have excluded the possibility of other forms of imperial-ism—even in modern times—arising from that kind of ex-treme nationalism which commits a whole people to expan-sionist policies, or from the directly political aims of the rulers of a state acting as an independent force, in the manner that Hilferding began to analyse in his later work. Thus the Austro-Marxist conception of imperialism, it seems to me—though in this case too it is necessary to recognize some diverg-ences between different thinkers—has as one of its great merits, from the vantage point of the late twentieth century, that it allows us to conceive of the coexistence of diverse forms of imperialism in a given period, and indicates the possible sources of these different forms.

---

[103] op. cit., p. 110.

[104] op. cit., p. 128. This view has some similarities with the analysis made by Veblen in *Imperial Germany* (1915).

[105] For example, that whereas the period of colonial expansion should coincide with the stage of mature capitalism, its heroic period was in fact that of early capitalism.

6. The Politics of Austro-Marxism

It was a distinguishing feature of the Austro-Marxist school, as I have made clear from the outset, that its members were all deeply engaged in party politics. Otto Bauer became the acknowledged leader of the S.D.P. in the period from the end of the First World War to 1934, Karl Renner was the principal representative of the more reformist tendencies in the S.D.P. and was on two occasions President of the Republic, Max Adler was active in the party conferences and in educational work, and Rudolf Hilferding became a leading figure in the German S.D.P., serving on two occasions as finance minister in social democratic governments. Austro-Marxism, therefore, can be said to have embodied, during three turbulent decades in European history, that unity of theory and practice which is often proclaimed but rarely attained; and its development provides the material for an exceptionally interesting case study of the relations and reciprocal influence between theoretical conceptions and practical policies.[106]

Some of the principal themes of Austro-Marxist thought have already been outlined, and in their application to political issues upon which the S.D.P. had to take a position they can be summarized in the following way (leaving aside the national question which ceased to have the same immediate importance after 1918): the role of the state; the class structure of capitalist society and the situation of the proletariat; and the nature of the transition from capitalism to socialism. The main political events of the period which affected the circumstances that the theory had to comprehend and elucidate, and which at the same time posed new problems for theoretical reflection, were the First World War, the Russian Revolution, and the rise of Fascism.

---

[106] In this introduction I can give only a brief sketch of some of the principal features. More comprehensive accounts will be found in the memoirs of participants, such as Renner's *An der Wende zweier Zeiten* (1946), in studies of individual members of the school, such as Jacques Hannak, *Karl Renner und seine Zeit* (1965) and Julius Braunthal, 'Otto Bauer: Ein Lebensbild' in *Otto Bauer: Eine Auswahl aus seinem Lebenswerk* (1961), and in more general studies of the socialist movement in Austria, among which the following are particularly useful: Charles A. Gulick, *Austria from Habsburg to Hitler* (1948), Norbert Leser, *Zwischen Reformismus und Bolschewismus* (1968), and the section on 'The Socialist Camp' by Adam Wandruszka in Heinrich Benedikt (ed.), *Geschichte der Republik Österreich* (1954).

'War and revolution,' Otto Bauer wrote, 'dissolved the Austro-Marxist school.'[107] But this is not entirely true. There was indeed a division among the Austro-Marxists in their attitudes to the war, especially in the period before the Russian autocracy was overthrown; and their political allegiances within the international socialist movement became diverse. Yet they remained in the same party after the war, and they all insisted (as Bauer goes on to remark in the article from which I have quoted) upon the overriding importance of the unity of the working-class movement, represented by a single party within which more reformist and more revolutionary tendencies could both find a place.[108]

It would be true to say in fact that all the Austro-Marxists wanted some kind of combination of reformist and revolutionary action. This outlook is revealed, from one aspect, by the efforts that they devoted to the introduction and extension of social policies which directly benefited the working class. In the period immediately following the First World War, when the balance of power between social classes in the country as a whole favoured the socialists, the S.D.P. introduced an array of measures dealing with hours of work, conditions of employment, works' councils, health, education, and housing which changed substantially the condition of the working class; and in Vienna, where the socialists were in power until 1933, their achievements in providing working-class housing, health and welfare services, and cultural facilities, and in introducing

---

[107] See below, p. 46.

[108] The terms 'reformist' and 'revolutionary' are bandied about in an extremely loose fashion, not only in political discourse, but very often also in what purports to be scientific social analysis. In the discussion in the text I shall attribute to these terms the following sense: 'reformist' describes a view in which an existing social system (in the present case, capitalism) is accepted, but various modifications or reforms in its organization and functioning are advocated; 'revolutionary' describes a view in which an existing social system is rejected and its replacement by a new, quite different system is advocated. This seems to me close to Marx's usage, since Marx meant by a social revolution precisely (and only) the transition from one type of social system to another. The matter is, of course, more complicated than this; for reformism may acquire the sense (by an extension of the original notion) of a policy directed toward bringing about a change from one system to another by means of an accumulation of reforms. But in this case the gap between reformist and revolutionary action narrows, since both aim at the same end. It is also necessary to insist, in order to avoid further confusions, that 'reformist' and 'revolutionary' are not to be equated with 'peaceful' and 'violent'. The question of the role of violence in social life requires a separate analysis, and is discussed below.

educational reforms, made the city a showplace of social democracy.[109] These reforming activities were obviously guided to a large extent by the Austro-Marxist view of the positive role of the state, and the possibility of using the existing state machinery to accomplish the transition to a socialist society; and their idea of the transition itself conformed with Otto Bauer's conception of the 'slow revolution', according to which the conquest of power by the working class had to be accompanied by a gradual, patient construction of socialist institutions. This outlook as a whole might be characterized as one of 'revolution through reform'. Clearly, it differed greatly from the Bolshevik idea of revolution, and from the model provided by the Russian Revolution. The Austro-Marxists were critical, from an early stage, of the course taken by the revolution in Russia, and they firmly opposed attempts to engage the Austrian working-class movement in revolutionary uprisings that aimed at establishing a 'dictatorship of the proletariat'. It was Otto Bauer who was chiefly preoccupied with the consequences of the Russian Revolution, not only in terms of the type of society that was being created in Russia, but also from the aspect of the division in the international working-class movement to which Bolshevik policies had given rise. Initially, he did not regard the revolution in Russia as a socialist revolution, and he did not consider that the Bolshevik dictatorship was capable of establishing a socialist society, but these views were somewhat modified in his later writings, especially in his analysis of the First Five Year Plan, which he thought might lead to an improvement of living standards so that 'the terroristic dictatorship would become unnecessary ... the Soviet regime could be democratized ... [and] state capitalism could be transformed into a socialist organization of society'.[110] Later still, after the rise of Fascism, and writing in exile, he saw the Soviet Union as constituting, despite the dictatorship and the absence of democracy, a basis for the development of

---

[109] There is an account of the immediate postwar developments in Bauer, *Die österreichische Revolution*, and a good general review of the social policies of the S.D.P. in Gulick, *Austria from Habsburg to Hitler*, vol. i, Chapters 10, 13–16, and 18.

[110] Otto Bauer, *Kapitalismus und Sozialismus nach dem Weltkrieg* (1931), p. 223 *et seq.*

socialism and a necessary support for the international working-class movement in its struggle against the most recent
forms of capitalist domination.[111]

Nevertheless, Bauer continued to insist—and others among
the Austro-Marxists did so even more strongly—that '. . . the
working class in the industrial countries of Europe and North
America would have to follow quite a different road to socialism'.[112] This road, as he conceived it, would be that of parliamentary democracy, by which means a more or less peaceful
transition to socialism could be accomplished with the declared support of a majority of the population. Bauer's conception, however, did not wholly exclude extra-parliamentary
means of struggle,[113] or the use of violence in particular circumstances. The S.D.P. had its own armed organization—the
Schutzbund—which had been created, and was led, by Julius
Deutsch; and the party leaders always took into account, in
considering their political strategy, the possibility of an armed
insurrection. This question was debated very thoroughly at
the Linz party conference in 1926, and the programme approved by the conference contained a section outlining the
conditions in which the working-class movement might be
obliged to resort to 'defensive violence' in order to protect
the civil, political, and social rights which it had gained by
democratic means under the republican regime.[114]

Between 1927 and 1934 the issue of violent class struggle in
Austria became steadily more acute, as the armed bands of the
Heimwehr and other organizations (which had been developing in an ultra-conservative direction since 1920) became increasingly active, and as the pressure upon Austria from the
German National Socialists on one side, and Mussolini on the
other, grew more intense. In this situation the Austro-Marxists and the leaders of the S.D.P. were not only divided be-

---

[111] Otto Bauer, *Zwischen zwei Weltkriegen?* (1936). See also the study of Bauer's
views by Melvin Croan, 'Prospects for the Soviet Dictatorship: Otto Bauer', in L.
Labedz, *Revisionism* (1962), pp. 281–96.

[112] Bauer, *Kapitalismus und Sozialismus nach dem Weltkrieg*, p. 223.

[113] Indeed, in *Die österreichische Revolution* he emphasized the important role of
'extra-parliamentary social organizations' in the political changes of the postwar
period.

[114] See Winkler, *Die österreichische Sozialdemokratie*, pp. 54–6.

tween more radical and less radical groups, but more important, all of them had to make very difficult political decisions—
in the light of Austria's internal and external circumstances,
and on the basis of a *shared* outlook which attached them firmly
to democracy and led them to recognize all the dangers of civil
war, from economic disorder and impoverishment, to foreign
occupation or the establishment of an authoritarian form of
socialism on the Russian pattern—about the precise conditions in which an armed uprising would be justifiable or unavoidable. These difficulties were rendered more acute by the
rapid expansion of Fascism in Europe after Hitler's seizure of
power, which increased the isolation and weakness of Austria,
and at the same time imposed upon the S.D.P. two different,
and partly antithetical, courses of action; one being to sustain
and defend by every possible means the existing democratic
system, and the other, to prepare in the last resort for a violent
resistance to Fascist violence.

In the end a civil war was forced upon the Austrian working
class in February 1934 by the actions of Dollfuss, who became
Chancellor in May 1932, and yielding finally to continued
pressure from Mussolini undertook to suppress the whole
Social Democratic movement. It was a civil war fought in the
most unfavourable conditions. The general strike which was
to inaugurate the armed resistance was a failure, largely as a
consequence of prolonged high unemployment and the reduced militancy of workers; the *Schutzbund* was disorganized,
and many of the Socialist leaders had already been arrested; a
considerable number of party members and leaders had hoped
until the last moment to avoid an armed struggle and entered
upon it, if at all, with the greatest reluctance. In Julius
Deutsch's words, the Austrian workers 'had been forced to
wage a revolutionary battle in a non-revolutionary situation'.[115]

There was much subsequent controversy about the causes
of this defeat, and about the whole doctrine of defensive
violence, and some of those who belonged to the left wing
opposition in the S.D.P. argued that an insurrection might
have been successful at an earlier time. Thus Ernst Fischer,

[115] See his pamphlet, 'Putsch oder Revolution?' (1934). See also, for a general
account of the events of that period, Gulick, op. cit., vol. ii.

who left the S.D.P. and joined the Communist Party after the 1934 defeat (and was later expelled from the Communist Party, in 1969, after a period of increasing disillusionment with Soviet society and Soviet policy from the time of the East European revolts of 1956 up to the military occupation of Czechoslovakia in 1968) wrote in his memoirs:

Had an armed insurrection taken place [in March 1933] it would almost certainly have brought about the overthrow of the Dollfuss Government. What would then have ensued was neither predictable at the time nor can it be retrospectively construed . . . None the less, we ought to have joined battle, as Otto Bauer himself was later to admit. A victory for the working class, even if only transitory, even in a country as small as Austria, would have encouraged and strengthened anti-Fascist forces throughout the whole of Europe.[116]

But as Fischer concedes there can be no definitive interpretation of the events and actions of that time, and the policies of the Austro-Marxists can equally well be seen as sensible and realistic in the prevailing circumstances, when Austria was largely at the mercy of the major European powers, assailed by Germany and Italy, and only weakly defended by Britain and France, whose leaders were already vacillating and ready to embark upon the road of appeasement.

On a longer view, in any case, the general orientation of socialist politics in Austria can be seen to have some measure of historical justification. Such progress as there has been toward socialism in the advanced capitalist societies has resulted from the attainment of political power by working-class parties through parliamentary majorities in a democratic system (aided of course by 'extra-parliamentary' forces, just as the maintenance and perpetuation of capitalism itself depends upon such 'extra-parliamentary' forces), and from a gradual transformation and extension of the activities of the state in economic regulation and planning, and in the provision of welfare services, rather than from any attempts to 'destroy' the bourgeois state. This slow and complex process of change arises from the class struggle, and it is animated principally by the working-class movement; but as the

[116] Ernst Fischer, *Erinnerungen und Reflexionen* (1969. English trans. 1974), pp. 215–16.

Austro-Marxists recognized, the conditions of class struggle have themselves been altered with the development of new middle strata, especially the 'service class', which have to be attracted to the socialist movement if a real social transformation is to be accomplished.

The Austro-Marxist conception of 'defensive violence', which had a particular significance in the political conditions that prevailed in Europe in the 1920s and 1930s, also has a wider bearing, for it defines in a clear and comprehensive way the attitude of a democratic socialist movement toward the use of force in bringing about a revolutionary transition to a new society. The Austrian socialists rightly emphasized the costs of civil war, in terms of the economic disorder and suffering that it would entail and the considerable risk of an authoritarian regime emerging from such a conflict; and they argued consistently in favour of peaceful change, brought about with the declared support of a majority of the population and on the basis of a social and economic structure which had already evolved toward socialism as a result of the developmental tendencies of modern capitalism itself and the cumulative effects of the reforms in institutions and policies achieved by the working-class movement. But at the same time they recognized that the class struggle could always erupt in violent forms, because of the extreme readiness of dominant groups and classes to resort to violence in defence of their privileges; and they also insisted, therefore, that the working class had to be prepared, in such conditions, to defend by force its own gains and its prospective attainment of socialism. The whole history of the twentieth century, from the revolutions of 1918 through the period of Fascism and the postwar national liberation struggles up to the most recent events—the war in Vietnam, the military coup in Chile—is one continuous illustration of this propensity of ruling groups to employ every kind of violence to maintain their domination. The Austro-Marxist analysis needs only to be supplemented now by a recognition (and they had indeed already warned against such possibilities) that those who rule the authoritarian socialist societies are prepared to use violence in exactly the same way to maintain the existing social system against the kind of liberation movements that have emerged in Eastern Europe since 1956.

In every respect the Austro-Marxists can be regarded as occupying a place precisely between Bolshevism and reformism. The scheme of thought that they developed was a theory of society, open to criticism and correction, not a dogmatic creed such as Bolshevism became. On the other hand, unlike the reformist labour parties in other capitalist societies, they *had* a social theory which informed and guided their political actions; they did not have to depend upon scraps of doctrine gathered from the most diverse sources and haphazardly utilized in each particular situation. Their practical achievements in Vienna were very great, and they might well have been extended successfully to the whole country if the S.D.P. had attained the majority in parliament that it was always seeking. In the theoretical sphere they made acute analyses of the problems of Austrian society, and undertook pioneering studies of the changing character of twentieth-century capitalist society; of the economic structure, the development of social classes, and the changes in law and the state. Their intellectual work and political activity together reveal the possibilities that are still to be found in Marxist social science as an instrument of human liberation and of the rational, humane ordering of social life.

I. General View of Austro-Marxism

OTTO BAUER, *What is Austro-Marxism?*[1]

For some time now 'Austro-Marxism' has been a favourite catchword of bourgeois discourse, referring to what is seen as a particularly malign variety of socialism. Nowadays, one can read in the bourgeois press the most varied and amusing opinions as to whether, at the Party Congress, Austro-Marxism was finally buried or whether it has won all along the line. Is it not about time to tell these gentlemen, who know nothing—absolutely nothing—about the nature and history of socialism, what Austro-Marxism really was and is?

We heard the word for the first time a few years before the war, from the mouth of an American socialist, L. Boudin,[2] and it was then quite rapidly diffused. A group of young Austrian comrades, active in scholarly research, were at that time labelled 'Austro-Marxists', the best known among them being Max Adler, Karl Renner, Rudolf Hilferding, Gustav Eckstein, Otto Bauer, and Friedrich Adler. They were united not so much by a specific political orientation as by the particular nature of their scholarly work. They had all grown up in a period when men such as Stammler, Windelband, and Rickert were attacking Marxism with philosophical arguments; hence they were obliged to engage in controversy with the representatives of modern philosophical trends. Whereas Marx and Engels began from Hegel, and the later Marxists from materialism, the more recent 'Austro-Marxists' had as their point of departure Kant and Mach. On the other side, in the universities these 'Austro-Marxists' had to come to terms with the so-called Austrian school of political economy, and this controversy too influenced the method and structure of their thought. Finally, living in the old Austria rent by national struggles, they all had to learn to apply the Marxist

[1] 'Was ist Austro-Marxismus?' *Arbeiter-Zeitung*, 3 November 1927, pp. 1–2. Published anonymously as a leading article. [Eds.]

[2] See the discussion of Boudin in the Introduction, p. 1 above. [Eds.]

conception of history to very complicated phenomena which defied analysis by any superficial or schematic application of the Marxist method. Thus there developed within Marxism a narrower intellectual community which has been called 'Austro-Marxism'. This name is intended precisely to distinguish its members on one side from the generation of Marxists represented above all by Kautsky, Mehring, and Cunow, and on the other side, from contemporary schools of Marxism in other countries, above all the Russian and the Dutch schools, which both developed under essentially different intellectual influences. These origins must be remembered in order to grasp the humorous side of all the attempts by some village ignoramus to annihilate Austro-Marxism.

It is true that war and revolution dissolved the 'Austro-Marxist' school. In the controversies during and after the war, those who had belonged to this school were in different and often opposed camps within the international socialist movement. Consequently the term 'Austro-Marxism' took on a different meaning. Our opponents acquired the habit of simply insulting the Austrian social democrats by calling them 'Austro-Marxists'. That was of course nonsense, the nonsense of the ignorant who confuse a political party with an intellectual orientation. It was precisely our opponents' witchhunt against 'Austro-Marxism' that made the term attractive to many of our comrades, with the result that some of the younger ones began to use the expression 'Austro-Marxism' to denote those theoretical orientations to the great postwar controversies which gradually developed in Austrian social democracy, and were summarized and expressed in the Linz programme.[3] Used in this sense, what is the specific meaning of 'Austro-Marxism'?

Austrian social democracy has succeeded in preserving its unity through all the storms of the postwar period, while the workers' parties in most other countries have split. We owe our success in this matter to certain advantageous circumstances. In particular, the powerlessness of Austria, the dependence of her economy on other nations, made it especially clear to Austrian workers in the stormy period of the revolution that any attempt to establish a dictatorship in this country

[3] Adopted at the Party Congress in Linz, 1926. [Eds.]

could only end in disaster. The terrible experience of Hungary has shown the Austrian workers what a catastrophe communism would have been for them too. Above all, the economic facts and the lessons of history immunized the Austrian working class against the communist attempts to divide their movement, and thus the intellectual legacy of our party has in fact made an essential contribution to resisting communism. Victor Adler, who in the 1880s brought the radicals and moderates together in *one* party, and for two decades, in the midst of the delirium of national struggles, understood how to hold the German and Czech, Polish and Ukrainian, Slovenian and Italian social democrats together in *one* united party, handed down to us the will—and even fanaticism—for unity, and the great art of keeping the most diverse sections of the working class together in a living unity. Thus, the unity of the working class was maintained. This unity now determines the specific intellectual position of our party within the International.

Otto Bauer formulated this outlook at the party conference: where the working class is divided, one workers' party embodies sober, day-to-day *Realpolitik*, while the other embodies the revolutionary will to attain the ultimate goal. Only where a split is avoided are sober *Realpolitik* and revolutionary enthusiasm united in *one* spirit. This synthesis, exemplified in the Linz programme, is what may be called, if one wishes, 'Austro-Marxism'. It is the product of unity. The only explanation of the particular intellectual position of our party, as compared with the social democratic parties of other countries, is that the Austrian workers have never allowed a split to occur. At the same time it is an intellectual force which maintains unity. For the fact that we can bring together the capacity for realistic adaptation of all our day-to-day struggles to the particular conditions of time and place, and a constant orientation of all partial struggles to the great goal of the seizure of power by the working class, and thereby to the great inspiring goal of socialism—this synthesis of the realistic sense of the workers' movement with the idealistic ardour for socialism—protects us from division. 'Austro-Marxism' today, as a product of unity and a force for the maintenance of unity, is nothing but the ideology of unity of the workers' movement!

Our opponents sense this instinctively, and it makes them very angry. How glad they would be if a split were to weaken the workers in our country too! The bourgeoisie would be very glad to subsidize the communists here! But the workers also feel that to maintain unity is the most important thing! In this respect the Linz conference has certainly not broken with Austro-Marxism. Coalition? Disarmament? In the end, these are tactical questions. The conference affirmed that the preconditions for both are lacking; but it did not prejudge the future, did not reject a re-examination of these questions if our opponents should create a new situation. But these are all particular tactical questions, questions of expediency, which can be answered according to the requirements of the prevailing situation. They do not go to the heart of the matter; they are irrelevant! It is more than a matter of tactics that we always formulate policies which bring together *all* sections of the working class; that we can only get *unity*, the highest good, by combining sober realism with revolutionary enthusiasm. This is not a tactical question, it is the principle of class struggle, the principle formulated at Linz, the principle of Austro-Marxism. Anyone who heard the stormy applause with which the whole conference placed the requirements of unity above all specific tactical demands, knows that the ideology of unity, the intellectual bond uniting us all, will remain unshakeable and unbreakable!

OTTO BAUER, *Max Adler: A Contribution to the History of Austro-Marxism*[4]

In the 1890s the disintegration of the old Austrian state was proceeding at an accelerated rate. The two historic parties of feudal clericalism and bourgeois liberalism, whose struggles had dominated the political life of Austria since the 1860s, were rapidly declining. They were displaced by the rise of the petty bourgeois Christian-Social movement on one side, and by intellectual nationalism on the other side. The rise of nationalism sharpened national struggles and thereby broke up the traditional state forms of the national states.

It was in this atmosphere of traditional state forms and

---

[4] From 'Max Adler: Ein Beitrag zur Geschichte des Austro-Marxismus', *Der Kampf* (N.S.), iv (August 1937), pp. 297–302. [Eds.]

party groupings that social democracy emerged. In the struggle against both the declining feudal and large-bourgeois parties, and the rising demagogy of the philistines, it represented the needs of the masses in industrial society, which was developing rapidly at that time in an Austria that was still petty bourgeois and agrarian. It attracted valuable forces from the university students. The young socialist intellectuals were greatly excited by the struggle between Marxism and revisionism, which dominated the intellectual life of all the socialist parties at the turn of the century.

At that time, therefore, there emerged from the socialist student movement in Vienna a new Marxist school whose most brilliant representatives at the end of the 1890s were Max Adler, Karl Renner, and Rudolf Hilferding. Somewhat later they were joined by Gustav Eckstein, Friedrich Adler, and Otto Bauer. In the academic field, having grown up in the midst of controversies about the new intellectual orientations in the universities during these years, these young Marxist scholars were closer to the current intellectual trends than was the older generation of Marxists: Kautsky, Mehring, Lafargue, and Plekhanov. The American Marxist, Boudin, was the first to call this new school of Viennese Marxists 'Austro-Marxism'. To be sure, war and revolution have broken up the intellectual community of the 'Austro-Marxist' school of that period; since 1914 and 1918 Renner and Hilferding have taken a different direction from Max Adler. In the original Austro-Marxist school Hilferding was the economist, Renner the theoretician of the state and law, and Max Adler its philosopher.

At that time Marxists everywhere were preoccupied with philosophical questions. Since the German bourgeoisie had capitulated before Bismarck's empire, the Hohenzollern authoritarian state, the Junkers, and the church; and German capitalism had bypassed free competition to develop directly in the form of cartels, state intervention, and organized capitalism, while its political parties had bypassed *laissez-faire* to go over to protectionism, authoritarian social policy, and imperialism; the bourgeois intelligentsia had given up militant liberalism along with militant materialism. The development of natural science had overcome the mechanistic materialism of the mid-nineteenth century. In the universities it was replaced partly by neo-Kantianism, partly by the empirio-criticism of Mach and Avenarius. As the mechanistic phase of development had been transcended, many thinkers held that the dialectical materialism on which Marx and Engels grounded their conception of science and society was also obsolete. The Marxist school was therefore obliged to take issue with the problems raised by contemporary academic philosophy. Plekhanov and Lenin defended materialism against its critics. Other Marxists sought to link the Marxist science of society partly with neo-Kantianism, partly with empirio-criticism. The development of Max Adler's philosophical work must be understood in terms of this historical situation.

It is of great interest today to compare the philosophical achievement of Max Adler with that of his most significant opponent in the field of the controversy between Marxism and philosophy—Lenin. In Russia, Marxism exercised an extremely strong attraction upon the bourgeois intelligentsia until the revolution of 1905. They were attracted by the Marxist recognition of the fact that Russia too would have to pass through the stage of industrial capitalism, that the development of a bourgeois industrial capitalist society was also a necessity for Russia, even though a transitory one. In Marxism they found a weapon against the ideologies of pre-industrial, pre-bourgeois Russian society; the weapon of bourgeois-industrial Westernism against the Slavophils and Narodniks.

Until 1905 the Russian bourgeois intelligentsia was also drawn to Marxism by its revolutionary character. As long as Russia still stood before its bourgeois revolution, and the bourgeois intelligentsia was still in revolutionary struggle against Tsarism, it still succumbed to the attraction of Marxism. But after the bourgeois intelligentsia saw the revolutionary proletariat stand threateningly before it in the bourgeois revolutions of 1905 and 1906, and after the revolution was suppressed, it turned away from Marxism. The critique of the philosophical foundations of Marxism furnished the bourgeois intelligentsia with a justification for deserting the ideology of the revolutionary proletariat. In the controversy between materialism and its opponents at that time, a complete separation took place between the ideologies of the revolutionary proletariat and the bourgeois intelligentsia which split from the proletariat and opposed the proletarian revolution (*Struve*). In this particular historical situation, Lenin's defence of materialism against the empirio-critics and neo-Kantians meant the revolutionary class separation between proletarian and petty bourgeois ideologies.

On German soil the philosophical discussion developed under quite different historical conditions. Here the separation between proletarian and bourgeois ideology did not need to be completed; it had taken place decades ago. The bourgeois intelligentsia had never been Marxist. In Germany the workers' movement developed quickly with the extremely rapid industrialization from the beginning of the 1890s; but once freed from the chains of the Anti-Socialist Law, developing in a non-revolutionary situation, and profiting from the prosperity of the second half of the 1890s by conducting successful struggles to raise wages and to extend social legislation, German social democracy gradually took on a reformist character.

The bourgeois intelligentsia believed that they could detach the working masses from all revolutionary objectives and reduce the workers' movement to the mere representation of the economic interests of the working class within capitalist society; win the workers as allies of bourgeois liberalism; and integrate them, as well as the liberal bourgeoisie, into an authoritarian state which would democratize itself peacefully. A highly sophisticated criticism of Marx developed from these aspirations. As the bourgeois intelligentsia no longer had to provide arguments for the suppression of the workers' movement by force, but aimed to win over the working class, to pacify the socialist movement, and eliminate its revolutionary character, it now scorned the old vulgar criticism of Marx. It recognized the historical achievement and scientific importance of Marxism, but at the same time of course it sought to detach socialism from its previous revolutionary ideology. The neo-Kantianism which was dominant in the universities provided it with arguments and methods. From Stammler through Rickert to Kelsen, there developed a criticism of

Marx which used Kantian epistemological arguments to dispute the possibility of a social science which would provide a causal account of the development of society. By this means, it was claimed, Marx's theory of the historical inevitability of social revolution was undermined, and socialism was reduced to an ethical postulate, a simple maxim for value-judgements and action within the existing social order.

This bourgeois criticism of Marx, at a new level of sophistication, gained a predominant influence on the theoretical revisionism within German social democracy which developed along with the reformist practice of the workers' movement. Conrad Schmidt, Staudinger, Eduard Bernstein, and Kurt Eisner adopted neo-Kantianism and sought to link the ethical justification of socialism through Kant's categorical imperative with Marx's scientific justification of class struggle.

Adler too accepted neo-Kantianism; he never had to cut the umbilical cord which tied his thought to the ideology of the bourgeois intelligentsia, and he was never able to recognize the social roots of Kant's philosophy in the bourgeois-individualist eighteenth century, and of neo-Kantianism in the bourgeoisie's rejection of the militant liberalism of its youth. But he accepted neo-Kantianism in a sense quite different from that of his socialist predecessors, without succumbing to the bourgeois criticism of Marx, overcoming the criticism of Marx by Stammler, Rickert, and Kelsen on its own battleground, that of Kantian or neo-Kantian epistemology. He accepted neo-Kantianism, not in order to link it eclectically with Marxism, as the revisionists did, but in order to defend the Marxist science of society against all revisionist dilution with the help of the Kantian critique of knowledge, and to distinguish it sharply from the ethical justification of socialism.

Editorial Introduction to the first issue of 'Der Kampf' [5]

[...] The task of our journal is to take part in these great struggles of a world experiencing the birth pangs of a new society, and to fashion weapons for the battle, so far as we

---

[5] From *Der Kampf*, i (1907–8), pp. 3–5. *Der Kampf* was founded, and initially edited, by Otto Bauer, Adolf Braun, and Karl Renner. The editorial statement was probably drafted by Otto Bauer. [Eds.]

are able, in the modest smithy of our thought. That is why we call it *Der Kampf*.

But we are only one detachment in the great fighting force of the proletariat. In no way do we wish to close our eyes to the whole; we do not want to deny ourselves the opportunity of debate with any member of the 'great general staff', but we fear that little time or space remains for the major problems of the whole proletariat. Fate has placed the Austrian corps of the International on a quite specific terrain, and has burdened it with tasks which are so singular, so intricate, and indeed so bizarre that we have our hands full dealing with our own problems. Moreover, the solution of our distinctive problems may become extremely significant, and even set a precedent, for the whole International. We are more likely to find ourselves in the position of asking advice from the General Staff of the International, than of giving it. We are obliged therefore (and this is what we wish) to restrict ourselves to our own problems, to the problems of Austria.

Every proletariat develops its own particular virtues as a result of the nature of its tasks. If the Germans, as the children of a nation of poets and thinkers, became masters of theory, the English pioneers of trade union organization, the Belgians outstanding in the co-operative movement, the French pathfinders of revolutionary and parliamentary tactics, and the Russians wonderful exemplars of a spirit of sacrifice and struggle (although the tendency of capitalism to produce more homogeneous conditions has brought about, in recent years, an exchange, generalization, and supplementation of these merits) so one particular role was reserved for the Austrians. Above all we had, and have, the difficult task of translating the idea of internationalism into living reality. We can only do this by means of struggle; it does not surprise us that no ready solution falls into our laps, we do not despair because we have to wrest from each other what will be, in the end, to everyone's advantage. As students of historical materialism, how could we expect it to be otherwise?

There is also a second task. Every other proletariat—even the Russian—confronted a well-defined typical form of the state. But in Austria we have to deal with a chaotic state, with state laws which do not die and state institutions that cannot live; with an association of states (Austria and Hungary) which can neither remain together nor break apart; with autonomous feudal domains which seek to disrupt nations; and with unorganized, legally non-existent nations which seek to disrupt the domains. A community of states, the state, feudal domains, nations—not one of them is fully born or finally dead. They are all mixed creations of birth and death, with which we must grapple openly, because our opponents are obsessed by them. Hence, everything remains perpetually in question: will this kingdom, the dual state of Austro-Hungary, survive, will the half of it on this side of the Leitha continue to exist or will the whole structure dissolve and the various pieces be absorbed by its neighbours? How should these portions be carved up among these neighbours? All the bourgeois parties which we are fighting exist on the basis of one or other of these partial issues, and consequently we must take up a position on them. This quandary obliges us to enter into rather tedious constitutional and administrative questions, and forces us into juridical casuistries and petty tactical artifices. It makes us, against our will and inclination perhaps, the constitutional experts of the International.

A motley diversity of economic and cultural stages of development corresponds, partly as cause, partly as effect, with this multiplicity of nations and state institutions. In spite of regional differences, every great Western nation comprises people who think and act in similar ways. But our case is different. German Bohemia is at the level of economic development of Saxony; Upper Austria is at the level of old Bavaria; by contrast, East Galicia has agrarian relations like those in the land of the Wallachian boyars or in many areas of Russia, while the coastal region, with its tenant farmers (*Kolonat* and *Kontodinat*) is reminiscent of Italy. In the Austro-Hungarian monarchy there are examples of all the economic forms to be found in Europe, including Turkey. It is only natural that the state administration, particularly municipal administration which is the most closely connected with economic development, in spite of the similarity of legal structure, should vary widely from one region to another. The light of socialist propaganda now shines everywhere in the midst of these divergent economic and political conditions. This creates a picture of extreme diversity. There are social democrats as a result of the maturity of capitalist development, as in Bohemia, or in consequence of its backwardness, as in East Galicia. What exists in the International as a chronological development—the socialism of artisans, journeymen, workers in manufacture, factory workers, and agricultural workers, which undergoes alterations, with the political, the social, or the intellectual aspect of the movement predominating at any given moment—takes place contemporaneously in Austria. This economic and political profusion of the Austrian movement has not yet been fully expressed, because the political struggle for the right to vote absorbed all our energies. In the future it may confuse us, or if clearly grasped, it may spur us on, both intellectually and politically, and make possible a remarkable advance. If we want to profit from this diversity, we must first of all study it and master it theoretically.

It will be seen that we have so many problems in our country that we are concerned about the possibility of being able to master all of them. It is not enough simply to adopt received formulae from the outside. We bring to this work only a method, certainly not any preconceived conclusions. We must first investigate in detail how national life and national struggles arise on the basis of economic facts; how law and the organization of the state can dominate these problems; how such great cultural differences in the proletariat can be integrated and co-ordinated in the party, in its programme and policies. We cannot impart our conclusions to the movement, but only learn from it and give to what exists and what is becoming, the accessible form of language, of conceptual expression. Being determines our consciousness, but it only determines it clearly and precisely when the new content of consciousness has become a concept, a word, or indeed a slogan.

The knowledge we acquire should enter immediately into the service of the movement, just as it was born from the movement. That is why representatives of all three branches of the organization should participate in *Der Kampf*. The political party which intervenes decisively in our politics, our trade union movement which has become the great economic power in production, our co-operative movement which unites the proletariat as consumers and thereby prepares itself to organize economic consumption; in short, all three elements of our movement, all three battalions of our fighting corps, need a comprehensive scientific organ. As the Stuttgart Congress [1905] recognized with acclamation, there does not exist in any other country such a close and intimate collaboration between the trade union, co-operative, and political movements as in Austria, in spite of the economic and cultural differentiation of the country that we have emphasized.

This unity of the movement should find a means of expression in a journal which brings together, for an exchange of experiences and mutual improvement, all the intellectual forces that are at work in these three fields of activity. The workers' education movement, the libraries of the workers' associations, the artistic aspirations of the proletariat, and its cultural endeavours as a whole should be critically and sympathetically discussed in this journal. *Der Kampf* should thus provide a mirror image of the economic and political aspirations of the whole Austrian proletariat, and of the cultural life of the German-speaking Austrian workers in particular.

It should be worthy of taking its place alongside the journals of other nations and countries, and show its comrades in arms that this detachment of the great army of the International understands and is carrying out its specific tasks at the same time as it faithfully fulfils its general obligations. It should make known to its brethren abroad that we, like them, are fighting on courageously, that we are determined to live and struggle until class domination is abolished along with ruling classes, in our own country and throughout the world, and peace reigns between the peoples, between man and man. All of us, however many different tongues we speak, fight together for the 'complete restoration of man', and we shall be reborn in the universal humanity which knows struggle and domination only with respect to nature, while among individuals and peoples there are only equal rights, and equal shares in the riches of the spirit and the joys of the earth.

II. The Theory and Method of Marxism

MAX ADLER, *The Sociological Meaning of Karl Marx's Thought*[1]

It was, therefore, the concept of society which prepared the way for that new attitude of scientific thought according to which human processes can be conceived in the same manner as natural processes. What still presented an obstacle was the fact that the specific interrelation of men in the unity of society posed a problem for the thinkers of the seventeenth and eighteenth centuries, though initially only as a question about the true, rational organization of the state, and hence in an individualistic formulation concerning the significance and purpose of the state for the individual. In this way, precisely what needed to be elucidated by conceptual analysis—society itself, this enigmatic association of men in a unity—was overlooked. For whether this unity was deduced from a divine command, from man's rational interests, or from an innate social impulse, the emphasis was always on the individual rather than on society. The individual simply associated with others, united himself with them, while the fact of this solidarity and unity, their nature and ground, remained unproblematic. Even at the pinnacle of thought, in classical German philosophy, where this unity for the first time sought conceptual expression and where such great and enduring insights into the question were acquired—so that this philosophy could be described as the doctrine of the social character of the human mind—it had still only found a formulation which obscured this character instead of allowing it to emerge clearly. Hence, in Kant it took the form of the mind establishing universal laws, in Fichte and Hegel of a process of the development of reason characteristic of the species; but in the first case it leads to what seems to be a purely

[1] From *Der soziologische Sinn der Lehre von Karl Marx*, pp. 11–18. [Eds.]

individualistic critique of knowledge, and in the second case to a mysterious universal metaphysics.

The remarkable and fundamental reorientation of thought which is concerned to discover the basis of men's social solidarity only reaches its conclusion with Feuerbach. He showed that the realm of ideas, above all that of religious ideas, is only a product of a universal psychological lawfulness of human mental life, the core of which he discovered in the species being of man. The highest being, whose emanations the religious man distinguished from himself, in awe and wonder, as the work of a deity, the thinking man as the rule of world reason, proved to be nothing but the essence of man himself, which could manifest its own character, going beyond the individual, only in this way, through a natural process. For 'the essence of man exists only in the community, in the unity of man with man ... the community of man with man is the first principle and criterion of truth and universality'.[2] 'That is why the new philosophy has as its principle of knowledge, its subject, not the Ego, the absolute, i.e. abstract, mind, in short not Reason for itself alone, but the real and whole being of man.' It 'makes man, including Nature as the basis of man, the sole, universal, and highest object of philosophy, and hence anthropology, including physiology, the universal science'.[3]

The enormous impact that Feuerbach's philosophy, with this real principle of the essence of man, had upon the whole thought of an age which was still under the spell of Hegelian speculation is well known. It can only be explained by the fact that it was perceived as an expression of reality, as a clear reference to a long-suspected truth. The young Marx also felt the liberating effect of this intellectual achievement, and provides such an eloquent testimony of this in his early writings that he has generally been regarded as being entirely under Feuerbach's influence during this period. But this is an error. Fundamentally, Marx was never a Feuerbachian, but from the outset felt the tremendous impetus he certainly received from Feuerbach only as a force propelling him along what was entirely his own path. Of course, at first his development

---

[2] Feuerbach, *Grundsätze der Philosophie*, paras. 59 and 41.
[3] Ibid., paras. 50 and 54.

appears to run in the direction of Feuerbachian thought, but it shows from the very beginning that characteristic critical attitude, which enabled him to transform the concept of human essence, which was still vague in Feuerbach, into a more precise new concept of human society. If this were not so then Marx would not have been capable of going beyond Feuerbach with such a clear understanding as he showed already in 1845 in the famous theses on Feuerbach. Here the new revolutionary idea of the socialization of man, as contrasted with the notion of the essence of a species being, is already clearly expressed, and the imperfections of Feuerbach's solution of the problem are demonstrated. 'The essence of man,' Marx argues against Feuerbach, 'is not an abstraction inherent in each particular individual. The real nature of man is the totality of social relations. Feuerbach, who does not enter upon a criticism of this real nature, is therefore obliged ... to conceive the nature of man only in terms of a "genus", as an inner and mute universal quality which unites the many individuals in a purely natural (biological) way.'[4] It is a matter of recognizing that this species being is not simply an affectual fact of nature, but is a mutual involvement and interrelationship of men continually created by themselves through their activity and the manner in which they work with each other and upon each other. The concept of human society is elaborated and defined here as the idea of an ultimate understanding of the necessary solidarity of man in a labour process in which the work of every individual is not only directed to every other man, but is inconceivable without them. That is the meaning of Marx's further thesis: 'All social life is essentially practical. All the mysteries which lead theory toward mysticism find their rational solution in human practice and in the comprehension of this practice.' This expresses clearly the difference between Marx's standpoint and Feuerbach's solution of the problem. In Feuerbach the basic concept is still man, but in Marx it is society. There is substituted for the essence of man the idea which Marx himself refers to as a new standpoint, that of 'human society or *socialized humanity*'.

It is very important to retain this fundamentally original

[4] *Theses on Feuerbach* (1845), thesis vi.

concept of socialized man, with the help of which, since Marx, the concept of society and of social life has emerged from the indeterminacy of a purely social nature of man and from speculation about its origins. The concept of sociation [*Vergesellschaftung*] expresses the character of human society in a way far removed from the intellectualism of a mere idea, or the crudeness of an animal drive; from the naïvety of a social contract, or the brutality of a coercive unification. Instead, it formulates a profound reality: the social character of human powers in the particular sense that they do not merely become social through their coexistence and interaction, but are from the beginning, in the individual activity of every single person, only modes of functioning of the species. For this reason, a true social standpoint is only attained, and the nature of man is only properly grasped, when, as Marx once put it, the real individual man 'as an individual man in his everyday life, in his work, and in his relationships, has become a *social being*, and when he has recognized and organized his *forces propres* as *social* powers . . .'.[5]

This perception enables us to investigate the causal regularities of social life by research into the particular nature and relations of causality of social forces. Hence it is Marx's concept of sociation with its more precise content which makes it possible, for the first time, to overcome the division between nature and society which has been developed in modern thought, and to bring them together in a single scientific conceptual scheme. Nature and society now comprise the causal regularity of events as a whole; the former, the purely physical events in and around men, the latter the purely mental events in and through men. In this way, everything physical, even if it concerns man as a species, is seen as purely natural, and everything mental, even though it only concerns the individual, is always perceived as social. Thus, for the first time, with Marx, a social scientific standpoint becomes possible which is logically on the same footing as natural science and extends the realm of science to twice its previous area.

But in order to understand fully the significance of the social scientific mode of thought newly created by Marx, which introduced in the middle of the century of the natural sciences

[5] *On the Jewish Question* (1844).

the even more hopeful era of the social sciences, it is necessary to evaluate a further element in this intellectual achievement. Another idea, which was first magnificently stated in Hegel's philosophy, becomes allied with the new conception of social life as the sociation of the individual; namely, the idea of *development*. With this notion, history, which had seemed previously to defy all scientific comprehension, entered for the first time into the centre of social scientific study. It was transformed from a mere chronicle of the past, or in the most favourable case, from a moral, political, or philosophical study, into an investigation of the causal interconnection of all social events.

Admittedly, in Hegel this conception is still concealed in a metaphysical disguise. The unity of man in society, this previously delineated peculiar intellectual sociation of men, still appears to him in the metaphysical form of their incorporation in an absolute spirit which bears the world within itself. Inside men's heads there operates a world reason which demonstrates its transcendence of every individual thought and plan by continually driving beyond all individual goals. Since every particular human activity in its encounter with other activities always produces consequences which could not be foreseen in any way, situations arise continually from the whole process of human action which are bound to lead on to new thought, plans, and actions, because their consequences are either favourable and can be used to advantage, or unfavourable and need to be averted. In this way, history becomes a process of intellectual creation, an uninterrupted movement which also necessarily leads to higher forms. For it really is the mind which is at work here and is obliged by what it perceives as contradictory to overcome the contradiction in a manner more conformable to reason, and consequently to progress to more perfect kinds of being. Thus one stage of development supersedes another by virtue of its greater reason: it cannot allow anything to exist which loses its reason, for although everything real is rational, it remains real only so long as it is rational.

The magnificent pioneering character of Hegel's philosophy of history does not reside only in the theory of absolute spirit which made so deep an impression upon his contemporaries and is today enjoying a remarkable renaissance, but in its conception of history as we have just encountered it. Here is the connecting link from which thought which was no longer metaphysically oriented, but was directed with the same passionate concern as Hegel toward the law-governed regularities of the cultural world, could proceed directly to a scientific mode of thought. This advance is indissolubly associated with the name of Karl Marx.

Hegel's conception of history already displays all the elements of a purely scientific understanding, in which history is conceived as a law-governed continuity no longer shaped by powers working outside or above it, but only by its own forces. In Hegel these are the forces of the absolute spirit, and they operate in a characteristic law-governed way which he calls the dialectic, according to which the development of spirit occurs through the unfolding and overcoming of its contradictions. Thus, history is conceived not only as causal connection, but at the same time as teleology, as goal-directedness, which is immanently accomplished through this causality. The meaning of history is no longer something laid down externally—by divine dispensation, for example—but is revealed as the causal product of the rational nature of the forces which achieve their development in history. In Hegel, therefore, history becomes a process, the knowledge of which no longer merely satisfies the needs of curiosity, an antiquarian interest, or a pragmatic attitude, but reveals theoretically for the first time humanity's mode of existence. Moreover, when this conception of history is transferred from is speculative Hegelian form into Marx's purely theoretical conceptual scheme, it becomes clear that history, not of course in its previously customary form of a collection of the biographies of rulers, the actions of states, or accounts of wars and revolutions, but as knowledge of the law-governed interconnection in the change and continuation of all the crowded images of the past, is bound to become the natural science of social being and events.

MAX ADLER, *The Relation of Marxism to Classical German Philosophy*[6]

In order to make clear at once the sense in which I refer here to a relation between Marxism and classical German philo-

[6] From *Kant und der Marxismus* (1925), pp. 135–90. [Eds.]

sophy, especially Kant, and to exclude, from the outset, any crude misunderstandings, it is necessary to emphasize very strongly the following point: I am not concerned in any way with a historical connection between the two systems of thought. I have already emphasized that a direct influence of Kant or Fichte on Marx and Engels is completely excluded. The fashionable theme, 'Kant and Marx', or even 'Fichte and Marx', is fundamentally quite different from that of 'Hegel and Marx', although this has not always been recognized. In the case of Kant or Fichte it is only a matter of showing logical or methodological agreements between them and Marx, not any historical influences. In short, the relation of Marxism to classical German philosophy, in so far as it is not mediated through Hegel—and even the meaning of this relation itself, which has necessarily come into consciousness—is to be found in the history of ideas, not in the history of the period. In this sense, there is a relation even where somebody was not at all aware of the ideas of Marx and Engels, and equally unaware of the ideas of his many disciples, the Marxists of earlier and more recent times. It is not a question, therefore, of which earlier ideas were consciously absorbed into Marxism from classical German philosophy, but which conceptual motifs of idealist philosophy actually persist in it, however much they may have assumed a materialist garb.

It follows that relating Marxism to Kant has nothing at all to do with the fashionable desire to 'supplement' Marx by Kant and, as it were, to provide a philosophical justification of socialism. Certainly Hermann Cohen, the inspirer of the Kantian revival, pointed out quite rightly that Kant's ethic represents a philosophical expression of the human aims of socialism. In fact the categorical imperative is the idea of a universal legislation by the will, in which there can be no more oppression of any willing subject. The requirement that no man should be regarded merely as a means, but that every man should be treated at the same time as an end, is an idea which excludes all exploitation. The idea of a realm of ends which makes all social unreason and oppression impossible, as inexpedient, is the idea of *solidaristic society* which no longer permits class conflict. These notions have also to be related to Kant's insistence upon regarding the idea of a perfected state of society not as an imaginary utopia, but as a moral task which must be tirelessly pursued, and which can be realized in historical development. Taking these ideas together, we can understand how Cohen could arrive at the claim that 'socialism is based upon ethical idealism', and that 'Kant is the real and authentic originator of German socialism'. In agreement with Cohen, a large number of thinkers—I will mention here only Stammler, Natorp, Staudinger, and Vorländer—have found the connection between Marx and Kant, between socialism and critical idealism, to lie in the fact that socialism is supplemented by the ethical justification of its goals provided by Kant's practical philosophy.

But this kind of relation must be decisively rejected from the standpoint of Marxism. Marxism is a system of sociological knowledge; it grounds socialism upon causal knowledge of the events of social life. Marxism and sociology are one and the same thing; that is to say, Marxism does not aim to be anything but the science of the laws of social life and its causal development. Consequently, it aims to deduce the development of socialism from capitalism as a matter of causal necessity. According to the Marxist conception socialism does not come about because it is ethically justified, but because it is causally produced. As we shall see later, it is in no way incidental, and for Marxists also no accident, that this causal product of social life is at the same time ethically justified. But this coincidence of the causal necessity of development with the ethical justification is a sociological problem which, within the Marxist scheme of thought, is only to be solved in causal terms. I shall show that this solution lies in the conception of socialized man, who is finally driven by formal-teleological causality to realize what he considers to be morally justified. The class struggle is the historical form in which this solution is achieved. I shall return to this point later.

The connection between Kant and Marx, to formulate our problem in a convenient and graphic way, does not lie in the fact that Kant was perhaps a socialist, if only a Utopian socialist. He was still quite remote from socialism, if socialism is understood as a matter of conscious and planned transformation of the economic system by the abolition of private property in the means of production, and the socialization of production. In this sense, Kant cannot even be called an ethical socialist, since the problem of the economic organization of society did not exist at all for him. The connection to which I refer lies at quite a different level. It is not a matter of linking the ethics of Kant and Fichte, and similarly Hegel's dialectic, with the economic and sociological theories of Marx and Engels, nor of forcing these thinkers' individual theories into a relationship with Marxist ideas, but of demonstrating an inner intellectual kinship in the method of working out the common basic problem, that is, the relation of man to his environment. It is here that the great alliance between Marxism and critical idealism is to be found. In this sense there is a straight line from Kant and Fichte via Hegel and Feuerbach to Marx and Engels. The latter appear as the true divine heirs in the pantheon of German thought ...

In fact, just as the critical philosophy starts, and must start, from individual consciousness but demonstrates in this consciousness a supra-individual, transcendental-social, *a priori* socialized character; so Marxism starts from man, a fact which has not yet received enough attention. However, it does not start from man as he conceives himself, as individual man, but from socialized man. More precisely considered, the central concept of Marxist sociology is not society but socialized man. Only in this way can an empirical-historical theory discover the epistemological fact that the basis of all sociation can only be found in individual consciousness. Consequently, the starting point for Marx is not society which in itself is an empty abstraction, if not a metaphysical supposition, and remains metaphysical even if it is given the modern name of universalism. For Marx society is not something which emerges from interaction between men, nor is it above men, nor has it come into existence through any sympathetic impulses or as a result of selection in the struggle for existence. Nor was it established by a 'contract'. It is simply there, that is to say, posited with the relation of man to man. As soon as man appears society is there, because man is empirically possible only among men. Similarly, the socialization of consciousness is simply given with the individual consciousness.

This is what Marx means in the classical passage where he briefly formulates his basic view:

In the social production which men carry on they enter into definite relations that are indispensable and independent of their will; these relations of production correspond to a definite stage of development of their material powers of production. The totality of these relations of production constitutes the economic structure of society. . . .[7]

Here, therefore, the social union is posited with men, and independent of their will; it constitutes the mode of their existence. In another passage there is a similar formulation:

In order to produce [men] enter into definite relations and conditions, and their influence upon nature, their production occurs only within these social relations and conditions.[8]

Here, too, there is no isolated man; not merely in the sense that men can only develop in society, but also in the stronger sense that from the Marxist standpoint man is not only impossible, but inconceivable, outside society. Robinson Crusoe is an epistemological absurdity just as he is a sociological absurdity. Marx himself expressed this very clearly:

Individuals producing in society—hence socially determined individual production—is, of course, the starting point. Man is in the most literal sense a *zoon politikon*, not merely a social animal, but an animal which can develop as an individual only in society. Production by an isolated individual outside society—a rare occurrence which may happen when a civilized person in whom the social forces are already dynamically present is cast by accident into the wilderness—is just as great an absurdity as is the development of language without individuals living and speaking together. There is no point in discussing this further.[9]

This is precisely a formulation of the transcendental relation, as I showed earlier, but expressed in empirical terms. It appears even more clearly in another passage from Marx, where he observes with regard to the nature of the value of commodities:

In a certain sense, the same holds good for man as for commodities. Since he does not come into the world either with a mirror or as a Fichtean philosopher who can assert 'I am I', he mirrors himself

[7] Preface to *A Contribution to the Critique of Political Economy* (1859).
[8] *Wage Labour and Capital* (1849), Section iii.
[9] *Grundrisse* (1857–8), Introduction.

at first in other men. Only through his relation to the man Paul as his equal does the man Peter relate to himself as a man. In this way Paul, as a being of flesh and blood, in his Pauline corporeality, is valid for him as the phenomenal form of the genus man.[10]

Thus socialized man is actually the real centre of Marxist theory, and Marx constructs social life only as a process of the activity of socialized man. The materialist conception of history is nothing without these ideas which are inherent in all its conceptions of man as active in the forms of socialization. The 'economic conditions' are really nothing but social conditions; that is, human conditions in which men produce, exchange, and consume. The productive forces, the development of which, according to the materialist conception of history, conditions the whole development of social life, are again not factual, mindless powers, but the forces of nature which men place in the service of their own goals, their social production. It is only by this means that the forces of nature (land and soil) become elements of human labour and acquire an economic character, becoming economic factors or forces. In general, therefore, the materialist conception of history is concerned simply with the activities of the human mind by which it establishes and develops the conditions of life through social labour. It is a formulation of the fundamental determinants of socialized human activity considered from its economic aspect. Thus it is not the case, as so many of its opponents think, that according to the materialist conception of history, man is sacrificed to alien and dominant economic laws, which confront him, as it were, with cold inevitability. Instead, man is sacrificed only as long as he has not understood these laws. For the true nature of this law-governed process is not its passivity at all, but its activity, which Marx called revolutionary praxis. . . .

Classical German philosophy was certainly not socialism, any more than Marxist socialism is critical idealism. But if the philosophical foundation of socialism is seen to lie in anti-individualism, that is to say, in the view that man in general cannot be conceived as an isolated being, then the correct name for German classical philosophy is the philosophy of

---

[10] *Capital* (1867), vol. i, Chapter i.

socialism. We must eventually get used to understanding it in this way, or we shall not have understood it at all. Marxism is still not part of this philosophy, but remains what it is; namely, sociology, the science of society and its development. It then becomes clear that the admirable critique of knowledge contained in the Kantian theory, was carried out not only for natural science, but also for social science, and that Marx stands in the same relation to Kant as does Newton. Critical philosophy is no more a completion of natural science and technology than it is of Marxism and socialism. But just as natural science gains from the critique of knowledge an increasing clarity about its methods, and above all a greater confidence in its findings, so too does Marxism, in which the materialist conception of history and the theory of social progress derive their meaning and their certainty from the concept of socialized man, or as we now understand, of socialized consciousness.

Furthermore, this relation of Marx to Kant goes beyond that of Newton to Kant. For in physical nature, a connection is established in which men are not co-determining partners, whereas the laws of social nature are only realized through the agency of men. There man suffers his fate, here he shapes it. A social science serves not just to explain but to transform Nature. By its logical character natural science is stationary, but social science, by its character, is revolutionary. That is the profound, little-understood meaning of the inner connection between Marxist theory and the socialist movement, between sociology and social revolution. At the same time this provides a connection with classical German philosophy which, likewise, as a philosophy of social consciousness, can only be revolutionary. German classical philosophy always aspired to be a philosophy of action. But it could only achieve this in idea; Marxism gave it the scientific knowledge that allowed it to realize this action historically. If the idealism of Kant and his followers was the philosophy of the conceptual possibility of socialism, the scientific socialism of Marx becomes the theory of the actual reality of idealism.

MAX ADLER, *A Critique of Othmar Spann's Sociology*[11]

... [Sombart][12] spoke in a somewhat sceptical tone about a sociology which is not very closely connected with any particular field of research; for example, with economics, law, art, and so on. I cannot share this scepticism, and it is not my view that there cannot be, in sociology, any universally valid theoretical statements. It is an unsatisfactory feature of sociology, which still discredits it in the eyes of many scholars, that the subject can be regarded as no more than the adoption of a particular attitude to social phenomena; so that there must be as many different sociologies as there are conceivable points of view. That is, however, a completely inadequate standpoint. As Sombart's first guiding principle rightly stresses, precisely because sociology is a wholly empirical science, it can and must be pursued in just as rigorously objective a manner as any other intellectual discipline that claims to be a science. It is then necessary to look more closely at its real object, which is not provided only by the particular empirical spheres of social life, but is already constituted by the fact of social association. It follows that the object of sociology is to investigate the nature, forms, and changes of social association. This science, as general sociology, is the foundation of the sociological treatment of the particular spheres of experience to which Sombart referred. This general sociology can be a completely rigorous objective science, though only if its basic concepts and method are correctly defined. There is still no other means except epistemology to emerge from the much lamented chaos of the very diverse opinions and ideas which everyone has of sociology. Only in this way will it be possible to overcome the scandalous situation that sociologists continually use the same words—for example, experience, law,

[11] 'Zur Kritik der Soziologie Othmar Spanns', *Der Kampf*, xx (1927), pp. 265–70. This paper was contributed to the Fifth German Sociological Conference, held in Vienna in 1926, and was originally published in the proceedings of the Conference. The opening and concluding paragraphs have been omitted in this translation. Othmar Spann (1878–1950) taught at the University of Vienna from 1919 to 1938 and expounded a theory of society as an organic unity, a *Gemeinschaft*, based upon eternal norms. Catholic in inspiration, his views had some affinity with the idea of the 'corporate state' and attracted attention with the rise of Fascism in Europe. [Eds.]

[12] Werner Sombart (1863–1941), economic historian and sociologist, is best known for his studies of modern capitalism, especially his major work *Der moderne Kapitalismus* (rev. ed. 1927). [Eds.]

causality—in entirely different senses, without any attempt to arrive at an agreement about the meaning of these terms. Only epistemology can provide a clear agreement of this kind.

Hence I subscribe to both of Sombart's theses: first, that sociology is an empirical science, and second, that it is a cultural, i.e. an interpretative, science. The epistemological problem emerges already at this point, for it is not immediately self-evident what experience means in the sociological field. Here, experience is something different from the experience of nature, for otherwise sociology would not be a specific kind of science compared with natural science. The expression 'cultural science' also needs to be grounded upon an epistemological analysis, as is indicated by Sombart's use of a further explanatory term, 'interpretative' science. For 'interpretation' is usually understood in the sense given to it by Max Weber, who was in fact the originator of this term and is generally regarded as the founder of this whole trend in sociology. I may perhaps point out that Weber's concept of interpretation is still predominantly psychological, and that many years ago in my book *Causality and Teleology* (1904), and frequently since that time, I referred to the fact that all 'understanding' in the psychological sense already presupposes a definite constitution of the individual consciousness, in which the immanent interrelatedness of self-consciousness depends on the consciousness of others; so that social association is already transcendentally given as a category of knowledge of consciousness. All understanding rests on this transcendental social character of consciousness, as I have termed it. If sociology is to be called an interpretative science, but is not to be absorbed into social psychology, then this 'understanding' must be epistemologically conceived and developed.

After these very sketchy preliminary remarks let me now consider Professor Spann's arguments. He began with a vigorous rejection of a naturalistic-mechanistic conception of social science. On this point I completely agree with him, and although I am an adherent of the Marxism which Professor Spann deplores I have combated naturalism since my earliest writings, not, as we shall see, from a purely metaphysical position like Professor Spann, but from an epistemological one. Even if Professor Spann does not like to rely on me as an ally in his refutation of a natural-scientific sociology I am surprised that he gives up the advantage of a much more powerful support for his rejection of naturalism, namely the social-theoretical standpoint of Marx and Engels. Of course, it would then be necessary not to identify their ideas with naturalism and social atomism, out of sheer ignorance, as Spann usually does. In short, one should first grasp the ideas before disparaging them. And if one sees in classical German philosophy, as I do, the fundamental development which made social science possible, but does not regard the German spirit which produced this as coming to an end with Bader—after which there is nothing more until Professor Spann's doctrine of categories—and instead, sees in Hegel's great pupil, Marx, the vigorous continuation of this German spirit, then one will attain a different conception of Marxism. Only in this way is it possible to ensure that sociology will continue to develop as an empirical science, as the critical philosophy was concerned to assure, and not in a metaphysical direction, as happens with Spann.

Before I go on to discuss, very briefly, this metaphysical aspect I must refer to another point which marks a fundamental difference from Spann's standpoint. He is as right to reject naturalism in social science as he is wrong to reject the causal character of sociology. The fact that social science cannot be tackled by natural science methods does not mean that it does not also have rigorous causal connections as its object. The lamentable ambiguity concerning basic concepts, which I mentioned at the beginning of my paper already begins here. One should establish an agreement about the notion of science, and as Kant already insisted, only speak of science in the strict sense where causal knowledge is possible. Of course, a normative scheme can also be called science; but it is then clear that the point of departure is a quite different logical structure and it cannot be maintained that this system is the only possible science until it has been shown that a causal scheme is unrealizable. Marxism proved to be so epoch-making for sociology precisely because, while it rejected the natural-scientific view of social phenomena, and substituted for it a historical conception, it did not bring into question the methodological foundation of all empirical science, causality. According to

Marxism, sociology is an empirical science, not a normative discipline or a teleological doctrine.

Professor Spann's rejection of causality rests on a specific, completely unfounded simplification of causality, as emerges clearly from his exposition today, which he himself described as programmatic. In general, he equates causality with mechanism. But this is a mistake even from the standpoint of natural science, and however much I oppose naturalism in social science I must come to its defence in this case. The view that all natural causality is simply mechanical causality belongs to those conceptions of a primitive materialism which are contradicted by natural science itself. Even in the sphere of physics, optical, magnetic, and electrical phenomena can no longer be explained merely by mechanical causes, and in chemistry and biology this is quite impossible. That is why one of the most famous representatives of sociological thought, Auguste Comte, whom Professor Spann would surely count among the naturalists, constructed a hierarchy of the sciences, in which the individual sciences are subordinated to one another—for example, chemistry to physics, physiology to chemistry, and sociology ultimately to chemistry—but cannot be deduced from one another. The basis of this idea is the correct conception, which is of decisive significance for the methodology of social science, that in the whole realm of being there is a single causality, which, however, is not of one kind, but displays various types of connection between cause and effect. It was a representative of German thought, Schopenhauer, who in his much underrated book *On the Fourfold Root of the Principle of Sufficient Reason* drew attention to the diverse basic forms of the causal relation.

I cannot pursue this question here, though I have discussed it at some length in my book *Marxist Problems* (1913), and must be content merely to point out that besides physical causality, which itself takes various forms, there is also physiological and psychological causality. While physical causality proceeds without consciousness, physiological causality occurs only *in*, and psychological causality *through* consciousness. In consequence the latter can only become effective within the forms of human consciousness. The transcendental judgements in which every content of consciousness is experienced belong to these forms. Human causality, which means the same as social causality, is so far removed from being mechanical causality that it is only realizable through human judgements and aspirations. This disposes of the extraordinary statement which Professor Spann emphasizes so strongly, and which he evidently regards as a basic principle of his sociology: 'There is not a single causal law in economic theory and social theory.' For according to his argument, if tariffs really do have an effect on prices, the connection between tariffs and prices is still not causal, i.e. mechanical. Here the catastrophic confusion between causality and mechanism is revealed in its purest state. It is difficult to know what to say about this. Who has ever conceived the effect of tariffs on prices in such a way that 'tariffs' act as a kind of physical force upon 'prices' as a kind of substance? In which naturalistic sociology is causality represented in such a way? Certainly not in Marxism, which Professor Spann regards as naturalistic. The main critical achievement of Marxism is precisely that it has dissolved the fetishism of the economic ideas of bourgeois political economy, this reification of all its concepts, and has revealed as the real agents behind these concepts socialized men involved in production and consumption. Is it possible to understand the effect of tariffs on prices, or for example Thünen's law,[13] in any other way than in terms of the average mass motivations which can be deduced as typical, according to the principle of psychological causality, from the given conditions of life; that is, which must emerge as causally necessary judgements and aspirations?

I turn now to an exposition of the metaphysical character of Spann's sociology. The statement that sociology must start from the whole of society sounds very good and persuasive, compared with the false atomism of social theories which is almost obligatory today. But what is this whole? Above all, where is it? When Professor Spann says that the elements can be regarded as being meaningfully arranged, we may agree, but what guarantee do we have that they are so arranged?

[13] Johann Heinrich von Thünen (1783–1850), gentleman farmer and economist, in his major work *Der isolierte Staat* (Part I, 1826; Part II, 1850), propounded a theory of rent and of the location of industry, and a marginal productivity theory of wages and interest, which influenced the Austrian marginalist school.

Particularly as these elements may be understood in two
senses: sometimes as elements in men's minds, at other times
as individual men themselves as elements of society. Now it
is true that the whole of the *individual* mind—the Ego—is a
fact of experience, an immediate event. But is the whole of the
social mind, of which men are supposed to be the elements,
this comprehensive whole which is supposed to have its own
meaningful unity just like that of the individual mind, such
a fact of experience or is it not perhaps merely an idea, a construction by the individual? It is immediately obvious that no
conclusive demonstration leads from the meaningful unity of
the part to the meaningful unity of the whole; and this is only
the old analogy which Plato had already put forward. So in
fact, as was already the case with Plato, the whole becomes
either a merely regulative idea, or if the reality of the whole is
asserted it becomes a metaphysical essence. If Fichte's Ego
begins with self-positing, this is not a detour into metaphysics
because this self-positing is in fact only a philosophical
expression for the original datum of the activity of consciousness. But on the contrary, if sociology begins with the self-
positing of the meaningful unity which 'articulates' itself in its
elements—this process being equivalent to 'organic growth or
community'—then this, despite its extremely clever formulation, is fundamentally a thoroughly naïve metaphysics which
solves all its problems by representing them as original
essences: the alien consciousness, the connection of the Ego
with this other consciousness, and the organic unity of the
whole. Totality and organic unity do not only take the place
of mechanism, which Professor Spann claims as a virtue of his
theory, but also take the place of an epistemological orientation for which totality and organic unity themselves are first
of all problems and not essences.

If the relation to totality is not to be understood metaphysically, but only as an analogy, I must say that I prefer the
analogy with the organism. Since it is by no means self-evident
how 'articulation', 'integration', 'organic growth', and 'community' are equivalent, I get a much more concrete orientation from the empirical idea of an organism and the functional
interrelation of its parts, then from that of organic unity,
which does not enable me to understand the connection of the

'I' with the 'you' which, on the contrary, can only be understood from the primary experience of this connection.

I believe, on the other hand, that it is Marxism which makes possible a more consistent development of the epoch-making trend of German philosophy, in which the unique character of social consciousness was elaborated. The means to do this is the basic concept of *socialized* man which Marx developed. Sociology, if it wants to remain an empirical science, must seek and find society where all experience is alone possible, namely in the individual consciousness. Hence, even sociological science cannot start from a totality, but must begin with the individual. This individual, however, is socialized man, that is to say, in Marx's sense, an individual who only makes his historical appearance associated with other men in relations of work and social intercourse. I have already shown that the historical socialization of this socialized man is only possible where the individual consciousness is already transcendentally socialized, that is to say, that an Ego-consciousness is only possible where there is an immanent relation to an indeterminate multiplicity of knowing subjects, with which every individual consciousness sees itself connected. Community, or as Professor Spann calls it, organic unity, is a form of the individual consciousness itself; and the conditions of our experience are constituted not only by space, time, and categories, but also by other consciousnesses. Social association is not a universal essence, nor merely an analogy, nor simply a universal conception, but a transcendental condition of experience. Thus, social experience is grounded as experience of *being* in exactly the same way as experience of nature, and there is no need for us to become victims of naturalism. The modern sociology of Marxism appears as a ripe fruit of classical philosophy, a theory in which the basic conceptions at the same time take up and develop Kant's critique of knowledge.

Finally, I would like to point out that the metaphysical foundation of Spann's conception results from the high value that he attributes to the Aristotelian proposition: 'The whole is prior to the part.' Unless this is intended merely as a method of scientific work, such a primacy of the whole over the part is only possible as a metaphysical essence. Even as a method this notion is far inferior to the dialectical conception of Marxism, that the whole and the part are relational concepts, which are mutually determining and continually change places in socio-logical research. Only in purely formal-logical thought is the whole prior to the part. On the contrary, in that thought which goes beyond the formal-logical rigid finiteness of concepts to infinite thought, as Leibniz already attempted to do, and as Hegel in particular succeeded in doing—that is to say, precisely in the thought of the classical German spirit which Spann is so fond of invoking—the whole is only given at the same time as the part, and provides an example of the dialectical movement of thought. It is precisely this dialectic which Marxism has taken over, and in this respect too has recognized the German philosophical spirit as one of its major sources. . . .

MAX ADLER, *Causality and Teleology*[14]

The dispute between the causal and teleological conceptions of science and about the proper demarcation of natural science from the so-called cultural sciences could only be settled by establishing a rigorous conception of science as the arbitrator. But this solution of a complex dispute provided a rare example of both sides achieving victory. For if the teleological view had to relinquish its claim in the field of science, it appeared as the unrestrained master in a much wider and more significant domain. This study would be misleading, and would give rise to a false conclusion, if it did not briefly examine this point. The deliberate one-sidedness of a view which made possible a rigorous notion of science should not be upheld to such an extent that it prevents us entirely from seeing those things which are bound to remain unobserved from this perspective.

The very fact that we have to exclude the notion of teleology completely from the standpoint of science gives us an insight which cannot be stressed too often or too strongly in face of the presumptions of vulgar materialism and of broken-winded self-sufficient positivism, which are still influential today; namely, that science can only reveal one side of existence as a whole, including cultural and social life, that aspect which can be grasped in the form of objects, abstracted in universal con-

[14] From *Kausalität und Teleologie im Streite um die Wissenschaft* (1904), pp. 430–3. [Eds.]

cepts, and subsumed under laws. All science involves abstraction, in which we can never grasp the total reality of the world.
The point of view which acknowledges and desires only
science always remains one-sided in the strongest, most
dangerous sense of this term, just because it always confronts
only *one* aspect of the world.

The aim of this study has been to show that the complete
reality of our being actually resides only in the will, and that
consequently man's real law-constituting activity, in relation
to his practical life, is carried out in the sphere of the will, a
law-giving activity which, as we have seen, requires him first
of all to admit truth as an obligation and to cultivate science.
The person who has fully understood this will never again
allow the sphere of science to be disturbed by the concept of
value; but he will regard science itself only as a means for the
ends of morality, as a value to be realized. That is the real
primacy of practical reason, which should not be confounded
with the sphere of logic, but should comprehend the latter—a
closed value-free system, undisturbed by any evaluation—as
possessing value. This is the simple meaning of that persistent
doctrine of the primacy of the practical.

Man is first of all a practical, conative, and goal-setting
being. His real being resides wholly in this sphere of activity,
and not, as people have often wanted to make him believe, in
the intellectual sphere of theoretical judgements. 'To know
in order to live' must be the authentic motto of science, by
which alone, from being an undertaking that is otherwise
almost ludicrous, it attains the nobility of a *truly* human enterprise, and as such must be in every respect an instrument of
the Ideal. 'To know in order to live'—with this phrase science
assumes control of humanity's moral and social spirit, in
whose ever-growing strength the full force of reality lives
much more powerfully than in the development of the intellect. The teleological relation, which could not have any significance in constituting the domain of scientific knowledge,
becomes a practical act in the consciousness of the real individual (who acknowledges the whole of his real life) in so far as
he develops science for his own ends, in order to shape the
world in his own image. If man constitutes the laws of nature,
in the theoretical domain, precisely by rigorously excluding

all teleological conceptions—because it is only the necessary forms of thought operative in the regularities of his cognition which establish the rigorous order that science then reproduces as the regularity of nature—so in the practical realm, to the extent that he creates an external validity for the regularities of the will, as they are expressed in the moral law, he becomes the new creator and transformer of the terrestrial world. The leap from the realm of natural necessity into the realm of freedom is only accomplished by the practical action which deliberately subordinates the comprehended regularities of nature to man's own self-imposed goals.

It is no accident, then, that the further development of the great doctrine of the primacy of practical over theoretical reason—which even the teleological conception thought it could use as one of its supporting arguments, and which my criticism has not only questioned, but also placed in the proper light for the first time—was undertaken precisely by those thinkers who were the outstanding pioneers of natural-scientific thought in the domain of social life. Auguste Comte's whole philosophy has avowedly no other object but 'savoir pour prévoir', the culmination of all knowledge in a comprehensive politics. The life work of Karl Marx, carried out with an extraordinary energy in the sphere both of thought and action, was to elicit this politics from the forces of humanity itself, and to make it a vital, combative, consciously self-determining reality. It was simply a pregnant expression of the doctrine of the primacy of practical reason when Marx at the outset of his creative intellectual work, formulated the phrase which should henceforth be the maxim guiding all scientific work: 'The philosophers have only interpreted the world in different ways; the point is to change it.'

OTTO BAUER, *Marxism and Ethics*[15]

When Kautsky[16] criticizes Kant's foundations of ethics, he evidently intends to oppose those who substitute for the discovery of the developmental tendencies of capitalism sermons on the immorality of capitalism and the morality of socialism,

---

[15] From 'Marxismus und Ethik', *Die Neue Zeit*, xxiv. 2 (1905–6), pp. 485–99. [Eds.]

[16] In *Die Ethik und die materialistische Geschichtsauffassung* (1906).

and hence retrace the path from science to Utopia, and who propose to abandon Marx's great achievement. I want to investigate whether socialism is really threatened by this danger from Kant. If socialist society is not regarded as the social order which the working class necessarily strives for, in unavoidable class struggle, and eventually wins by force, but is conceived only as one possible social order to be evaluated from a moral point of view, then socialism is characterized only by a juridical feature, namely the legal institution of social property in the instruments of labour. This idea includes the notion that society as proprietor rules and directs the means of production. Such a society can be of various types.

At one time private ownership of the means of production meant that everyone would be protected in the possession and enjoyment of what he himself had acquired by working. Later it meant that those to whom society had entrusted the function of directing production have the power to rule over others, to command and forbid others, to appropriate to themselves a part of the produce of labour. Finally, in a society based upon the highest stage of development of the private ownership of the means of production, one class, on the basis of the merely historically given fact of its property, has the possibility of exploiting the other classes in society without exercising any function in the production process. The norm has remained unchanged—for the normative system of property is in every case the same—but the economic function of private property has completely altered. It is transformed into its opposite: from the defence of the worker in the possession of the product of his labour to the defence of the exploiter in his claim to the labour of others. Karner [Renner] calls this phenomenon the functionlessness of the legal institutions. What is valid for individual property is also valid for social property. Social ownership of the means of production can function in various ways; it exists in those paradisiacal forms of society which the great Utopians have depicted, but also in the dismal Utopias in which socialist society is described as a barracks or a prison. Even if we think of democratic socialism, which characterizes the socialist order of society not only by social ownership of the instruments of labour, but also by a specific type of education of the will of society as a whole, social property can still work in quite different ways.

Democratic socialism does away with class conflict, but this does not mean that all conflicts, not even all conflicts of interest, are eliminated. When society appropriates the power over the instruments of labour which until now has been entrusted to the property owners, then it is faced with entirely new tasks, and with new struggles. For example, today there is no conflict about where a new shoe factory should be built. But in a socialist society, vigorous conflicts could break out over the choice of a new place of production. Some would choose to build the new factory in a region where coal and iron is available, so that superfluous labour for transport can be saved, and society can satisfy its need for shoes with a lesser expenditure of labour. Others will visualize a beautiful location among splendid woods by the sea, which would make the life of the members of society working in the shoe factory more pleasant than in the coal and iron region. Here the interest of society as a whole conflicts with the interest of those working in the shoe factory; economists and technicians would make a different choice from that of people concerned with health or education. Will the economic interest of the whole decide? Will the special interest be strong enough to prevail? Will a fair compromise be arranged?

Social property can function in various ways; a pessimistic Utopia can be counterposed to every optimistic one. Who would argue that in a socialist society it could no longer happen that a man, or a group of men, is treated only as a means, and not at the same time as an end? Or would our ethical theorists use the statistical method and seek to prove that this happens more frequently in present-day society than under socialism? Utopian socialism founders upon the fact that the same legal order may embrace quite different functions of the legal institutions, so that it is impossible for any legal order in itself to represent the realization of the moral law.

If, therefore, we want to establish socialism, we can follow no other path than that shown to us by Marx. Marx demonstrated that, in capitalist society, the proletariat was bound to *want* socialism as the only possibility of escaping exploitation; that it *can* attain its goal because the concentration of property has made possible the appropriation of the instruments of labour as social property; that the working class *will* attain its goal, because it becomes the overwhelming majority of the population. Now that is all that science can achieve. By enabling us to comprehend Being in its necessary form, science allows us to derive from it Becoming. It is not the business of science to make moral judgements; but such judgements must be preceded by science, which lays before us the great task of our age. By showing how, in our society, the struggle of the working class for socialism, and the opposition of the threatened property-owning classes, arise with similar necessity, it places before every one of us the question, which of the two great camps he wants to be associated with. Thus we no longer confront the question as to what kind of society could most effectively realize Kant's principle of practical reason, but the question which arises empirically from our society: whether to be with the proletariat for socialism, or with the possessing classes against socialism. Science confronts us with this question, but by itself it can give us no answer. For the recognition that socialism will come into existence does not yet lead me to fight for it. If we regard the social question no longer as a scientific issue, but as one involving a practical attitude, then it is certainly a moral question. Only science must come first, before we can successfully pose the moral question.

Do we only need to teach the still hesitant and undecided individual the formal laws of the will, so that he can decide which of the contending classes he will join? In the vast majority of cases, certainly not. If we only make him realize that the proletariat necessarily fights against exploitation, that with the development of capitalist society the fight against exploitation necessarily leads to a struggle for the socialist mode of production, we give him the material for a decision, and the decision itself will then be the correct judgement on the rightness of his will. Without ever having heard of Kant's categorical imperative, he will immediately judge the maxims flowing from the class interest of the proletariat differently from· those of the classes defending their property. He will judge as immoral the maxims of those who have to defend a social order which can only exist if it represses the overwhelming majority of the members of society, either by force, or by deceiving them about their real interests by means of a false ideology. He will recognize the universally valid imperative in the maxims of those who necessarily fight for a social order which is not so much the realization of the moral law—there is no such social order—but which makes it possible to fight for the correct decision in every particular case where the will of society as a whole is faced with a decision. Only teach men to understand the tendencies of development of capitalist society, as discovered by Marx, and they themselves will already know how to establish the criterion for universal law-giving in the class maxims, without ever having heard of the principle of practical reason. It is not necessary to tell anyone who wishes to pursue science that he must establish the unity of the manifold forms of experience by means of the pure forms of conception and thought; just give him the opportunity to see, to hear, to learn, and in general allow the regularities of consciousness to take care of the fact that his consciousness will not rest until he has established that unity.

What service, then, can Kant's doctrine still provide? Is it not in practice completely useless? Not entirely. It is the final bastion to which we can retreat whenever ethical scepticism obstructs the naïve moral judgement of class maxims discovered by science. That is not a rare event at the present time. The bourgeoisie, which can no longer hope to establish its maxims as an imperative, diffuses ethical relativism through its theory—the 'historical school' in economics and jurisprudence—and likewise through its political practice—the cult of *Realpolitik*. That is the way of thinking which believes it has justified a maxim when it grasps it as an outcome of historical development. The materialist conception of history might easily turn out to be looking after the affairs of the enemies of the working class, as it is today in many cases, in its concern with Darwinism, if it abandoned its claim to distinguish sharply between the task of understanding a maxim scientifically, and the question of which of the contending maxims is supposed to guide us. If anyone misled by ethical scepticism thinks that there is no criterion of choice for him, because he knows the necessary will of all classes, we recall to his attention the formal law-governed character of his will, we provide the criterion which enables him to distinguish the will of the working class from that of the bourgeoisie in terms of its value, and so guide him into the camp of the fighting proletariat.

I hope that my analysis will not have the misfortune to be confused with the attempt of some revisionists to import Kant's principle of practical reason into the justification of socialism. For their attempt rests on a persistent confusion between the theoretical and practical points of view. This is really the most serious offence which can be committed against the spirit of Kantian philosophy, for nothing lay closer to Kant's heart than the task of delimiting the realm of practical reason from the empirical realm. If we make socialism an object of science, and if we also investigate the tendencies of development of capitalist society, then of course we must speak of ethics. For the driving force of class struggle is not only class interest, but also the class ideology which arises from its particular conditions of life. Consequently, it is not so much Kant's basic principle which underlies all ethics, but rather the class ethic of the proletariat which has a specific content. The student of moral ideas as the driving force of working-class struggle has to study not Kant but the proletariat. His method cannot be that of the critique of practical reason—for this never leads to a knowledge of the substance of the will—but that of the materialist conception of history. He will show how, from the social conditions of existence of the proletariat, its position in the production process, in the state, in the national cultural community, there arises a specific way of judging phenomena, and how this specifically proletarian ethic is effective in the class struggle, how it influences its goals, methods, and forms.

If we regard socialism no longer as a question of science, but of life, and if we also seek an answer for the waverer who asks us whether he should be a socialist or not, we do need Kant's ethics. But before we can go on to judge the diverse maxims of different classes, we must know what they are. The discovery of the tendencies of capitalist development must precede the practical attitude to capitalism. It is a sign of painful confusion if someone thinks he can *replace* even a single line of Marx's work by the categorical imperative.

The immediate occasion for Kautsky's study was the

well-known conflict with the former majority of the editorial staff of *Vorwärts*. For Kautsky it was a matter of showing that if we want to educate socialists, we need the 'historical-materialist', not the 'ethical-aesthetic', method. We should not preach morality but investigate the tendencies of development of the capitalist mode of production and diffuse knowledge about this process. In this practical matter I am of one mind with Kautsky. A teacher of science must make the material of experience accessible to his pupil, not give lectures on the conditions of possible experience. Likewise someone who wants to spread socialism must teach men to understand the present social order; lectures on the formal law-governed character of every moral will are not sufficient. It is also my opinion that we need economic and social science rather than moral preaching. But what separates me from Kautsky is the conviction that we cannot renounce Kant's critique of reason; time and again it is able to protect us from the stream of scepticism unleashed by the enemies of the working class. For us, the critical philosophy is a solid barrier against the invasion of scepticism which aims to transform our knowledge into deceptive appearance and our moral action into the play of blind chance.

RUDOLF HILFERDING, *The Subjectivist Outlook in Economics*[17]

It is precisely the phenomenon of variations in the price of production which has shown us that the phenomena of capitalist society can never be understood if the commodity or capital is considered in isolation. It is rather the social relationship in which they exist, and changes in that relationship, which dominate and account for the movements of individual capitals, which are themselves no more than parts of the total social capital. But the representative of the psychological school of political economy fails to see this social context, and hence he is bound to misunderstand a theory which intends precisely to reveal the social determinism of economic phenomena, and whose starting point therefore is society and not the individual. He always subordinates the concepts and terms of this theory to his own individualistic outlook and so he finds contradictions which he ascribes to the theory, whereas

[17] From *Böhm-Bawerk's Marx-Kritik* (1904), pp. 51–61. [Eds.]

they are in truth ascribable solely to his conception of the theory.

This incessant *quid pro quo* is to be found at all stages of Böhm-Bawerk's polemic. Even the fundamental concept of the Marxist system, the concept of value-creating labour, is understood in a purely subjective manner. For him, 'labour' is identical with 'trouble' or 'effort', and making this individual feeling of distaste the source of value naturally leads us to see in value a purely psychological fact, and to deduce the value of commodities from our evaluation of the labour they have cost. As is well known, this is the basis which Adam Smith always adopts for his theory of value, for he is always inclined to abandon the objective standpoint for a subjective one. Smith writes: 'Equal quantities of labour must at all times and places be of equal value to the labourer. In his ordinary state of health, strength, and spirits, in the ordinary degree of his skill and dexterity, he must always lay down the same portion of his ease, his liberty, and his happiness.'[18] If labour regarded as 'trouble' is the basis of our personal estimate of value, then the 'value of labour' is a constituent, or a 'determinant' as Böhm-Bawerk puts it, of the value of commodities. But it need not be the only one, for a number of other factors which influence the subjective estimates made by individuals take their place beside labour and have an equal right to be regarded as determinants of value. If, therefore, we identify the value of commodities with the personal estimate of the value of these commodities made by this or that individual, it seems quite arbitrary to select labour as the sole basis for such an estimate.

Hence, from the subjectivist standpoint, on which Böhm-Bawerk bases his criticism, the labour theory of value appears untenable from the very outset. And it is because he adopts this standpoint that Böhm-Bawerk is unable to perceive that Marx's concept of labour is totally opposed to his own. Already in *A Contribution to the Critique of Political Economy* Marx had defined his opposition to Adam Smith's subjectivist outlook: '(Smith) fails to see the objective equalization of different kinds of labour which the social process forcibly carries out, mistaking it for the subjective equality of the labours of

[18] *Wealth of Nations*, bk. 1, Chapter 5.

individuals.'[19] In fact, Marx is entirely unconcerned with the individual motivation of the estimate of value. In capitalist society it would be absurd to make 'trouble' the measure of value, for generally speaking the owners of the products have taken no trouble at all, whereas the trouble has been taken by those who have produced but do not own them. With Marx, in fact, every individual relationship is excluded from the conception of value-creating labour: labour is regarded, not as something which arouses feelings of pleasure or its opposite, but as an objective magnitude, inherent in the commodities, and determined by the degree of development of social productivity. Whereas for Böhm-Bawerk labour seems merely one of the determinants in personal estimates of value, in Marx's view labour is the basis and the connective tissue of human society, and the degree of productivity of labour, and the method of organization of labour, determine the character of social life. Since labour, viewed in its social function as the total labour of society of which each individual labour forms merely an aliquot part, is made the principle of value, economic phenomena are subordinated to objective laws that are independent of the individual will and controlled by social relationships. Beneath the husk of economic categories we discover social relationships, relationships of production, in which commodities play the part of intermediaries, the social relationships being reproduced by these intermediate processes, or undergoing a gradual transformation until finally they require a new type of mediation.

Thus the law of value becomes a law of motion for a definite type of social organization based upon the production of commodities, for in the last resort all change in social structure can be referred to changes in the relationships of production, that is to say, changes in the productivity and the organization of labour. Thus, in striking contrast with the outlook of the psychological school, we are led to regard political economy as a part of sociology, and sociology itself as a historical science. Böhm-Bawerk has never become aware of this contrast. In a controversy with Sombart as to whether the 'subjectivist method' or the 'objectivist method' is the proper method in economics he concludes by saying that each method must

[19] Kerr ed., p. 68.

supplement the other; when in fact the issue does not concern two different methods, but contrasting and mutually exclusive outlooks upon social life as a whole. So too it comes about that Böhm-Bawerk, invariably carrying on the controversy from his subjectivist and psychological standpoint, discovers contradictions in the Marxist theory which seem to him to be contradictions only because of his own subjectivist interpretation of the theory.

If labour is the only means for estimating value and thus the only measure of value, it is only logical from the subjectivist standpoint that commodities should exchange solely in proportion to the equal quantities of labour embodied in them. Otherwise it is impossible to see what would induce individuals to deviate from their personal estimates of value. If, however, the facts do not conform to these premises, then the law of value loses all significance, even if labour is no more than one determinant among others. This is why Böhm-Bawerk lays so much stress upon the contention that commodities are *not* exchanged on the basis of equal quantities of labour. This necessarily appears to be a contradiction when value is conceived, not as an objective quantity, but as the outcome of individual motivation.

Marx's outlook is entirely different. In his view, the fact that goods contain labour is one of their intrinsic qualities; that they are exchangeable is a quite distinct characteristic solely dependent on the will of the possessor, which presupposes that they are owned and alienable. The relationship of the quantity of labour to the process of exchange does not come into consideration until goods are regularly *produced* as commodities, produced that is to say as goods specifically destined for exchange; thus this relationship makes its appearance only at a definite stage of historical development. The quantitative ratio in which they are exchanged thus becomes dependent upon the time taken to produce them, and this in turn is determined by the level of social productivity. Thus the exchange relationship loses its fortuitous character and ceases to be dependent upon the caprice of the owner. The social conditions imposed upon labour become objective limitations for the individual and the social complex controls the individual's activities. . . .

The exchange relationship between commodities is no more than the material expression of the social relationships among persons, and what is actually realized in the exchange relationship is the equality of the agents of production. Since, at the stage of simple commodity production, equal and independent workers, each of whom possesses his means of production, confront one another, exchange takes place at prices which tend to correspond to the values. Only in this way can the mechanism of the simple production of commodities be maintained, and the conditions needed for the reproduction of the relationships of production be fulfilled.

In such a society the product of labour belongs to the labourer. If, as a result of permanent deviation from this rule (chance deviations compensate each other), a portion of the product of labour is taken away from the labourer and assigned to another person, the basis of the society will be modified; the former will become a wage labourer (engaged in domestic industry) and the latter a capitalist. This is actually one of the ways in which simple commodity production is dissolved. But it cannot finally cease unless a modification of social relationships has occurred, accompanied by a modification of exchange, which is the expression of social relationships.

In the capitalist process of exchange, the purpose of which is the realization of surplus value, the equality of the economic units is once more reflected. These units, however, are no longer independent producers, but owners of capital. Their equality finds expression in the fact that exchange is only normal when the profits are equal, when they are average profits. The exchange which expresses the equality of the owners of capital is of course determined in a different way from that which is based upon equality in the expenditure of labour. But just as both societies have the same basis—the division of property and the division of labour—and just as capitalist society can be conceived simply as a higher, modified form of the earlier type of society, so also the basis of the law of value is unchanged, for it has merely undergone certain modifications in its realization. These result from the specific mode of capitalist competition, which brings about the proportional equality of capital. The share in the total product, whose value remains directly determined by the law of value, was formerly proportional to the individual's expenditure of labour, but now becomes proportional to the expenditure of the capital that is needed to set labour in motion. In this way the subordination of labour to capital is expressed. It appears as social subordination; the whole society is divided into capitalists and labourers, the former being owners of the product of the latter, the total product determined by the law of value, which is divided among the capitalists. The capitalists are free and equal; their equality is shown in the price of production $= c$ (cost) $+ p$ (profit), where p is proportional to c. The dependent position of the labourer is shown by the fact that he appears as one of the constituents of c, along with machinery, lubricating oil, and beasts of burden; this is all he means to the capitalist as soon as he has left the market and has taken his place in the factory to create surplus value. Only for a moment did he have a role in the market, as a free man selling his labour power. This brief glory in the market and the prolonged debasement in the factory illustrate the difference between legal equality and economic equality, between the equality demanded by the bourgeoisie and the equality demanded by the proletariat.

The capitalist mode of production socializes mankind to a greater extent than did any previous mode of production; this is its historical significance, and the reason why we can regard it as a preliminary stage on the way to socialist society. That is to say, capitalism makes the existence of the individual dependent upon the social relationships in which he is placed. It does so in an antagonistic form, by the formation of two great classes, making the performance of social labour the function of one of these classes, and enjoyment of the products of labour the function of the other. The individual is not yet a 'direct expression' of society; that is, he does not yet have a direct relationship to society, for his economic position is determined by his position as member of a class. The individual can only exist as a capitalist because his class appropriates the product of the other class, and his own share is solely determined by the total surplus value, not by the surplus value which he individually appropriates. The significance of class reveals the law of value as a *social* law. The theory of value would only be refuted if it were shown to lack confirmation *in the social domain*.

In capitalist society the individual appears as ruler or slave according to whether he belongs to one or other of the two great classes. Socialist society makes him free, by abolishing the antagonistic form of society, and by promoting socialization in a conscious and direct manner. At that stage, social interrelations are no longer concealed behind enigmatic economic categories which seem to be the natural qualities of things, but manifest themselves as the freely willed outcome of human co-operation. Political economy then ceases to exist in the form which we have known so far, and is replaced by a science of the 'wealth of nations'.

Inasmuch as the productive power of human society, in the specific organizational form which society confers upon it, is for Marx the fundamental idea of political economy, he portrays economic phenomena and their modifications in terms of their law-governed regularities, and as causally dominated by the changes in productive powers. In his demonstration, following the dialectical method, conceptual development runs parallel throughout with historical development, since the development of the social powers of production appears in the Marxist system, on one side as a historical reality, and on the other side as a conceptual reflection. Moreover, this parallelism furnishes the strictest empirical proof of the correctness of the theory. The commodity form is necessarily the starting point; it is the simplest form, and becomes the object of economic observation, as the object of a specific science. For in the commodity form there already emerges that illusory appearance which results from the fact that the social relationships of individuals assume the aspect of material qualities of things. It is this illusory material appearance which so greatly confuses the issues of economics. The social functions of individuals masquerade as material qualities of things, just as time and space, the subjective forms of perception, masquerade as objective qualities of things. In so far as Marx dispels this illusion, discloses personal relationships where previously material relationships had been seen, and social relationships where individual relationships had been seen, he succeeds in providing a unified and consistent explanation of the pheno-

mena which the classical economists had been unable to elucidate. The failure of the classical economists was inevitable,
for they regarded bourgeois relationships of production as
natural and unalterable. Marx, having demonstrated the historical conditioning of these relationships of production, was
able to take up the analysis at the point where the investigations of the classical economists were bound to stop.

But the demonstration of the historical transitoriness of
bourgeois relationships signifies the close of political economy
as a bourgeois science and its foundation as a proletarian
science. Only two ways now remained open to the champions
of the bourgeoisie if they wanted to be anything more than
simple apologists, adopting an uncritical eclecticism to shore
up the crumbling pillars of their harmonious systems. They
might, like the historical school in Germany, ignore theory
and try to fill the gap with a history of economic science; but
they would then be hampered, as the German historical school
has been hampered even within its chosen field, by the lack of
any coherent understanding of economic events. The psychological school of economics has chosen the other path. The
members of this school have endeavoured to construct a theory
of economic events by excluding economics itself from their
purview. Instead of economic or social relationships they have
chosen as the starting point of their system the *individual* relationship between men and things. They regard this relationship from the psychological aspect as one which is governed
by natural and unalterable laws. They ignore the determinate
social character of the relationships of production, and the
idea of a law-governed development of economic events is
alien to their minds. This economic theory means the repudia-
tion of economics. The last word in the rejoinder of bourgeois
economics to scientific socialism is the self-destruction of
political economy.

KARL RENNER, *Problems of Marxism*[20]
[...] Karl Marx's whole productive period falls within the
liberal epoch of society, the starting point of which is that

[20] From 'Probleme des Marxismus', a series of eight articles published in *Der
Kampf*, ix (1916), pp. 154–61, 185–93, 229–39, 275–81, 312–21, 354–9, 383–6, 417–
421. [Eds.]

people and commodities are free and the state does not intervene in their movements. This precondition must be historically given, in order for political economy to be possible as a science. For it poses the question: since the economic process is not regulated by the conscious will of society (not by state law), then by what unconscious order, by what law of nature is it ruled? As there are only private owners, private workers, private capital, private labour, private production and circulation, etc. how is society then possible? Karl Marx gave an answer to this question in a brilliant, incontestable, irrefutable way. The law of value is the demiurge of private enterprise.

In order to reveal this law its conditions must be constructed in pure abstraction. Conceptually, all state intervention must be excluded: capitalist and worker must always appear as individuals, and in legal terms as sovereigns; only in this way can the level and extent of their economic dependence through the law of value be systematically established, and the economic relation 'capital' be revealed in its pure form. Free competition, that is the legally unhindered self-movement of all agents and factors of production, completely free trade over the whole surface of the earth, absolute legal equality of persons and commodities, are conceptually necessary for the system. This logical rigour enabled Marx to discover and describe the social natural law of the human economy.

In Marx's time this was not simply a conceptual assumption, for the freedom of occupations and labour internally, the freedom of commerce and trade externally, both connected with the bourgeois economy, had just become intellectually and politically victorious in Europe; the logical assumption was at the same time the practical one. Only in the evening of Marx's life, five years before his death, did the free trade ideology suffer its first blow (1878).[21] Since Marx's death a generation and a half of unprecedented intensity has elapsed and we can now ask what occurred during this period. First, we must establish the following: Marx investigated and described those individualist-anarchist economic forms in order to negate them, to make the brilliant discovery that 'freedom' signifies universal social constraint, and strives from within to substitute for the blind laws of nature the conscious direction of

---

[21] When Bismarck adopted a protectionist policy. [Eds.]

production by organized society. The dictatorship of the united organized proletariat of the world was supposed to assume control over world production, and liberal society was to change abruptly into socialism. There is scarcely any indication, in Marx's work, of transitions or intermediate stages, in which the already existing state powers have a role to play. Nor did he experience any such stages: the protectionist movement of 1878 might seem to be merely a reversion to pre-liberal epochs. Marx saw both the starting point and the goal of future development, and he was right about both of them. He could not survey the road between the two, just as we cannot foresee this even today. He set the goal in immediate proximity to the starting point: the internationally organized working class takes over the world and the passion of the fighter shortens the way. We all thought in this fashion, and although the revisionists undermined some people's confidence, without illuminating the way forward, on the whole the orthodox Marxists, like the revisionists, still adhered to the idea. Despite some reactionary protectionist experiments, we live in the liberal world and have to replace it with socialism.

I confess that it was the economic phenomena of the war which made me puzzled about the development of capitalism from 1878 to 1914. I feel that we Marxists have partly overlooked, partly underrated, and in any case have failed to incorporate in the Marxist conceptual scheme, fundamental changes which have taken place in the structure of society. Capitalist society, as Marx experienced and described it, no longer exists! The theorems of trigonometry remain valid even if they are applied to a rectangle instead of a triangle: they simply have a changed and mediated application. If such a change has taken place in society, we do not necessarily have to modify a single proposition of Marx, but only to apply the old Marxist method to a new society. Nothing needs to be revised in Marx. The problem is: to what extent are we faced with a new society?

The operation of the war economy has produced conflicting opinions: some have called it war socialism, others war capitalism, while most perceive it as an exceptional state which has to be suffered as one of the necessities of war, although an

obscure instinct revolts against this. Among socialists the
traditional world of ideas revolts against this notion, and in
particular our conception of the tasks and limits of the positive
state, of the present state, upon which we do not wish to
confer any special role as the demiurge of our future state.
But even in the camp of our opponents those who were until
now passionately enthusiastic about the state power, who saw
in it a religious institution, the realization of the ethical idea,
the original source and guarantee of law, are bewildered by
the idea that the sovereign state now has the function of selling
potatoes and trading in livestock. The roles are exchanged
precisely in this respect, that we demand, and our opponents
contest, the new tasks. Against our will, we stand in our hearts
on the side of the state, our opponents against it, so far as
welfare administration is concerned.

Thus we observe that in spite of all the counter-agitation,
there survives in the depths of the bourgeois soul the conviction, which almost a century and a half ago Adam Smith
raised to the level of a system of political economy, that the
economy must be carried on as a private affair, that the production, circulation, and consumption of commodities must
be free from state interference and remain private, that the
state economy itself is only derivative. The state economy
rests upon taxes and duties levied on private establishments;
these taxes are absorbed by the state and are then distributed
to the public services. Only gradually has the bourgeoisie
learnt to tolerate the fact that the state does not merely (to
use Lassalle's phrase) perform the services of a night-watch-
man, so that the private economy will not be disturbed by
criminals, but also intervenes here and there. However, all
these encroachments have scarcely shaken the ruling idea that
economic activity is a private, individual matter; above all it
has been an absolutely incontestable dogma that the household, consumption, hearth, table, and dwelling were the most
extremely personal and holy of all the spheres of individual
life. As yet the world outlook of liberalism is practically un-
shaken for the overwhelming majority of men. It is precisely
now, when the well-known spectre of liberalism, the unlimited supreme power of the state, has gained a foothold in
all countries because of the needs of war that the old liberal

idea of the 'limits of state power' becomes more powerful every day, particularly among the bourgeoisie. They want to return by force from 'authoritarian constraint' to the realm of 'freedom', of unregulated commerce, trade, and consumption; the half-forgotten expression 'state-slavery' is becoming current again, and many a 'social thinker' (professorial or Christian) of yesterday has become a real 'liberal' overnight. But the socialist still sees in the state the executive committee of the capitalist class, and protests against social functions being transferred to it; many a socialist, who yesterday still fought against the 'anarchy of the mode of production and exchange' is on the point of fleeing from such an excess of order and regulation back to the disorder of economic anarchy, as soon as he realizes that the capitalist and militarist state is now supposed to provide the worker even with his daily bread.

It will be seen that the consequences of the war economy revive the basic problems of all human economic life in a quite unsuspected fashion. With justified anxiety capitalists and socialists alike ask themselves whether the phenomena are permanent, and which developmental tendencies they serve. Is there a way back to the previous, predominantly liberal private economic order? If not, what is the goal of the new development? Future developments can only be revealed if past origins are considered along with present forces. If we want to be sure of the order in which development proceeds, we must take as our starting point the individual-anarchist economic system which Marx described. It is true that this system is still generally dominant in thought, but the facts have long been different. As is so often the case, the consciousness of society lags behind social facts. The epoch of the individual entrepreneur operating in a situation of completely free competition is already farther away than we think. Here I am not so much concerned with the fact of the numerous nationalizations, which only make the state a private owner and change little or nothing in its social character. It is a question rather of the penetration of the private economy down to its elementary cells by the state; not the nationalization of a few factories, but the control of the whole private sector of the economy by willed and conscious regulation and direction, hence precisely what Marx's system logically and practically excluded. Let us call it 'state penetration' of the economy, employing this neologism in order to avoid confusion. If such a development has taken place on an increasing scale it is obvious that its sequel can neither be demonstrated nor disputed by Marx, since it clearly lies outside his system. We must first show that this development is taking place, and then go on to evaluate it. . . .

At first the state intervened only timidly and shyly under the slogan: 'Protect the Weak.' Each state did this in a different way from others. It did not as yet undertake the functions of management, but only 'regulated' the private sector of the economy. This era of protectionism began in the mid-1870s and operated in the same way internally as it does externally. Internally, the artisan is protected against free competition by qualifications and guilds, by licences and concessions, and the peasant is protected by legislation concerning debtors, rights of entail on farms, and so on. Externally home industry is protected by initially moderate tariffs. In each state the economy slowly becomes more distinctive through the elaboration of a particular economic constitution which, in itself, contradicts free competition and free trade, diverges from the single, undifferentiated, natural-law world economy envisaged by Marx, and artificially distorts the conditions of economic life and the life of the masses. Nevertheless, initially the economy remains a private enterprise economy.

This period from 1878 to about 1890, which I would call the era of minimum protectionism, proved not to be simply a temporary relapse into pre-liberal methods which occurred in particular circumstances, although it was initially seen in this way by social democracy. It was, rather, the beginning of a specific new development. Meanwhile a new motive force appeared. Private enterprise created its own organizations to restrict competition and establish a uniform economy. This socialization does *not* arise from the intervention of the state, but is carried through at first against the state's opposition, and results from the tendency to concentration of capital itself. This is entirely within the scope of the Marxist system, although it has given rise to many misunderstandings which I will now discuss. This development always takes place within the framework of a definite, and often decisive, system of legislation and administration in a given state, which runs counter to, and distorts the economic factor. To a large extent it is because of differences in legislation that cartels, co-operatives, and trade unions have developed differently in England and Russia, in Germany and America, sometimes becoming too powerful, sometimes declining. State laws run counter to economic influences, and it is questionable which is the stronger. The organization of the economy becomes differentiated through the activity of the state!

If one looks at the dates when these business associations were established it is surprising to find that, although all types of association and coalition occasionally appeared in earlier periods, and many attempts were made and failed, the organizations really began to establish and consolidate themselves from about 1890. Cartel after cartel arose, most of which lasted for some years, and not a few already have a stable history of twenty years. They are, therefore, no longer experiments but economic institutions. At the same time the workers' trade unions grew rapidly, maintained themselves in spite of the fiercest resistance, and we are now celebrating one-quarter-century jubilee after another. The commodity and labour markets have organized themselves within the framework established by the state, and for a generation now Adam Smith's law of free competition has not been valid; it is not eliminated but is severely limited. Alongside these coalitions are the associations. The agricultural co-operatives have been extensively and successfully built up in the last generation. The farmer is still two-thirds a private entrepreneur, but with respect to his raw materials, the sale of his products, his credit relations, he no longer works as an individual, but in common, co-operatively. Ten years later, but still twenty years ago now, the German working class created a co-operative organization; nine-tenths of the workers' households are still private, but certainly one-tenth are socialized through the consumer co-operatives and wholesale societies. The purely capitalist factories grow beyond the scope of private wealth, and are transformed increasingly into companies, the larger ones into limited liability companies. The enterprise takes the place of the entrepreneur and

becomes semi-public. Only with reservations do people still
speak of the 'private capitalist mode of production'. The expression needs to be qualified, for we are in the epoch of
organized private enterprise economy which is determined by
the state and has become a thoroughly state-dominated
organization.

In this development the Marxist concentration process has
quite rightly been recognized. But the misunderstanding lay
in the fact that we saw in concentration only the growth of
giant factories and immense wealth. Alongside the concentration of wealth and factories a third form has developed.
Wine-producing peasants can maintain their small property
and small-scale enterprise, and concentrate simply upon one
or a few functions such as the supply of auxiliary materials or
the sale of products (all mercantile functions), or upon one
part of the production process (storage and refinement of the
wine). Here the process of socialization has taken a third
course, which Marx could observe or predict only to a limited
extent. A closer investigation shows that this course is bound
to produce a new economic situation and social psychology,
about which we have not yet become clear. The activity of the
state essentially determines all forms of organization, although
the state power at first reacts with a lack of understanding, or
with hostility, to the newly emerging powers. The state per-
secutes the trade unions, endures the co-operatives, regards
the limited liability companies with suspicion, and (at least
in public) rejects the cartels. The economy as a whole is not
its economy, and it feels itself elevated above it as a God-
willed sovereignty. However, this is only for a time. The process of capitalist organization is decided from above by finance
capital. It is only a short time ago that the banker stood aloof
from industrial and mercantile enterprises and merely supplied them with credit. The joint-stock bank, which controls
finance and establishes industrial and mercantile enterprises,
has taken the place of the banker. The growth of banking
capital began ten or fifteen years ago, and now, from the most
remote co-operative bank to the banks of the capital, credit is
integrated into a single system. The banks rule the whole
realm of the state economy and shape it uniformly in accordance with rates of interest and commodity prices. The econo-

mic sphere and the sphere of the state coincide; externally, the economic system of a particular state is clearly distinguished from those of other states, while internally it constitutes a specific organic unity.

This situation diverges greatly from the uniformly conceived world economy of Marx. The old private capital of the individual has been absorbed, like many organizations, into the single national capital, over which a small number of great banks have decisive control. They direct it into new industries, or like the French banks, stake the whole amount on the single card of the Russian national debt. In a certain sense the private enterprise economy has become a national economy. The Marxist idea that capital is international possesses only an extremely limited and conditional truth. This process of the nationalization of capital, with its manifold extremely interesting and significant features, has scarcely been investigated by Marxists up to the present time as it should have been.

At this stage, however, the relation between the state and capital changes rapidly. Capital did, of course, influence the state power earlier, but never saw in it more than the necessary and costly evil of a police function, the provision of security, both internally and externally. But now organized national capital uses the state power precisely as a positive economic agency. The frequent movements of personnel from the bureaucracy to the banks and vice versa, which were formerly rare, are only a symptom of this. The state power serves capital by substituting the defence of the strong for the traditional 'protection of the weak'. It is the epoch of imperialist defence. The state deliberately assists in the concentration of capital; the gigantic iron works and shipping firms are now acknowledged as the pride of the nation and the apple of the state's eye. High protective tariffs separate national territories completely from each other, and for every particular area a closed organism is created. We socialists still lack a basic analysis of the 'closed economic region', of its organs and functions, although this is of the highest importance for the condition of the working class. State power and the economy begin to merge; the state's area of domination and the national economic region coincide; the national economy is perceived as a means of state power, state power as a means to strengthen the national economy, in spite of their overtly proclaimed separation. It is the epoch of imperialism. The age of free trade in the world is far behind us; the law of value of commodity exchange is only valid in the 'last instance'; the private, individual economy exists in complete purity only in the household of the private man.

The difficulty of new research arises from the fact that the roles of all economic agents have been fundamentally transformed. Nevertheless, I will venture to single out *some particular features* of this change and put them forward for discussion. It is enough to note here that in this course of development, even before the war, the economy had already become highly concentrated around the state power, and since then it has been increasingly and more effectively subordinated to the state. The war has not thrown it off course, has not introduced anything peculiar, but has merely accelerated an already apparent line of development. The state has placed the existing cartels under its own sovereignty, thus creating central sugar and brandy authorities, and in conformity with such models it has assumed the management of cotton, wool, flax, metals, fats and oils, fodder, and even breadfruit. In Germany it forces the livestock trade into compulsory guilds and organizes them in meat departments of the Reich. It is a step further, nothing more! Following the era of protectionism, of the organized private enterprise economy, and the imperialist national economy, we have entered an era of state economy in which, along with its political and juridical activity, the state has taken over the tasks of an economic department, though entirely within the framework of the capitalist economic order. Counter-posing the beginning and the end of this process one might say that *laissez-faire* capitalism has changed into state capitalism or is well on the road to doing so. The progressive, thoroughgoing state intervention is temporary in some spheres, but in the most important branches of the economy it has advanced to the direct state management of the economy.

Socialization, which Marx regarded as inevitable, has thus taken a course which was not to be foreseen. For the time being, the place of the dictatorship of a united world proletariat has been taken by all-powerful national states. Socialism can no longer be related to the *laissez-faire* economic order; we face entirely new and different problems. To orient ourselves intellectually to a situation which no longer exists, means wanting to march backwards into the future. We have to start right at the beginning, not with propositions, but with the investigation and ordering of economic facts; with the old Marxist method, but not with the old quotations; not revising the old, but establishing the new. The truth which is compelling and unifying can only be discovered by the peaceable co-operative work of all Marxists. Nothing would be more pernicious for the whole school than self-righteous sectarianism!...

III. Nationalities, Nationalism, and Imperialism

OTTO BAUER, *The Concept of the 'Nation'*[1]
In conclusion, I should like to support this attempt to define
the nation by comparing it with some earlier theories. I have
already referred to the *metaphysical* theories—national spiritu-
alism and national materialism—and later on I shall consider
the *psychological* theories, which seek to discover the essence
of the nation in the consciousness of, or the will to, solidarity.
Here, therefore, it is only necessary to consider those attempts
to enumerate a number of elements, which are supposed, by
their interrelationship, to constitute the nation. The Italian
sociologists adduce the following as such elements:

1. A common territory.
2. Common descent.
3. A common language.
4. Common mores and customs.
5. Common experiences, a common historical past.
6. Common laws and a common religion.

It is clear that this theory puts together a number of characteristics which cannot simply be ranged side by side, but
can only be understood in their relations of dependence upon
each other. If we disregard for the time being the first alleged
element of the nation, a common territory, then the fifth—a
common history—stands out among the remainder. This is
the one which determines and produces the others. A common
history first gives common descent its determinate content, by
deciding which qualities will be inherited, which excluded; a
common history produces common morals and customs, common laws, and a common religion, and hence—to use our own
terminology—a common cultural tradition. Common descent
and a common culture are merely the tools which the common
history employs in its activity, in its work of constructing the

[1] From *Die Nationalitätenfrage und die Sozialdemokratie* (1907), pp. 130–8. [Eds.]

national character. The third element—a common language—cannot be ranged with the others: it constitutes a second order means. For if a common culture is one of the means through which the common history effectively forms the national character, then in the same way a common language is a means through which the common culture operates, a tool which creates and maintains the cultural community, as an external regulation of the form of social co-operation among individuals who form a community and are continually recreating this community.[2]

Thus, in the first place we substitute for a mere *listing* of the constituents of a nation a *systematic conception*: a common history as the effective cause, common culture and common descent as the means by which it produces its effects, a common language as the mediator of the common culture, both its product and its producer. We can now understand the relation of these elements to each other, for what previously caused such great difficulties for those who developed theories about the nation, namely the fact that these elements could manifest themselves in very diverse interrelationships, with now one, now another element being absent, becomes comprehensible. If common descent and a common culture are both instruments for the same effective factor, it is clearly not important for the concept of the nation that both instruments should be operative: that is why the nation can be based upon common descent, but need not be, while common descent alone establishes only a race, never a nation. These considerations also lead to a conclusion about the relation of the various elements of the common culture to each other: common laws certainly are an important means of forming the common character, but the latter can exist or develop without them, provided that the other elements are effective enough to unite the individuals in a cultural community. Diversity of creed can make two nations out of peoples with the same language, where the diversity of religion is an obstacle to cultural

---

[2] Language, of course, is not simply a means of transmitting a culture, but is itself an element of culture. A Frenchman does not differ from a German only because his language conveys a different culture, but also because the language itself is a cultural element which has been transmitted to him and determines, by its specific qualities, his speech, thought, and character. The difference between French and German rhetoric is due in part to the difference of language.

community. A common religion is the basis for a common culture, as it was with the Serbs and Croats; but the Germans remained one people despite their religious divergences, because the religious division could not prevent the development and persistence of a universal German cultural community. Finally, in this way we can also understand the relation of language to the other elements of the nation: without a community of language, no cultural community and consequently no nation. But a community of language still does not produce a nation where diversity in other respects—for example the diversity of religion in the case of the Serbs and Croats, or the diversity of descent and of social and political conditions in the case of the Spaniards and the Spanish-speaking South Americans—prevents a community of language from becoming a cultural community.

We have still to consider the first 'element' of the nation: a common territory. I have noted repeatedly that territorial separation disrupts the unity of a nation. The nation as a natural community is gradually destroyed by national separatism, because the diverse conditions of the struggle for existence breed different characteristics in the spatially separated parts of the nation, and this diversity cannot be compensated by any ethnic mingling. The nation as a cultural community is similarly destroyed by spatial separation, because the spatially distinct parts of the nation which carry on their struggle for existence in isolation from each other, also differentiate their originally unitary culture, and in the absence of intercourse between them the original unitary culture dissolves into a number of diverse cultures. This appears very conspicuously in the differentiation of the language into different languages, as a result of the inadequate bonds of intercourse between the spatially separated parts of the original nation. Just as spatial separation disrupts nations, so a common territory is certainly one of the conditions of existence of a nation; but only in so far as it is the condition of a common destiny. To the extent that a cultural community, and so far as is conceivable a natural community, can be maintained in spite of spatial separation, then the latter does not constitute an obstacle to a common national character. The German who continues to be influenced by German culture in America

—even though this is only through German books and news-papers—and who gives his children a German education, remains a German in spite of spatial separation. Only in so far as a common territory is a condition of a community of cul-ture, is it also a condition of the nation's existence. In the age of printing, the post and telegraph, railways and steamships, this is much less the case than it was formerly. If, therefore, a common territory is conceived not as one of the 'elements' of the nation along with others, but as a condition for the others to operate, then the necessary limits of the frequently uttered proposition, that a common territory is a condition for the existence of a nation, can easily be shown. This conception brings us no small advantage; for our understanding of the relation of the nation to its most important constituent body, the state, rests upon our idea of the relation of the nation to a territory. We shall need to return to this question and to illus-trate our solution by some specific examples. Here, however, we are concerned only to show how this theory of the nation is able to comprehend the various factors, which the older theory merely juxtaposed as 'elements' of the nation, as the effective forces of a system, in their mutual dependence and their interaction.

But the worth of the theory has still to be shown in one task in which earlier attempts to determine the essence of the nation failed; that is, the demarcation of the concept of the nation from the narrower communities of locality and descent within the nation. To be sure, a common destiny has bound the Germans together in a community of character. But does this not apply equally to the Saxons or the Bavarians, the Tyroleans or the Styrians? Or indeed to the inhabitants of each particular Alpine valley? Have not different ancestral destinies, the diversities of settlement and land distribution, of the fertility of the soil, and of climate, created strongly marked communities of character among Zittertalen and Passeirern, Vintschgern, and Pusterern? Where does the boundary lie between those communities of character that we regard as autonomous nations, and those that we see as narrower associations within the nation?

We should remember here that we have already become familiar with these narrower communities of character as products of the disintegration of the nation resting on common descent. From the time that the descendants of the primitive German people became territorially separated from each other, were bound to the land by agriculture, and led separate lives without social intercourse or intermarriage, they became increasingly diversified. It is true that they started from a common natural and cultural community, but they are in the process of forming autonomous, clearly distinctive natural and cultural communities. There is a tendency for a distinct nation to come into being from every one of these narrower associations which have emerged from a single nation. The difficulty of demarcating the concept of these narrower communities of character from that of the nation is therefore, a consequence of the fact that they represent stages in the development of the nation.

As we have seen, there is a counter-tendency, which strives to bind the nation more closely together, working against the tendency to disintegration. At first, however, this counter-tendency is only effective in the case of the ruling classes. It binds the medieval knights, and the educated classes of the early capitalist period, into a close-knit nation, sharply distinguished from every other cultural community, brings them into close economic, political, and social intercourse, creates a uniform language for them, and enables the same intellectual culture, the same civilization, to affect them. This bond of a common culture links the ruling classes to a particular nation. No one can be in any doubt whether an educated person is German or Dutch, Slovene or Croatian; national education, the national language, mark off from each other even the most closely related nations. By contrast, the question as to whether the peasants of some village or other should count as low Germans or as Dutch, as Slovenes or as Croats, can only be decided in a somewhat arbitrary fashion. Only the citizens of each nation are clearly distinguished from each other, not the peasants and small farmers.

Modern capitalism begins gradually to distinguish the lower classes in each nation more sharply from each other, for these classes too gain access to national education, to the cultural life of their nation, and to the national language. The tendency toward unification also affects the labouring masses.

But only socialist society will bring this tendency to fruitic
It will distinguish whole peoples from each other by t.
diversity of national education and civilization, in the same
way as at present only the educated classes of the different
nations are distinguished. True, there will be narrower communities of character within the socialist nation too; but there
will be no autonomous cultural communities, for every local
community, as a result of cultural intercourse, and the exchange of ideas, will itself be under the influence of the whole
national culture.

Thus we arrive at a comprehensive definition of the nation.
*The nation is the totality of men bound together through a com-
mon destiny into a community of character.* Through a *common
destiny*: this characteristic distinguishes the nation from the
international character groupings, such as an occupation, a
class, or the members of a state, which rest upon a similarity,
not a community, of destiny. The *totality* of the associated
characters: this distinguishes them from the narrower communities of character within the nation, which never create
a natural and cultural community that is determined by its
own destiny, but only one that is closely connected with the
whole nation, and consequently determined by the destiny of
the latter. In the period of tribal communism the nation was
sharply delimited in this way; the totality of all those de-
scended from the original Baltic people, whose cultural being,
through natural inheritance and cultural tradition, was determined by the destiny of that ancestral stock, constituted the
nation. In socialist society the nation will again be sharply defined in this way; all those who share in national education
and national cultural values, whose character is therefore
shaped by the destiny of the nation which determines the content of these values, will constitute the nation. In a society
which is based upon private ownership of the means of labour,
the ruling classes, once the knights and now the educated
classes, constitute the nation as the totality of those in whom a
similar upbringing resulting from the history of the nation,
and a common language and national education, produces an
affinity of character. But the popular masses do not constitute
the nation: they do so no longer, because the age-old
community of descent no longer binds them closely enough

together; and they do not yet do so, because they are not fully incorporated in the developing system of education. The difficulty of finding a satisfactory definition of the nation, upon which all earlier attempts came to grief, is therefore historically conditioned. People tried to discover the nation in our present class society, in which the old sharply defined community of descent has disintegrated into an immense number of local and descent groups, while the growth of a new community of education has not yet been able to unite these small groups in a national whole.

Thus our search for the essence of the nation reveals a grandiose historical picture. At the outset, in the period of primitive communism and of nomadic agriculture, there is a unitary nation as a community of descent. Then, after the transition to settled agriculture and the development of private property, the old nation is divided into the common culture of the ruling classes on one side, and the peasants and small farmers on the other, the latter confined to narrow local regions produced by the disintegration of the old nation. Later, with the development of the capitalist mode of social production and the extension of the national cultural community, the working and exploited classes are still excluded, but the tendency to national unity on the basis of national education gradually becomes stronger than the particularistic tendency of the disintegration of the old nation, based upon common descent, into increasingly sharply differentiated local groups. Finally, when society divests social production of its capitalist integument, the unitary nation as a community of education, work, and culture emerges again. The development of the nation reflects the history of the mode of production and of property. Just as private ownership of the means of production and individual production develops out of the social system of primitive communism, and from this, again, there develops co-operative production on the basis of social ownership, so the unitary nation divides into members of the nation and those who are excluded and become fragmented into small local circles; but with the development of social production these circles are again drawn together and will eventually be absorbed into the unitary socialist nation of the future. The nation of the era of private property and individual production, which is divided into members and non-members, and into numerous circumscribed local groups, is the product of the disintegration of the communist nation of the past and the material for the socialist nation of the future.

Hence the nation proves to be a historical phenomenon in two respects. In terms of its material content it is a historical phenomenon, since the living national character which operates in every one of its members is the residue of a historical development; in the nationality of the individual member there is reflected the history of society, whose product is the individual. From the point of view of its formal structure it is a historical phenomenon, because diverse broad circles are bound together in a nation by different means and in different ways at the various stages of historical development. The history of society does not only decide which given characteristics of the members of the nation are to constitute the national character; the form in which the historically effective forces produce a common character is also historically conditioned.

The national conception of history, which sees the driving force of events in the struggles of nations, strives for a mechanics of nations. According to this view, nations are regarded as elements which cannot be reduced any further, as fixed bodies which clash in space, and act upon each other by pressure and collision. But my conception dissolves the nation itself into a process. For me, history no longer reflects the struggles of nations; instead the nation itself appears as the reflection of historical struggles. For the nation is only manifested in the national character, in the nationality of the individual; and the nationality of the individual is only one aspect of his determination by the history of society, by the development of the conditions and techniques of labour.

OTTO BAUER, *Socialism and the Principle of Nationality*[3]

Every new economic order creates new forms of state constitution and new rules for demarcating political structures. How will communities be separated from each other in socialist

---

[3] From *Die Nationalitätenfrage und die Sozialdemokratie* (1907), pp. 509–16, 520–521. [Eds.]

society? Will the nationality of the citizens determine the limits of the community in this case too?

In order to answer this question about the relation of socialism to the political principle of nationality, we must start from the fact that only socialism will give the whole people a share in the national culture. With the uprooting of the population through social production, and the development of the nation into a homogeneous community of education, labour, and culture, the more circumscribed local associations will lose their vigour, while the bond which unites all members of the nation will become increasingly strong. Today the Tyrolean peasant is closely linked with the fellow members of his province through the distinctive peasant culture of the province and is sharply distinguished from the Germans outside the province. This fact of national life is reflected in national consciousness. The Tyrolean peasant feels himself to be first of all a Tyrolean and only rarely remembers that he is a German. The Tyrolean worker is already quite different; he has little share in the particular way of life of the Tyrolean peasants, and he is linked with the German nation by much stronger bonds. By making every German a product of German culture, and by giving him the opportunity to share in the benefits of the progress of German culture, socialist society will, for the first time, abolish particularism within the nation. There is no doubt that this development will strengthen the principle of political nationality.

Another group of phenomena have a similar influence. The peasant masses are completely bound by tradition; the household possessions of their ancestors are dear to them, while everything new is hateful. Their love for the values of the past also has political consequences; it is the root of their attachment to the church, their local patriotism, their dynastic loyalty. We have seen the significance of this fact in our investigation of the forces which assure Austria's stability; the peasants who cannot free themselves from the chains of centuries-old tradition are one of the supports of this state. If on the one hand the socialist mode of production integrates the masses for the first time into the national cultural community and thereby strengthens their national consciousness, so on the other hand it destroys their attachment to the ideologies of past centuries which is an obstacle to the full realization of the nationality principle. It not only increases the driving force of the nationality principle, but also clears away the obstacles from its course.

Nevertheless, all this only prepares the victory of the nationality principle. It will only be achieved by that flood tide of rationalism which will submerge all traditional ideologies as soon as the dam of capitalism is broken. In the great period of transition from capitalist to socialist society, in which everything old is destroyed, all old authorities are overturned, and the old property relations are finally eliminated, what is old and traditional loses its sanctity. Only now will the masses learn to overthrow the old in order to create on its ruins new structures to serve their purposes. This revolution in the consciousness of the masses will be consolidated by the everyday praxis of socialist society, which gives the masses for the first time the power to determine their own destiny, to decide by free discussion and resolution their own future, and thus make the development of human culture a deliberate, intentional, conscious human act. It will be made possible by socialist education, which will provide every individual with the cultural objects of the whole nation and indeed a good part of those of the whole human race. Only in this way can the individual be liberated from the traditions of restricted local circles, broaden his views, and be enabled to establish his own ends and make an intelligent choice of the means to those ends. No state boundary which past ages established for their own purposes will be sacrosanct for the people living in socialist society. Only now will all peoples be ready to confront the question which, in the nineteenth century, was only a question for the educated, concerning the relation between the internal community and external power, which appears in the antagonism between nation and state. While the narrow local associations within the nation become weaker, the national cultural community embraces more closely the people as a whole, and the national community becomes for them a certain and unalterable fact; but they conceive external power as a means serving human ends, which must adapt itself to human ends. So there comes to life in them the basic idea of the nationality principle, the principle of the adaptation of external power to inner community.

The content of the nationality principle is the rule that the external power should consolidate and serve the internal community. But this principle will only become causally effective as a motive when the transformation of the techniques and conditions of labour makes the traditional forms of the state which do not correspond to this principle insupportable. So it was at an earlier time, that when the traditional small states no longer corresponded with its need, the bourgeoisie inscribed the principle of nationality on its banner. It will be so again, as soon as the transformation of social production from its capitalist to its socialist form changes the human spirit, destroys old cultural values, and prepares to confront the question of the 'natural' limits of the state.

But if the masses see the free national community as their goal, socialism also shows them the way to this goal; for socialism is necessarily based upon democracy. Even such a democratic community will compel minorities to bow to the will of the whole; it is unimportant whether it does this by direct compulsion or by excluding them from their share in the process and profits of labour. But such a community will never be able to incorporate whole nations which do not want to belong to it. How could nations in which the masses are in full possession of the national culture, provided with the rights of participation in legislation and self-government, and armed, be compelled to bow to the yoke of a community to which they do not wish to belong? All state power rests on the power of weapons. The present-day people's army is still, thanks to an ingenious procedure, a tool of power in the hands of an individual, a family, or a class, just like the armies of knights and mercenaries in the past. The army of the democratic community in socialist society, made up of highly cultivated men, who no longer obey the command of a foreign power in their workplaces, and are called to full participation in political life, in legislation, and administration, is no longer a separate power, but is nothing more than the armed people itself. With this vanishes all possibility of rule by a foreign nation.

At present, the situation of the nationalities in our society is not based only on the fact that whole nations do not have the power to achieve the national state to which they aspire, nor only on the fact that large sections of many nations, under the influence of the ideologies of past epochs and as a result of their exclusion from the cultural community of the nation, resist the idea of national unity and freedom. The thorough-going implementation of the principle of nationality is also impeded by the fact that the modern state is at the same time an economic region. Should it not strive, therefore, to embrace an area which can, at least to some extent, be economically independent? Would not the productivity of labour fall, if a socialist community, in order to implement strictly the principle of national demarcation, desired only to encompass a small economic region, without regard for production?

We should remember here, in the first place, that only socialism will be able to implement successfully the international division of labour. Simple commodity production greatly increased the productivity of labour, by extending the division of labour, at first within a limited area, in a town and its surrounding trading region. Capitalism subsequently promoted the division of labour within large economic regions, and in this way again greatly increased the productivity of labour. This process already laid the basis for an international division of labour. Classical political economy then established theoretically the proposition that the productivity of labour and wealth increase in every economic region when the inhabitants of each region produce only those goods for which the conditions in their region are favourable, and obtain the other goods they need by exchange. This idea is not to be disputed theoretically. Nevertheless, capitalist society has not achieved and now never will achieve a free exchange of commodities and an international division of labour. For the goal of capitalist economic policy is not the greatest possible increase in the productivity of labour, but the greatest possible augmentation of profits. It seeks to attain this goal not by allocating productive capital to those individual branches of production which would make possible the greatest increase in the productivity of labour, but by accelerating the flow of unused capital into the sphere of production, and extending continually its markets and spheres of investment. Only where the requirements of the international division of labour happen to coincide with the requirements of capitalist economic policy—as was the case in England until recently— is freedom of trade realized in capitalist society.

In socialist society, on the contrary, where the means of production is no longer capital, capitalist economic policy no longer has any sense. Socialist society, therefore, will be able to achieve for the first time an international division of labour and the corresponding distribution of labour. Of course, this will not happen at a single stroke. If a state has developed an iron industry behind protective tariffs, instead of making use of the richer iron ores of other countries through a free exchange of goods, socialist society could not suddenly shut down the existing furnaces and steel works. But the number of workers, and the productive apparatus of society, grows every year; and the new workers, the new means of production, will regularly be applied to those branches of production which enjoy the most favourable conditions, and their products will be exchanged for those of other countries. In this way the socialist community will be able to accomplish, in a few decades, the division of labour between states that classical economics advocated.

Thus, for the first time, the greatest obstacle to the implementation of the nationality principle will be eliminated. For then even the smallest nation will be able to create an independently organized national economy; while the great nations produce a variety of goods, the small nation will apply its whole labour-power to the production of one or a few kinds of goods, and will acquire all other goods from other nations by exchange. In spite of its small size it will enjoy all the advantages of large-scale enterprise. Even those peoples whose territory has been most meagrely endowed with natural resources will be able to establish an independent economy; after all, Ricardo showed conclusively that even the economic region least favoured by nature has a role in the international division of labour, namely to produce those goods in the manufacture of which the superiority of all other countries is proportionately least, and to exchange these goods for the products of all other economic regions. Hence, through the international division of labour, the whole of civilized humanity becomes a great organism; and precisely by this means the political freedom and unity of all nations becomes possible. In a society in which each community is supposed to be autarchic and to supply its own needs, the full implementation of the nationality principle is impossible; national freedom is necessarily denied to the small nations, the nations whose territory provides less favourable conditions for production. As soon as the international division of labour embraces all peoples, the most important barrier preventing the reconciliation of the political division of humanity with its incorporation in historical cultural communities, falls.

Even the shifts within the organization of social labour assume an entirely new character in socialist society. The unregulated migration of individuals, dominated by the blind laws of capitalist competition, will then cease, and will be replaced by a conscious regulation of migration by the socialist communities. They will encourage immigrants where an increase in the number of workers will raise the productivity of labour; they will induce a part of the population to emigrate, where increasing numbers result in a declining yield. This deliberate regulation of immigration and emigration will give every nation, for the first time, control over its linguistic boundaries. It will no longer be possible for social migration to infringe again and again the nationality principle, against the will of the nation.

It is no accident that the realization of the nationality principle is linked with the victory of socialism. In the era of tribal communism, communities were, at least originally, nationally unified. Even where a tribe was subjugated by a foreign people, it did not initially lose its own political organization, but only became dependent as a community on the community of the victors, to whom it owed tribute. The political disruption of the nation first began with the disintegration of the old communist nation into narrow local associations. And foreign domination only became possible with class divisions, with the cleavage into members of the nation and those who are excluded. The opposition between rulers and ruled, exploiting and exploited classes, assumes the form of the domination of the historical nations over those without history. With the development of social production in the form of capitalist commodity production, political particularism is forced to retreat; the need to extend the division of labour within large economic regions creates great national states on the ruins of countless small states. But as a result of the same development foreign domination also becomes intolerable; the nations without history awaken to historical life and likewise strive to achieve a national state. Finally social production sheds its capitalist shell, and only then is a national cultural community attained. Only then does all particularism within the nation vanish and all rule of one nation over other peoples become impossible, only then does the division of labour embrace the whole of humanity, and there is no longer any obstacle to the political organization of humanity into free nations. The political organization of humanity reflects its national cultural being, which is determined in turn by the development of the techniques and conditions of labour. Political particularism and foreign rule are the political forms of an epoch which is characterized from the point of view of nationality by the division of the nation into members and outcasts, and by the disintegration of the nation into narrow local associations; and economically by settled agriculture, private ownership of the means of labour, and landlordism. The principle of nationality is the constitutional principle of the unitary and autonomous nation in a particular epoch of social production. The construction of the great national states in the nineteenth century is only the precursor of an era in which the principle of nationality will be fully realized, just as the extension of the cultural community by modern capitalism is the precursor of the full attainment of the national cultural community by socialism, and as social production in its capitalist form is the precursor of co-operative production by and for society. . . .

We have seen that socialism leads necessarily to the realization of the principle of nationality. But while socialist society gradually constructs above the national community a federal state in which the communities of the individual nations are once again incorporated, the principle of nationality changes into that of national autonomy, from a rule for the formation of states into a rule of the state constitution. The socialist principle of nationality expresses a higher unity of the principle of nationality and national autonomy.

Thus the socialist principle of nationality is able to combine the advantages of both the bourgeois principle of nationality and national autonomy. By organizing the nation as a community it gives it the right to legislate and to administer itself, power to dispose over the means and the product of labour, military power. But by incorporating the nation into a community of international law, established as a corporate entity, it secures for the nation power even beyond the limits of its territory. Let us suppose, for example, that socialist society could raise the productivity of labour in Germany by reducing the number of workers on German soil, while raising the productivity of labour in South Russia by increasing the number of workers. It would then seek to transfer a part of the German population to South Russia. But Germany would not send its sons and daughters to the east without assuring their cultural independence. So the German colonists would not enter the community of the Ukraine as individuals, but as a corporate legal entity. If the national territorial bodies first unite in an international community, there now arise, as a result of planned colonization, foreign-speaking associations of people within the national communities, associations which are legally bound, in many respects, to the territorial bodies of their nation, and in other respects, to the community of the foreign nation. Socialist society will undoubtedly present a variegated picture of national associations of people and territorial bodies; it will be as different from the centralized, atomistic constitution of present-day states as from the equally varied and complex organization of medieval society. I do not intend to outline here a fantasy of the coming society. What is said about it here is the result of sober reflection upon its nature. The transformation of men by the socialist mode of production leads necessarily to the organization of humanity in national communities. The international division of labour leads necessarily to the unification of the national communities in a social structure of a higher order. All nations will be united for the common domination of nature, but the totality will be organized in national communities which will be encouraged to develop autonomously and to enjoy freely their national culture—that is the socialist principle of nationality.

KARL RENNER, *The Development of the National Idea*[4]

The enormous changes in the map of Europe which were accomplished in the nineteenth century and transformed the world of states, are characterized by the fact that great nations appear as actors on the stage of history. Even before the French Revolution there were states and peoples on the European mainland, but the states were the property of dynasties, and the peoples were only the objects of their rule—objects and not subjects of the state administration. The dynastic state can, without reproach, unite unconnected regions and fragments of peoples with different languages: the English dynasty owned Hanover on German soil, the Prussian Neuchâtel in Switzerland, the Habsburg, in addition to its inherited German lands, Hungary, Galicia, some areas of South Germany, the Aarau Canton, parts of Alsace and present-day Belgium, parts of Italy. The nations were there, existing corporeally in their millions of members and spiritually in their common language and culture, but not as political personalities, that is, not as legal entities, as communities organized in states. They united for the first time in circumscribed state territories by means of warlike revolutions and revolutionary wars, and through their ruling classes they seized state power either directly or indirectly. This process of the formation of nation states can be regarded as the political law of motion of the nineteenth century. It is based upon the economic transformation of simple commodity production into the capitalist mode of production, a development which transforms the old feudal class system, with its various estates, and leads to the triumph of the bourgeoisie. The nation state is the state idea of rising capitalism; the basis of the state is not the economic region, but the region of national settlement.

Historically this idea of the state bears the name 'the principle of nationality'; it claims that 'every nation should form one state, and every state should embrace only one nation!' According to this view, the map of Europe has to be redrawn; the circumscribed areas of settlement of the nations should be organized as states—national unity! Within its boundaries the

[4] From *Marxismus, Krieg und Internationale*, pp. 139–41, 142–4, 148–54, 157–8. [Eds.]

nation should not be subject either to foreign rule (opposition to domination by a foreign, non-national ruler), or to absolutist princely rule (opposition to the internal absence of rights) —national freedom! In this dual form the concept of the nation became the decisive political idea of European bourgeois democracy (Mazzini) in the mid-nineteenth century. This occurred simultaneously with the appearance of the *Communist Manifesto* and the foundation of the International Working Men's Association, and it soon developed into a conscious opposition to these world-historical founding deeds of international proletarian socialism. . . .

Long before the nation emerged as a political factor it existed unconsciously as national character, semi-consciously as national feeling, and finally as a clear national consciousness. The feeling, and awareness of the feeling, that someone who has the same language and culture belongs to us, that 'we' are different from 'foreigners', that we have to stand with our own people and against foreigners, is naïve nationalism: that primitive, certainly genuine, and in a sense, eternal impulse in the life of the emotions. No analysis of human society is needed in order to explain it, but by the same token it does not explain the simplest facts of more highly organized societies; neither hospitality, nor the preference shown by particular classes for foreign culture, nor the preference of ruling classes for foreign languages, nor the historically frequent imitation and acceptance of foreign customs by the masses. That indefinite feeling of rejection of what is foreign has always been misused by the ruling class without any difficulty. How the pre-1848 German democrats despised those who wanted to justify the unbearable political conditions in Germany as an emanation of the 'Christian-German spirit of the people'; how they despised the national-historical school, 'a school which justifies the infamy of today by the infamy of yesterday'. (Marx, 'Contribution to the Critique of Hegel's Philosophy of Right. Introduction.')

This high valuation of the nation has always been dear to all conservative classes. 'There is no class which is intrinsically more emancipated from all national values than the proletariat, which has been totally liberated from tradition by the disruptive, destructive power of capitalism, and excluded from enjoyment of the national culture; and which rises up in struggle against all the historically given traditional powers.'[5] Like every aspiring class, like the bourgeoisie which in its time also rose up against the feudal powers, it searches the whole world for the intellectual and material means of release from its domestic misery. When it belongs to a historical nation, it professes at first an unreflective naïve cosmopolitanism, which is quite different from conscious internationalism. But in nations without history, whose ruling classes speak a foreign language, capitalist exploitation does not appear as an economic necessity, but as national coercion, as foreign rule; in such nations, the awakening proletariat is seized by a naïve nationalism fortified by class hatred, and this obstructs, for a long time, the penetration of socialist ideas.

A later stage of development is represented by that cultural nationalism which is not yet engaged in dominating and shaping the state. Remote from, and hostile to, the state it devotes itself to improving its own people intellectually and morally, develops the national language, literature, and art, and to this end gathers together with loving care all that is best from the most distant past and from all peoples. It is a nationalism which is at the same time humanism, and is characteristic of our classical period. But it too precedes the age we are concerned with; it does not yet touch the core of the national question, the relation of the nation to the state. Our classical philosophy of the state deals with the state in all periods, and for all peoples, without any regard to language, neither demanding a single language nor rejecting the polyglot state; it is quite indifferent to the nation. Only in Fichte's *Addresses to the German Nation*[6] does the nation appear as a factor which forms states and therefore politics; he introduces the German nation as a unity and totality into German history, in a theoretical manner, although his conception of the historical vocation of the nation diverges widely from all the ideas of the nationalists. . . .

The political psychology of the period from 1870 to 1890 was not determined by the liberal bourgeoisie, by the manufacturer (the industrialist) who, with his factory, personally

[5] Renner provides no reference for this quotation. [Eds.]
[6] Delivered in Berlin 1807–8. [Eds.]

accomplishes the transition from handicraft to machine production, as the pioneer of a technological transformation. At
this time, and certainly after 1873, he was the most maligned
person in the nation. It was the victorious Junkers, as economists and bureaucrats, who determined the national ideal and
the national mode of thought. The country estate and the
peasant village, not the factory or the town, were regarded as
the basis of national life. The essence of the nation resides in
the peasant's bones. Neither shipping nor world trade, least
of all free trade, make the nation healthy and strong. Commodity exchange and a money economy are regarded as hag-
gling and usury rather than as productive labour, the main
forms of which are agriculture and handicrafts. 'Protect
national labour' is the slogan of the epoch. The future of the
nation does not lie on the sea, nor in colonies, nor in world-
political adventures. The whole of the Balkans are not worth
the bones of a Pomeranian grenadier, and colonial politics are
a senseless adventure of people who want to be Jacks-of-all-
trades. The national state is politically self-sufficient. In order
to satisfy its own needs, it must have economic autarchy. The
protective tariffs which serve this autarchy are not just
temporary measures but are intended to keep the realm
permanently independent of the world economy.

According to the outlook of the age, the 'new spirit' of
liberalism threatens great harm to the people; the task of protecting them devolves upon the socially minded monarchy,
and the professorial socialists are its prophets. Protection and
insurance for the workers, defence of the middle classes, protection of national production, economic autarchy, the
authority of royalty, of the state power, of the master in the
factory—in short a paternalistic system in every respect—
these are the guidelines for the nation. The class interest of
the rulers is embellished with ethics and science, and gilded
with historical memories and the glory of victorious battles;
it becomes the national ideal.

This reorientation of ideas is not peculiar to the Germany
of 1870 to 1890. Even in England liberal industrialism was
superseded by social Toryism, whose intellectual founder and
leader was Benjamin Disraeli. From liberal industrialism to
social Toryism is, economically and politically, at least as great

a step as the previous one from mercantilism to the physiocrats; fundamentally it is the same step at a historically higher
stage of development. Here we are not so much interested in
economic change, as in the revaluation of the national idea
which flows from the economy of the period. For this age the
principle of nationality, the democratic, nay revolutionary
principle of the unity, freedom, and self-determination of the
nation, is over and done with, externally as well as internally.
It is not 'the nation' as a basic and primary phenomenon which
uses the state as its tool; the primary fact is the state, and the
nation is the object of its patronage. . . .

Capitalism is now passing from its industrial into its
finance-capitalist stage. The entrepreneur has been displaced
by the enterprise, the industrial capitalist by the loan-capi-
talist, by the bank. Under the sway of finance capital the protective tariff has changed its function a third time. It is no
longer List's[7] temporary tariff for the purpose of catching up;
no longer the 'protection of national labour' of social Toryism,
which is supposed to make the state economically autarchic
and hence independent of foreign nations; it is a means of
establishing the monopolistic exploitation of national labour
and by this means conquering the world market. It is a cartel
tariff, which is intended not so much to hinder foreign imports, as to facilitate exports. By contrast with the free trade
period of industrialism it is not so much manufactured goods,
commodities, use-values, that are to be exported, as capital
itself. Of course, the export of commodities continues and
perhaps still exceeds in volume and value the export of capital,
but it is the latter which is vitally necessary for capitalism at
this stage. . . .

How does the national ideal change in this period? Initially,
the state and the economic region protected by tariffs, not the
national settlement region, is responsible for this latest development. The state has increasingly separated itself from
its original basis, the nation. A situation which as a general
rule can only be grasped conceptually, appears in Austria with
dazzling clarity. Only a decade ago the national impulse of the
Magyars was so strong that they aspired to a separate state and
their own customs area. The reality of the great common

[7] Friedrich List (1789–1846). [Eds.]

economic area has prevailed and today they passionately defend their economic and national existence within the framework of the state as a whole; they defend themselves by defending the empire. What an abrupt and fundamental change! It shows us that among the ruling classes the interests of statehood have long since triumphed over the old ideal of the nation; that it is now no longer a matter of preserving the national idea, but of defending economic interests and traditional economic communities. But aside from Austria–Hungary the great states of Europe are nation states; consequently with them nation and state coincide, and for that very reason the national idea, in the last generation, has been totally inspired by the needs of statehood and the economic requirements of the state. The nation state needs exports, a merchant fleet, foreign markets. It needs penal tariffs to protect the cartels, so that it can dump its own goods in foreign states. But it needs still more. Foreign markets and trading posts as they existed in the free trade period are no longer adequate. A market is only really profitable when it is monopolized, when there are preferential tariffs or no tariffs, and that can only be achieved if the market is also dominated politically. . . .

Suddenly the national spirit has been torn from the confines of landed estates and villages, from semi-feudal romanticism and Teutonic dreams of Odin, and led on to the world stage. 'Germany's future depends upon the sea.' A different romanticism continues the crusades of the old German emperors; Kaiser Wilhelm visits the Caliph in Constantinople, the holy sepulchre in Jerusalem, and the Sultan of Morocco. It is a question of the Bagdad railway and the copper deposits of Morocco. The Boxer rising in China gives an impetus to the acquisition of Chiao-chou. The German Empire seeks a place in the sun in every part of the world. . . .

This is the latest phase of bourgeois-national thought, the dominant national idea of our age. Although it has been illustrated here by the example of Germany, it is just the same among the French, English, Italian, and Russian bourgeoisie; it emerges in the capitalist mind as a necessary consequence of the fearsome development of capitalism itself. National imperialism today is simply the national idea of the ruling classes.

If you declare yourself for the nation—even though you may
mean only the cultural, the democratic, or even the Tory concept of the nation—the other person will take you for a
national imperialist, and nothing more; every qualification is
regarded as a betrayal of the nation. . . .

It would be an error and self-deception, and so would mis-
lead the working class, if one disregarded the circumstances
which give this war its specific characteristics. It is not a
national war in the sense of the principle of nationality; it is
the opposite of such a war, in the sense of the old, pure
national idea not yet thrown into confusion by class antagonisms. The International of the East dominated by Russia is
allied with the British and French International of the West
in order to deny to the middle European, middle Asiatic International access to the rest of the world and a future share in
ruling the world. It is a struggle between imperialisms for
world domination, for the right and the power to unify and
dominate other historical nations and peoples, or those which
do not yet have a history, which have not yet developed a
national consciousness. It is a struggle for the right and power
to subject international groups of servile peoples to the bourgeoisie of a dominant nation.

The ruling class of every such ruling nation (or one aspiring
to rule) calls this endeavour—imposed upon it by the economic needs of capitalism—'national' and regards it as the highest task of the nation, and therefore of all sections of the
people. I cannot investigate here whether and to what extent
the proletariat is involved in, or can escape, national imperialism; my inquiry concerns only the history of the idea of the
nation. This inquiry has led to a definitive judgement on one
branch of its development—the bourgeois-capitalist—which
both conceptually and historically presupposes the self-
enclosed, sovereign nation state.

At a definite stage of production, when the internal market
is saturated, national capitalism necessarily bursts through
the confines of the national state and drives toward the
creation of an international world state. But the latter is international only in a physical sense, in the variety of peoples who
compose it; not in a legal or cultural sense, for the community
of peoples in this world state is in greater or lesser degree un-

free and delivered over to domination and exploitation by the bourgeoisie of a ruling nation. Thus the principle of nationality is turned on its head, and that is the outcome of the development through three generations: national imperialism, this latest phase of bourgeois-national thought, brings with it the destruction of the national idea itself and abolishes the principle of nationality from which it arose. Capitalism develops from an internal to an external form in such a way that domination of a ruling class over all other classes in the nation will become in the future the subjection of all other nations in the world to a ruling nation which destroys their national existence. The principle of nationality aimed to create a community of independent nations, but national imperialism enslaves them under a common knout. The conflict among the rulers of the world seems to concern only whether this knout shall be English, Russian, or German.

MAX ADLER, *The Ideology of the World War*[8]

It is a triumph of scientific socialism—of course I mean its doctrine, which unfortunately has to be distinguished very sharply from the actual policies of the socialist parties at the present time—that its basic theory, the materialist conception of history, is the only one that makes possible a scientific analysis not only of nationalism in general, but of its world-historical product: imperialism and its World War. How often have we heard the opponents of the materialist conception of history emphasize with a triumphant air the significance of the national factor as an alleged refutation of the theory of the fundamental determination of history by economic conditions. Today even schoolchildren can learn from every popular and patriotic statement that this great war, despite all its frequently inflated national-cultural phraseology, is being conducted to defend the economic interests of their country; that it is the outcome of the economic rivalry between nations culminating in the conflict between English and German trade, which pushed everything else aside. Thus, a work of popularization such as that of Artur Dix[9] is quite right in

---

[8] From 'Zur Ideologie des Weltkrieges', *Der Kampf*, viii (1915), pp. 123–30. [Eds.]

[9] Artur Dix, *Der Weltwirtschaftskrieg* (1914).

calling this no longer the Great War or the German war, but simply the 'world economic war'. Without meaning to do so, he provides a revaluation, very revealing for our time, of Clausewitz's much quoted phrase that war is only the continuation of politics by other means, when he says: 'World wars are not only fought with weapons; they are also world economic struggles. This world economic war is also conducted in times of peace, and when the cannon begin to speak it merely assumes a more intense form.'

In fact, this confirms what we noted at the outset: this World War is only the armed continuation of a war which has already been conducted for a long time without arms in the bourgeois world—the war of capital, which has acquired a national character, for its profits. That is the ultimate goal for which this war is being fought; the nationalization of surplus value, its monopolization by each of the great economic regions which has entered the conflict. If the bourgeois poets and thinkers utter their resounding words about the freedom and honour of the fatherland and about the renewal and elevation of the people's consciousness they are quite honest and sincere in what they say. For the regrettable isolation of the bourgeois intellectuals from the real driving forces of social and political life (often lamented since the time of Fichte) has meant that they have no idea, especially in such stormy times when they are utterly captivated by the glittering exterior of events, that this drive and upsurge of nations is fundamentally about much more prosaic, if no less important, things. It concerns the elementary urge toward a secure and exclusive disposal over the basic trading commodities—iron, livestock and cereals, cotton and furs, petroleum and coal. The soul of the bourgeois epoch resides in these things, and the real content of the idea of national domination is to be found in the power over them. Artur Dix again expresses this very well, when he suggests the following hierarchy of national goals: world economy, world power, world culture. Culture comes last not only because the superstructure only arises on the foundations, but also as a luxury which can only be satisfied when the rest has been gained—God granting that time and strength remains for it.

One hears it said very often that this war has something so

peculiar and baffling about it that no one can say conclusively what its object really it. After all, each of the powers desires only to have the attacks of the others repulsed; hence all tear each other to pieces—from the defensive. The reason for this extremely curious phenomenon is that the people everywhere are prevented from attaining a clear understanding of the real goal of the war by the obscuring influence of ideology, which was mentioned earlier. Even in the proletariat it has only become clear to a few that the idea of the nation is only an imperialist expression for the increased commercial and industrial power of a part of the nation, the ruling classes, for their supremacy in the world market, and thus for their world profits. 'Who is to be lord of the earth?' That is, whom shall the capitalist world serve, and to whom shall all interest and profit flow? The whole world has been plunged into flames to decide this question; it was bound to be the fateful question of our age, because the age has not yet found a way of organizing economic life in any but capitalist forms, and so the peoples of the civilized world must now bear all the suffering and destruction of war. Certainly it is only a stage of a necessary economic development, prescribed by the immanent tendencies of capitalism, which is now being accomplished. But to understand this necessity does not mean that we must celebrate it as the high point of national progress or a popular renaissance.

Here only the Marxist standpoint, which has guided us safely through the vagueness of ideology and enabled us for the first time to give a real sense to such concepts as state, people, and similar general ideas, proves to have explanatory power. We began really to understand the nature of the state and the nation, and their transformations, only when the mysterious power of the state, apparently based upon the will of the whole people, was revealed as the organized will to power of one class over the other, and when its source was disclosed in the economic opposition of class interests. This could only be understood when the cosy picture of the unity of the nation was dissolved into that of a class struggle within the people that permeated every stage in the historical development of the state. The new and seductive feature of the idea of the imperialist state is that it no longer presents the old naïve ideology of a national community, innocently unaware of the economic conflicts which undermine it. Instead, it undertakes precisely to reconstruct this ideology from a powerful economic common interest, the common interest of all classes, as it believes, in the economic exploitation of foreign peoples and countries. Indeed, in this way it even succeeds in perceiving itself as the means by which the accommodation and reconciliation of class antagonisms can be achieved, through a common interest in dominating the world, which creates solidarity.

In order to demonstrate fully the deceptiveness of the ideology, we should now undertake an economic and social-psychological analysis of imperialism. It is impossible to do this here, and also unnecessary, for it has already been done brilliantly and comprehensively, in two works which are indispensable for an economic and political understanding of our age. I refer, of course, to Otto Bauer's book on the problem of nationalities, especially Section VI, and to Rudolf Hilferding's *Finanzkapital*. For our purpose, which is to elucidate the character of the war ideology, it is enough to present the conclusions of those studies.

In the first place, imperialism is not the creation of an ambitious ruler, or of a people bent upon conquests, but the necessary outcome of the peaceful work of the merchant, the manufacturer, the stockbroker, and the financier; in short, of the whole capitalist mode of production and circulation. It results from the insatiable and uncontrolled drive of capital to realize itself. At first it strives for realization, for the creation of surplus value, in peaceful trade, so long as foreign countries still represent markets, because their own industry is not sufficiently developed to meet their needs, or because they lack raw materials and semi-manufactured goods which can only be acquired through trade. In this period capital is interested in peace, for only peace ensures undisturbed trade. It is interested equally in the autonomy and strength of the other nations. For only a vigorous development of civilization creates and continually enlarges its market. Hence, in this period capital is peaceful, cosmopolitan, inspired by a love of freedom in all the goods produced by mankind. Free trade, political liberalism, the enjoyment of a cosmopolitan culture

—all are admirable, as well as necessary conditions for good business. This should not be misunderstood: men are sincerely enthusiastic about these ideals, but they have such ideals because they facilitate and promote their economic life.

But as free trade, political freedom, and cultural development achieve their aim of strengthening the state, so such states naturally develop their own economies. Through protection they eventually build up their own industries everywhere, and in this way the market area open to the competing economic regions gradually diminishes. But the capitalist drive for expansion not only remains unimpaired, but increases as a result of the ever higher organic composition of capital, that is, the continually more complex and expensive machines and other mechanisms of production which it has to introduce. Now begins that period in which we find ourselves when the capitalist system of each economic region attempts to substitute the export of capital for the export of commodities as a means of increasing its profits. Capital now gravitates abroad, even for expansion, in order to conquer the market from the inside, since it is sealed from the outside by tariff barriers. However, the safest form of this external investment of capital, which at the same time increases the influence of the whole domestic economic region, is the acquisition and exploitation of colonies. The greatest advantage is offered by subjugating geographical regions which previously had no ruler, or a weak ruler, of foreign race and belief, not belonging to 'our' cultural community. Through colonization such areas now provide not only new market opportunities, but more important in consequence of their mineral wealth and agricultural products, new possibilities of exploitation, the monopolistic control of which eventually opens up the necessary investment opportunity for new capitalist enterprises.

Thus it is no longer the old urge to trade which now dominates capitalism, but the new, much more violent desire for investment opportunities, for ever new sources of the production of surplus value, to which it has to yield, and which has radically and brutally transformed its earlier peaceful nature. For it now requires, in order to secure its ends, a state power which is militarily prepared, and above all an ever-ready, awe-inspiring navy, which is able to support its struggles and make a place for its interests even in the most distant places. With this emphasis upon the strength of each individual economic area, there develops national feeling which zealously nourishes everything that distinguishes and separates the peoples, and which assumes ever greater importance. The honour which emanates from the national flag, the respect it commands, and the fear that it can spread, now become preconditions for good business. A strong realm, a powerful army and fleet, national feeling, pride in one's own country whose power extends everywhere—all this constitutes a brilliant picture, but it is only the other face of the extremely prosaic, but extremely necessary, striving for expansion by capital. The arms race, which at once becomes a continual threat to peace, and only maintains peace because of uncertainty about victory, not through any lack of inclination to attack one's neighbour, has become the new interrelationship between the peoples, which we experienced in all its painful aspects up to the collapse of this system in the present war.

If the necessity for the warlike orientation of the new idea of the nation is recognized as having an economic basis, and if consequently the World War really depended upon the life conditions of the present stage of capitalist development, so that only the precise time and occasion of its outbreak was uncertain, but not the occurrence itself: then this necessity also teaches us something else. We saw that the expansion of capital was necessarily bound to appear to the ruling classes as a national concern, as an affair of the state which they dominate, as a matter affecting the honour and greatness of the fatherland, whose immediate beneficiaries they are in a material as well as an ideal sense. But how does it come about that it seems to be just as much the affair of the oppressed and dominated? How does it concern the proletariat? Here the historical and critical observer of events can see the unique distorting power of a national ideology in its strongest and most fateful form.

There is no doubt that in capitalist society the fate of the proletariat is bound to that of capital. This community of fate is unbreakable, especially on the bad side, in unfavourable circumstances. Every crisis, which means for the possessing classes only a restriction of their level of living, and often not even that, throws tens and hundreds of thousands of petty bourgeois and proletarian lives into the abyss of economic, and even physical, annihilation. So there is really no one who is more anxiously concerned for the business prosperity of the rulers than those who serve—the petty bourgeoisie and the workers. That applies to both small and large matters. In small matters it is a concern for the family, in large matters for the fatherland. In fact, every unfavourable change in the world-political position of a country, every limitation of its trade, every loss of one of its markets or hindrance to its production of raw materials, is not noticed so much by the possessing classes, who can still eventually make use of their property everywhere, as by the classes without property. For them, a restriction of the national economy means the direct constriction, or even abolition, of their means of existence. By contrast, a victorious national economy, a successful imperialism, brings an increase in marketing and investment opportunities for capitalism, hence a greater amount of work, and perhaps even here and there a rise in wages, but in any case a generally less depressed economic situation for the proletariat.

In this way, apparently in direct contradiction with the Marxist theory of class conflict, there arises on the ground of national politics a sudden community of interest between capital and the proletariat, which finds expression in an identical inclination of both classes to imperialism. What the economy divided, the idea of national power and glory unites. It seems that in this way the class struggle, from being an international means of overcoming class distinctions, is bound to become simply a means to improve as much as possible, within the capitalist class system, the situation of the proletariat. The struggle against foreign nations in order to bring about their economic subjection now appears one of the most promising ways of accomplishing this aim. The international struggle of the proletariat against the bourgeoisie is transformed into the national struggles of the bourgeoisie against each other, carried on with the support and participation of the proletariat. The proletariat no longer fights for the future state, but for the economic state.

This community of interest between the proletariat and the ruling classes, in the sense of following imperialist policies, is the real keystone which gives to the continually developing structure of the idea of national power that immense attractiveness and solidity which now sustains all the tremendous sacrifices of the World War, to the astonishment of the whole civilized world. But this community of interest is after all only a product of the national ideology which reflects in a quite peculiar way, that is not easily penetrated, the real conditions of the social order. For anyone who looks beyond the ideas and sentiments which reflect the momentary gains of the ruling classes to the necessities of social development as a whole, this ideology turns to be only a flattering, but all the more damaging, appearance. Of course, it is not merely an appearance without any substance, for as we are now experiencing it sets the peoples of the world, consciously and to some extent enthusiastically, against each other; but still it is an appearance in so far as it simulates for the various social classes a community of ends which, in reality, does not and cannot exist. Here the paths of bourgeois and proletarian conceptions, of capitalism and socialism, divide.

It is quite clear (and it could only be doubted from the standpoint of the ill-intentioned suspicions of the opponents of socialism) that the class standpoint of the proletariat does not in any way diminish its duty and its natural inclination to defend the fatherland. On the contrary, the recent widely quoted declarations of Bebel, Liebknecht, and Jaurès, and of others at various times, show that there was always a full recognition in the International that the proletariat has to defend the freedom and independence of its country, as inalienable preconditions of its own struggle for emancipation, and that every assault on these basic conditions of its free development will find in it the most resolute and self-sacrificing opponent. But this option of the proletariat for its own country and its own nation is something quite different from an identification with the power politics of individual classes in the state. It occurs in spite of, not on behalf of, imperialism, which has plunged it into this situation; and it requires, given the identical goal—defeat of the enemy—a clear distinction in the realm of ideas and feelings. When this distinction is made it becomes clear at once that the viewpoint which regards the well-being of the working class as linked with the success of an imperialist policy is fundamentally not socialist but capitalist, not proletarian but bourgeois. It abandons completely the independent goal of socialist development, and acquiesces in the existing state of affairs at its most traditional. To speak frankly, this is really the outlook of the servant who thinks in a patriarchial way: if things are going well for my master, then they are also going well for me. Such a viewpoint does not transcend the master–servant relationship, and is even very content with it so long as things go well.

This way of thinking is perhaps compatible with social development so long as it does not become necessary for the servant's well-being that he should take up arms, because the master's well-being can be secured or maintained in no other way. Once this is the case—and the general development of capitalism necessarily leads in that direction—then the proletariat loses on one side, as a result of the war and the preceding preparations for war, what it gains on the other side from this common interest, and the loss may be much greater than the gain. Just consider what sacrifices imperialist politics impose on the proletariat, even apart from the war. In order to obtain better working conditions through national economic expansion the country has to accept the terrible burden of continually increasing armaments, and this involves an increase in the tax burden and the national debt, for which ultimately the mass of the people have to pay, through indirect taxes on consumption. Furthermore, the unlimited growth of the war budget restricts all other cultural activities to a pitiable minimum; and as if that were not enough the growth of militarism means at the same time an increasingly evident restriction of democratic development and a growing threat to civil rights and liberties. Last but not least, there is the continual danger of war, accompanied by more frequent economic crises, the daily fear of possible catastrophes which could bury peace; until finally such a catastrophe arrives and adds the sacrifice of blood to all the economic sacrifices which this system has previously demanded.

Thus there emerges a simple calculation for every viewpoint other than the capitalist one; do the economic advantages achieved by the expansion of capitalism outweigh for the people as a whole, and in the first instance for the proletariat,

the losses which it already suffers in peacetime as a result of
all these burdens, and which increase quite dramatically in
wartime? The answer is that imperialist politics do not in
reality, represent the interests of the people, or the nation, as
they claim, but only the interests of one class, of the owners
of capital and masters of production and the market, which
pass themselves off as the interests of the people and hence as
universal. This is possible because the employed population
of every country does in fact have an interest in the strength—
and in the case of military conflict, in the victory—of its own
economic region. But this overlooks the fact that the people
are only interested in victory because they have found themselves forced into a situation of conflict by the prevailing
economic system; whereas the real interest not only of the
culture, but also of modern economic life, is already oriented
to the establishment and smooth functioning of an international organization which would make the conflict superfluous, rather than to national competition which perpetuates
it. . . .

Only by paying attention to the results of objective, dis-
passionate economic analyses, can we escape the spell of extremely confusing and deceitful ideas, in which an ideology
sustained by time-honoured prejudices has engulfed the
judgement of the self-directing intellectuals of our time. And
indeed, the desire for spiritual eminence, for orienting ourselves to high ideals, is not lacking here. It has become evident
that the real meaning of this war is that it is only an expression
of the most important economic phenomena of our age;
namely, that economic development has already outgrown the
present political and economic forms, that it requires an
organization of the world as a whole, a supra-national order,
which would regulate the economic antagonisms between
states and peoples, at first through international agreements
and ultimately through a new economic order which will only
be able to eliminate external conflicts at the same time as
internal conflicts are overcome. The fulfilment of the dream of
eternal peace is not deferred as a result of this terrible war, but
actually brought closer, because the war will not only perhaps
dissolve the rigid political forms which prevent its attainment,
by the realignment of national boundaries which will result

from it, but above all will leave such a spiritual upheaval in people's minds that they will apply themselves more resolutely than ever before to creating the real conditions for achieving this age-old ideal. For the world will not want to experience a second time all the horrors of such a war. When peace eventually comes and the people reflect upon what has been gained, even the victors—whichever is favoured by destiny—will find that the victory has imposed great sacrifices upon them, both to attain it, and to maintain it against the constant threat of a new war. When the people everywhere see that they have escaped from the war, but not from the even more intense preparation for war, because nothing in the organization of states has removed the sources from which the danger of war arises; and when the proletariat of all countries recognizes that despite all the unimaginable sacrifices of war, its general situation, even in the best case, has remained the same as before the war—the same economic dependence, insecurity, and lack of prospects—then even beyond these circles, even in the bourgeois world itself there will be a growing recognition that war is not an appropriate means for settling the differences and antagonisms even in this bourgeois world. Since these antagonisms will continue to exist, however, even after the war, and indeed will remain as threatening as ever, the ideas of all those who suffer from these conditions—and it will be an increasing majority of the people—are likely to turn to the only available alternative; namely the organization of the whole civilized world, and a new ordering of society through a transition from the inhumanity of capitalism to the humane realm of socialism. Once the seed which has been sown on the tear-soaked battlefields of the world germinates, the dazzling illusions of imperialism will be dispelled. The ideology of imperialism will disappear in face of the idea of socialism.

IV. Revolution and Counter-Revolution

MAX ADLER, *The Sociology of Revolution*[1]

The first decade following the violent upheavals in Russia and in Central Europe will naturally give ample opportunity to inquire into the historical significance of these revolutions, to describe the fate that has befallen them during this decade, to point out their inner complexity, and to estimate their possible further developments. In this essay, however, I shall not be concerned with these questions, nor with the description and criticism of any actual revolutions, but with a different issue. Although at first it may seem quite abstract, it has a very close connection with understanding precisely the actual historical process, and indeed throws a great deal of light on it. I shall deal with the *sociology of revolutions* in general.

A sociology of revolutions can be discussed in two ways:

1. One can examine the social determination and outcome of different revolutions, as they have occurred, or else consider their similarities and differences, and inquire into the causes of these. In this kind of investigation revolution is regarded as a historical event which can only be explained sociologically.

2. Another course to follow is to disregard initially every historical revolution, and instead raise the question whether revolution is in general a necessary or accidental feature of the social process; whether it is an essential element—or on the contrary a disturbance and interruption—of social causality. After all, the violent historical events called revolutions do really erupt into men's lives like an elemental social force, interrupting their otherwise peaceful course like a sudden feverish illness.

The second kind of investigation is the only one that we can

[1] From 'Zur Soziologie der Revolution', *Der Kampf*, xxi (1928), pp. 570–6. [Eds.]

call in the strict sense a sociology of revolution. The first is really more an application of the basic sociological knowledge acquired thereby to historical material. Looked at in this way, it is at once apparent that a sociology of revolution cannot be a self-sufficient special sociology, but is a part of general sociology itself; that is, the theory of the nature, forms, and necessary transformations of human social life. From this point of view the problem of a sociology of revolution is posed in such a way as to raise the question of the significance that revolutions have within a scientific conceptual scheme such as Marxism, which regards social events as constituting an economically determined, causally necessary development.

Furthermore, such an investigation is also very necessary from the point of view of the proletariat. For the opposed right-wing and left-wing tendencies which are emerging more and more sharply at present in the social-democratic movements of all countries, have had as a consequence that even within the party, revolution is often regarded as an interruption of the normal course of peaceful democratic progress and an arbitrary act of violence which runs counter to the normal process of reform. The opponents of Marxism fully support these ideas, and ever since Sombart they like to refer to the fatal dualism which has produced within Marxism an unresolvable schism between theory and political practice. According to the Marxist theory the development of society is entirely determined by necessary economic processes, and at no point does the theory allow any arbitrary intervention of political passion or social Utopianism. But in Marx's own work this revolutionary passion and fanatical longing for the millenium constantly recur in contradiction to his calm scientific reflections.

It is irritating to be obliged constantly to deal with such arguments, which display nothing more than a total incomprehension of Marxism. They make it necessary, however, to demonstrate again and again that, for Marx, *economic* necessity has a *social*, that is, a *cultural*, character. For sociation [*Vergesellschaftung*] is only solidarity among human beings, who are the bearers of all social processes, including the economic ones. Economic necessity never derives from anything but human knowledge, will, and actions, although these cannot be independently effective, but are determined both as to means and ends by the totality of conditions of production and distribution under which men live at the time. Hence there is no contradiction at all in Marxism between economic necessity and human will; they are only two different standpoints from which to observe. The same historical process which for the scientific observer is the result of economic determination, is for those who are not external observers, but are living and acting in the midst of it, a task for thought, will, and action. The bourgeois critics of Marx, and many of our comrades too, completely fail to understand what Marx and Engels indicated as their new standpoint: 'revolutionary praxis'. They characterized by this term a way of thinking which comprises the coincidence of the directly willed event with the simultaneous knowledge of its economic necessity. The Marxist as theorist does not stand in contradiction with the Marxist as politician. He is distinguished from the latter, who must set goals, and act in relation to them, only in so far as he has a theoretical insight into the necessity of the goal. Marx wrote about this in the *Communist Manifesto*, in brilliant phrases which expressed a view of politics which has subsequently become that of Marxism: 'The Communists . . . are theoretically in advance of the rest of the proletariat through their insight into the conditions, course, and general results of the proletarian movement. . . . The theoretical propositions of the Communists . . . are merely the general expression of the actual conditions of an existing class struggle, a historical movement taking place before our eyes.'[2]

This makes evident that conscious work for the revolution and for strengthening the will to revolution on one side, and the economic determination of social development on the other, need not be contradictory; so long as this conscious revolutionary activity is nothing more than making conscious those impulses which are the outcome of the economic process itself and require the transformation of what exists. The will to revolution, and the work of creating a revolutionary ideo-

[2] Unfortunately, it is not superfluous to recall that for Marx and Engels the term 'Communists' meant the same as our present term 'socialists'. Similarly, the 'Communist revolution', used later in this essay, is identical with 'socialist revolution'.

logy which orients the consciousness of the masses to new forms of social life, have only an accelerating effect on the causal process of social events. That is the real sense of Marx's famous phrase which characterized revolutions as the loco-motives of history.

But this only brings us to the threshold of the problem con-cerning the sociological meaning of revolution. So far we have only succeeded in showing that revolution *can* be a part of the necessary social process, not that it *must* be. At this point Marxist sociology makes an important conceptual distinction; between political and social revolutions. This distinction should not be regarded as political, although it has political consequences. It originates in a basic law of the social process; namely, its determination by economic development. In the famous sketch of the materialist conception of history which Marx gives in his Preface to the *Contribution to a Critique of Political Economy* we read: 'At a certain stage of their develop-ment, the material forces of production come into conflict with the existing relations of production, or—what is merely a legal expression for the same thing—with the property rela-tions within which they have previously moved. These rela-tions change from forms of the development of the productive forces into fetters upon them. An epoch of social revolution then occurs.'

This conception of social revolution is to be found also in the earlier writings of Marx, in fact if not in name; it occurs for the first time, notably, in the 'Critique of Hegel's Philo-sophy of Right', where it appears in the form of a distinction between human, and merely political, emancipation; and it underlies the whole train of thought of the *Communist Mani-festo*. According to the definition given above, the social revolution is that social transformation which emerges from the insupportable contradiction between the forces of pro-duction and the relations of production. Hence it does not refer merely to a political reorganization of the state, but to the reconstruction of the foundations of a given social order. Com-pared with this, a political revolution is, as Marx himself put it, one which leaves the pillars of the house untouched. It does not change anything in the economic foundations of the social order, and attempts simply to modify the structure by redistributing power and thus changing the circle of those who are entitled to profit from society.

In order to understand the full significance of this distinction it is particularly necessary to keep in mind what was said previously, that it is a sociological, *not a political*, distinction. In this way, the whole concept of revolution is changed from the merely political idea of the transformation of the state, into the social concept of an economic change in the bases of society. The political changes which were previously considered pre-eminent are now seen as subordinate, and in spite of the political progress associated with them, only provisional. But if, in this way, every revolution points beyond its political effects to changes in society which it has either produced or prepared, then the distinction between political and social revolution must not be conceived as a means of historical classification, as though some revolutions were only political, and others only social. This cannot be the case, because every revolution is directed against an existing state order, and to that extent must be political. The distinction is intended rather to characterize certain active historical tendencies which appear to varying degrees in every revolution. In so far as a revolution includes efforts to change the social structure, then an essentially political revolution is also, to this extent, a social one. This is particularly true of the French Revolution which, by eliminating feudal and guild economic forms, broke the most burdensome fetters on the capitalist mode of production.

It follows that the concept of social revolution, in the sociological sense, is not simply a revolutionary demand addressed to the future, nor a teleological conception, nor merely fanatical idealism. It also applies to the past and has already been realized, at various levels, in the very diverse types of revolution that have occurred. In every case, the level depended upon the economic conditions in which the revolution took place. In particular, the varying levels of maturity of these conditions mean that a social revolution cannot attain its goal —the solution of basic economic contradictions—when this is not yet economically feasible. Marx's further significant distinction between a *total* and a merely *partial* revolution derives from this; the former being that which he calls a *radical* or *communist* revolution. This new definition indicates that the concept of social revolution is not identical with that of a Communist revolution; but the latter is the completion of the former.

But is not this concept of radical revolution, in the end just an idealistic, even Utopian, political programme, which is directed by a fanatical will, not by the requirements of the real historical process itself? This question can be answered by returning to Marx's definition of social revolution, according to which revolution is the consequence of a conflict in the economic structure of society. Such a conflict is only possible when the means of production cannot be adapted to the relations of production, because private ownership by a section of society precludes their planned utilization by the members of society as a whole. This means that the concept of social revolution presupposes a society in which there are economic class antagonisms. Like all social concepts, it is partly historical; social revolution is not a form of social development in general, but only that form through which the development of a class society must pass. Certainly, there will be revolutions in classless society too; but when the solidaristic character of this future society has become thoroughly established as a result of several generations growing up in the new conditions, and has undergone a comprehensive development, these revolutions will assume more the character of those intellectual revolutions that the scientific world, for example, experienced in the transition to the Copernican system, or through Einstein's theory. As the social revolution is born from class antagonism it becomes a particular form of the class struggle which permeates the whole history of class society. It is no longer an accidental, but a law-governed phenomenon; namely, the determined and necessary goal of the class struggle. In a class society, the class struggle is the only means of social progress since its object is to eliminate all class injustice and class domination. Hence social revolutions no longer appear merely as the outcome of the passions of specific periods of history, but as a measure of the conscious achievement of the historical progress that was economically possible at that time. But although revolutions can be seen, in this way, as inseparable elements in the continuous process

of historical development, they do not thereby lose their character of a break with the present which can only be achieved
by force; even if this might occur in the future through a
simple democratic majority. In summary we can say: violent
revolutions are necessary elements of the social process, so
long as this proceeds through class antagonisms. Hence
revolution itself undergoes development, in so far as it pro-
gresses from an essentially political to an essentially social
form, and from a merely partial to a total transformation of
society. In its application to the present level of economic
development, in which the proletariat is the last economic
class, this means that in the future a social revolution can only
be a radical, that is, a Communist, revolution.

It remains to consider an important element in Marxist
sociology which completes the sociological concept of revolution. We have seen that the economic conflict between productive forces and relations of production, which revolutions
aim to resolve, forms part of the concept of social revolution.
But how is such a conflict to be resolved? In order to understand this, one must begin from the fact that according to the
basic conception of Marxism the economic structure is only
the base upon which there arises a superstructure of theoretical, legal, moral, etc. forms, which constitute what we should
call the ideology of an epoch. We know also that this does not
involve a dualism of two factors, one economic and the other
ideological, but that economics and ideology form a single
social complex. There is not a single economic process which
does not occur at the same time in an ideological, and especially legal form. In Marx's well-known sketch of the materialist
conception of history mentioned above, it is argued therefore
that this superstructure is more or less rapidly transformed
along with the changes in the economic base. Every change
in the economic conditions of life is therefore accompanied by
a change in man's opinions and evaluations; and it follows
that there must correspond to a period of social revolution—
that is, of a fundamental reorganization of social life—profound changes in the ideology of those who desire and carry
out this reorganization. An economic conflict will only be resolved if new concepts, sentiments, and values emerge in the
class which suffers from the conflict, are directed against the

old ideologies, and dissolve them. The social revolution intends to break with the existing political, economic, and cultural conditions; hence it must first and foremost break through that intellectual state of affairs in which the revolutionary class still thinks the thoughts of the old classes, and still aims to carry out its tasks with concepts and methods of the forms of life which are to be cast aside. This is what Marx called the 'reform of consciousness', which the proletariat has to accomplish within itself, and which he characterized in the *Communist Manifesto* as a radical break with the past. In the *German Ideology*, where so many of the basic ideas of Marxism are formulated with a clarity never subsequently achieved, it is argued that the precondition for a social revolution is not only the maturity of the forces of production, but equally 'the formation of a revolutionary mass which does not revolt only against particular conditions of existing society, but against the whole previous production of life itself'. The creation of a mass revolutionary consciousness, in which the proletariat liberates itself from the ideas of the ruling class, from the prevailing moral and legal conceptions, and especially from traditional political concepts and ideals, is therefore essential to a social revolution. Only by this means does the proletariat attain its full freedom of action.

This will at once become clearer if we visualize for a moment the kind of social ideology into which the proletariat has been born, and which at first it adopts unthinkingly for its own struggles. From the moral aspect it is the ideology of the general interest, to which every particular interest, and consequently class interest as well, has to be subordinated. In the legal and political sphere it is the ideal of the constitutional and democratic state, founded upon the idea of the equal worth of all citizens and the self-determination of the whole. So long as the bourgeoisie was a revolutionary class which attacked the privileges of the estates with the idea of the general interest, and set out to defeat absolutism with the ideal of the constitutional state and democracy, this ideology was a revolutionary force and expressed a historical necessity. But after the victory of the bourgeoisie this whole ideology has proved to be an illusion, in which the bourgeoisie itself does not believe any longer, as its passage from democracy to fascism, or at least its inclination toward fascism, demonstrates. In fact, there can be no question of the rule of a general interest in a society such as capitalism, where the most profound antagonisms exist with respect to the requirements of life and culture. Similarly, there can be no talk of democracy, in the sense of a self-determination of the whole for the equal benefit and enjoyment of all, when parliaments, the present bearers of democracy, and the supposed representatives of society as a whole, are everywhere increasingly divided into two class camps and heedlessly promote the domination of the stronger. So it is becoming ever more obvious that all the concepts belonging to the arsenal of traditional political idealism—the concepts of the state as a community of the people, and as the defender of the general interest and representative of the collectivity, as well as the concepts of democratic freedom and equality in the constitutional state, of the extension of democracy and the perfection of the constitutional state, etc.—are concepts entirely of the bourgeois world. At one time it used them to justify the necessary aims of its struggle, but everywhere today it has come into open contradiction with the moral content of these concepts. It is impossible to realize them in a society of class antagonisms, and consequently they are inappropriate to the ideas and feelings of the proletarian world, the aim of which is to overcome this contradictory bourgeois society.

In Marxist workers' education it is already very common to point out the economic contradictions of the capitalist economic system, and every enlightened socialist worker is familiar with the basic idea of Marxism, that the economic framework of capitalism has become too narrow for the development of social life. By contrast, much remains to be done before the contradictions of bourgeois ideology, embodied in concepts that are surrounded by the splendour of moral and political ideals, become clear to the proletariat. One particular obstacle to a better understanding of this issue is that in Central Europe especially, the proletariat has to assume the historical task of developing political democracy, which has been abandoned by the bourgeoisie, and to defend it against reaction and fascism. But it is all the more necessary—and this must constitute the main task of all socialist educational work—that

it should become clear, and even self-evident, to the proletariat
that the ideological framework of capitalism has also become
too narrow for the attainment of the cultural aims and ideals
which the bourgeoisie nominally acknowledges and celebrates.

So long as the proletariat carries on its struggle only with
the concepts of political democracy, parliamentarianism, and
state ideology, it has not yet found its own concepts. It speaks,
as it were, a foreign language—the language of its masters, of
the past, of the eighteenth and nineteenth centuries—not the
language of its own present and future. It still thinks entirely
in terms of a merely political revolution, while it wants to
make a social revolution; it has not become aware of the
radically new character of what it desires to achieve.

The nineteenth century has passed without bringing the
radical revolution of the proletariat for which Marx and
Engels hoped until the end of their lives; and even the violent
storms of 1918 were not able to attain this goal. And the whole
twentieth century may pass in the same way if the economic
strengthening of capitalism is not eventually opposed by the
resistance of a revolutionary class ideology of the proletariat.
We have now reached a stage of development in which the
cultural and intellectual orientation of the workers poses the
real question of power. Increasingly the problem is to draw
away from the economic and power apparatus of the bourgeoisie the hearts and minds of those who have served it
hitherto even where it has been directed against the workers
themselves. This can only be done if the purely political and
state-oriented (national) ideas of the working class are transformed into the ideas of international socialism, which are
required for a radical revolution. These would replace the
conception of peaceful democracy, in which a gradual development continually brings the classes and parties closer to
one another and is supposed to unite them in the notion of a
total state, by a conception of democracy based upon a class
struggle in which, as Marx argued in *The Class Struggles in
France*, the democratic victory of the proletariat can be nothing but the assertion of the 'permanence of the revolution, the
class dictatorship of the proletariat as the necessary phase of
transition to the abolition of all class differences, to the abolition of all the relations of production on which they rest, to

the abolition of all the social relationships corresponding to these relations of production'. The radical revolution of the proletariat cannot of course renounce the means of political struggle, and in particular the means of political democracy; nor will it do so. But here, finally, what Marx wrote about the relation of the new radical ideology to the old political ideology must be acknowledged: 'Revolution in general, the overthrow of the established power and the dissolution of the old conditions, is a political act. Socialism cannot be established without revolution. It needs this political act, in so far as it needs this destruction and dissolution. But where its organizing activity begins, where its own aims and soul appear, socialism casts aside its political shell.'

OTTO BAUER, *Political and Social Revolution*[3]

The political revolution has dethroned the Emperor, done away with the upper chamber, and abolished the privileged voting rights in all the provinces and municipalities. All political privileges have been destroyed. All citizens, without distinction of class, status, or sex now possess equal rights. But the political revolution is only half the revolution. It abolishes political oppression, but allows economic exploitation to continue. The capitalist and the worker are legally equal, they enjoy equal political rights, but the one remains a capitalist, the other a worker; the one is still master of factories and mines, the other poor and defenceless as a church mouse.

The political revolution does not abolish economic exploitation, but only makes it more palpable. Have we overthrown the omnipotent Emperor only to remain subject to the omnipotence of the capitalists? Have we broken the domination of the generals, the bureaucrats, and the feudal lords only to remain the slaves of bank directors, cartel magnates, knights of the stock exchange? The working masses are asking this question. The semi-revolution arouses the will to total revolution. The political upheaval awakens the desire for a social reorganization. The victory of democracy inaugurates the struggle for socialism.

The victory of democracy in Central Europe is the result of the war, the consequence of the defeat of the Central

[3] Excerpt from *Der Weg zum Sozialismus* (1919), pp. 6–9. [Eds.]

Powers. The war has destroyed the military forces of the two military monarchies, wrenched the means of coercion from the authoritarian state, and thereby led democracy to victory. But the same war has produced vast economic transformations, which make socialism an ineluctable necessity. For four and a half years the people have built no houses, but dug trenches; have manufactured no machines, but made shells and shrapnel; have not tilled the soil, but operated cannons. Our land has been deprived of foodstuffs, our machinery is worn out, our railways are neglected, our clothes and linen are in rags; the whole wealth of society has been destroyed. As a result of the war the people have become poor, unspeakably poor.

All peoples have become poor, but the peoples of Central Europe much more than the others. For we are the vanquished. We shall have to pay to the victors tribute and compensation for war damage. However poor we are, we shall still be obliged to pay a huge tax to the others, the victors, out of our poverty. We shall work; but for what? First of all we shall have to work in order to clear the neglected land of weeds, to replace the worn-out machines with new ones, to restore the impoverished railways. And then we shall have to work in order to produce all the commodities with which to pay our tribute to the victors. Under such circumstances, will there remain enough labour power to produce in sufficient quantities what we need for ourselves; food, clothing, linen, dwellings?

We shall be poor, unspeakably poor. In such poverty, can we afford the luxury of paying a tribute from the produce of our labour to corpulent prelates, haughty princes, opulent war profiteers, and idle *rentiers*? Can a people which has become so poor accept such an unequal distribution of the meagre product of its labour? We are too poor to continue sharing the fruits of our labour with capitalists and landlords. It is bad enough that we shall have to pay tribute to foreign capitalists in the form of war damages; we cannot remain tributaries of the capitalists at home in addition. There is only one way out of our economic plight: socialism! The war which has led democracy to victory has also forced us upon the road to socialism.

But how can we attain a socialist order of society? How can
we transform the factories and mines, the forests and building
land, the great properties which today belong to the capitalists
and landlords, into the property of the people as a whole? The
political revolution can be the work of a day. In place of the
monarchy, the republic; in place of the privileges of the few,
equal rights—that has always been the work of a moment, of
one great hour. Many believe that the social transformation
could be carried out just as quickly, just as suddenly as the
political revolution. One fine day the workers could take
possession of all the factories, mines, trading concerns, banks,
and landed property, and simply chase away the capitalists and
their managers; so that what was still the property of capitalists and landlords in the morning would be the property of
the people in the evening. Is it really so? Can the social revolution really be carried out so quickly and simply?

Our prosperity depends upon two things; first, on how
many goods are *produced* in the country as a whole, and second,
on how this supply of goods is *distributed* among the various
classes of society. Socialism aims first to change the distribution of goods. Today the idle capitalist who has inherited his
property from daddy receives a far greater share of the total
supply of goods than the most energetic and industrious
worker. In socialist society there will be no such distinctions.
Of course, it will not be possible to establish complete equality
in the distribution of goods; socialist society too will have to
pay the industrious more than the indolent, otherwise there
would no longer be many industrious people. It will also have
to pay higher wages to the inventor who contrives new techniques of work and to the energetic worker who suggests new
forms of economic production, than to the worker who carries
out his day's work in a routine fashion, or there would no
longer be many people concerned with perfecting the techniques of work. But only a real contribution to society, not
inherited landed property, not unscrupulously acquired capital, will justify a claim to a higher share in the product of
social labour.

Hence socialism will first transform the distribution of
goods in society as a whole. But that can only benefit the mass
of working people if, at the same time, the production of goods

is not diminished. For if, in a socialist society, only half as many goods were produced as under capitalism then the workers in that society would live no better, and probably much worse, than under the domination of capital; the most just distribution would be of no use if there were less to distribute. The task of socialism, therefore, is to institute a more just distribution of goods, without doing harm to the production of goods.

We have become terribly poor. As a result of the neglect of our whole apparatus of production, the lack of raw materials, the weakness of our undernourished labour force, we are producing much, much less than we produced before the war. But if we are producing less, then of course we can consume less. The smaller the product of social labour, the more limited its wealth, the less there is for each individual, even with the most just distribution, and the less he can consume and enjoy. In such a period we must be careful not to do anything which would ruin our productive apparatus even more, make the supply of raw materials even more difficult, limit still more our production of goods, and diminish further the total product of our labour. Our poverty obliges us to arrange the distribution of goods more fairly, but also to carry out this transformation in such a way that the production of goods does not suffer thereby.

Let us now imagine that the workers should suddenly take possession of the factories by force, expel the capitalists, their managers, and officials, and take over the management of the factories themselves. Such a transformation would only be possible, of course, in a bloody civil war; and it is self-evident that civil war would involve massive destruction of means of production, machines, and railway material, so that our productive apparatus, already terribly run down, would be still further impoverished. Foreign capitalist countries would deny us the raw materials we need and the credits without which we cannot obtain the raw materials; America and the *Entente* would maintain the blockade; the lack of materials would oblige our factories to work even shorter hours. Most of the managers, engineers, chemists, administrators, technicians, clerical staff, and commercial representatives, who alone have been able to acquire, in capitalist society, the knowledge necessary to manage great factories, would withhold their co-operation. Would the workers by themselves be able to find sources of raw materials, and to organize the complicated work process of a large modern factory, in which each worker carries out only a part of the work and consequently understands only a small part? The workers themselves, gripped by the passions of civil war, would have little time or inclination for work, and the productivity of labour would fall alarmingly. As a result far fewer goods would be produced than at present. True, the distribution of goods would be more just; but the individual worker would none the less get no more, and probably much less than now, because fewer goods would be produced and distributed. The people who expected from socialism an improvement in their condition, would be terribly disappointed, and this disappointment would drive them into the arms of the capitalist counter-revolution.

It is not in this way that we can attain socialism. We must adopt quite a different course. We must construct socialist society gradually, by planned organizing activity, proceeding step by step toward a clearly conceived goal. Each one of the successive measures which are to lead us to socialist society needs to be carefully considered. It must not only achieve a more equitable distribution of goods, but also improve production; it should not destroy the capitalist system of production without establishing at the same time a socialist organization which can produce goods at least as effectively. The political revolution was achieved by force; the social revolution can only be the product of constructive organizing activity. The political revolution was the work of a few hours; the social revolution must be the outcome of the bold, but well-considered activity of many years. This conception has nothing to do with the illusions of the narrow-minded revisionism and reformism of earlier times, which believed that society could 'grow' peacefully into socialism, without any need for a violent revolution. That was of course a mistake. For the social revolution presupposes the seizure of political power by the proletariat, and the proletariat could and can seize state power only by revolutionary means. But once this political power has been seized the proletariat faces an entirely new task, which can no longer be accomplished with the means appropriate to the political revolution. All that the political revolution can ever do is, as Marx said, 'to set free the elements of the future society'; but to construct the new society from these elements is a task which cannot be accomplished in street battles, or in civil war, but only through creative legislative and administrative work.

OTTO BAUER, *Two Revolutions*[4]

The Russian Revolution progressed rapidly to the dictatorship of the proletariat, which undertook, and is still undertaking, a vast and violent transformation of capitalist society into socialist society, at the cost of heavy sacrifices but also with prodigious success. The German Revolution came to a halt at the stage of bourgeois democracy; the republic established by the German working class in 1918 became a bourgeois republic which succumbed fifteen years later to the most brutal and barbarous type of Fascism. How is this divergence in the development of the two revolutions to be explained?

Present-day Communist propaganda has a ready-made answer: the Bolsheviks, under Lenin's inspired leadership, led the Russian workers to victory, while German Social Democracy betrayed the German workers. Friedrich Engels answered this kind of simplistic explanation long ago when he analysed the causes of the defeat of the 1848 Revolution:

It is an acknowledged fact that the sudden movements of February and March 1848 were not the work of a few individuals, but the irresistible, spontaneous manifestation of popular needs, more or less clearly understood, but felt very strongly by large classes in all countries; but when one looks for the causes of the success of the counter-revolution one receives from all sides the convenient response that it is Mr. A or Citizen B who has 'betrayed' the people. This reply may be true or not, according to the circumstances, but in no circumstance can it explain anything at all, or show how the 'people' allowed itself to be betrayed.

And he urged 'a study of the causes which necessarily produced both the latest uprising and its defeat, causes which are not to be looked for in the aspirations, talents, mistakes,

---

[4] From *Zwischen zwei Weltkriegen?* (1936), pp. 267–83. [Eds.]

defects, or betrayals of this or that leader, but in the general
social situation and conditions of life in each of the nations
affected by this upheaval'.[5]

The Russian Revolution and the German Revolution followed a similar course at the outset. In Russia, as in Germany,
the leadership of the revolution was initially in the hands of
the democratic socialist parties: in Russia, the Mensheviks
and the right wing of the Socialist Revolutionaries; in Germany, the Social Democratic Party. In both countries a
minority of communist workers attempted to gain the leadership; in Russia, the Bolsheviks and the left wing Socialist
Revolutionaries, in Germany, the Spartacus League (the left
wing of the Independent Socialists) and the 'revolutionary
delegates'. In both countries the revolutionary minority of
the working class tried to seize power by a coup, in July 1917
in Russia, and in January 1919 in Germany. The defeat of
these attempts at a coup was followed in both countries by a
considerable decline in the revolutionary movement, a
strengthening of reaction, and a period of persecution of the
Communist minority. But at this point the great divergence
between the two revolutions begins. . . .

In Russia the setback was overcome in a few weeks. From
August onwards support for the Bolsheviks revived; in September they became a majority in most of the urban Soviets,
while their allies, the left wing Socialist Revolutionaries,
gained a majority in a large proportion of the peasant Soviets.
In October, the Bolsheviks were already a majority in the
Congress of Soviets and they were able to seize power without
encountering resistance from the army at the front or from
the garrisons in the large towns.

It was quite different in Germany, where the Communist
movement took much longer to recover from the setback of
January 1919. The elections to the National Constituent
Assembly showed that the overwhelming majority of the
German working class supported social democracy. The
democratic regime had time to establish itself, and it was able
to resist without difficulty the subsequent Communist attempts
at an armed coup. Whereas the defeat of the Bolsheviks in

[5] Friedrich Engels, Preface to *Revolution and Counter-Revolution in Germany*
(1851–2).

July was only a temporary episode, the effects of which were overcome in a few weeks, the defeat of Spartacus in January was the battle of the Marne for the German Revolution.

How can this divergence be explained? However much importance one attributes to the conscious leadership in the development of mass revolutionary movements it is still not possible to explain the divergence of these two revolutions solely or even mainly by the difference in the quality of revolutionary leadership in the two countries.... The explanation is obviously to be found in the fact that there was lacking in the German Revolution a powerful motive force, acting with elemental violence and producing an upheaval in the consciousness, behaviour, and will of the masses, which would have enabled it to advance, as did the Russian Revolution, to the dictatorship of the proletariat.

A better understanding of this force will be gained if one remembers that the peasantry played quite a different role in the Russian Revolution from that which it played in the German Revolution. In a large part of Russia bourgeois property relations had still not been established in the countryside by 1917, and semi-feudal relations persisted. The great movement of occupation of the land, which accompanied the abolition of serfdom, had not yet been forgotten. The revolution awakened the peasant masses. Immediately after the collapse of Tsarism the peasants enthusiastically seized the land of the large landowners. Peasant insurrections began in Great Russia in March, and spread to the Ukraine at the end of the summer. The peasants appropriated the large estates, expelled the prisoners of war who were working on them, and took the harvest for themselves. Here and there country houses were pillaged and burnt down, the livestock and furnishings divided among the peasants. When the provisional government, after suppressing the July uprising, attempted to repress the mass movement of the peasants, it threw them completely into the arms of the revolutionary leaders. The series of peasant uprisings shook the foundations of the state and the social order, and produced an upheaval in the army, which was made up of peasants and the sons of peasants. It reinforced the revolution of the urban workers with tens of millions of peasants.

In Germany the situation was entirely different. The German

peasant had not been in conscious, revolutionary opposition
to the large landowners for a long time. On the other hand
the wartime requisitions and the war economy had intensified
the opposition between town and country. In the course of the
German Revolution not a single country house was burnt
down, no estates were occupied by the peasants, and there was
no pillaging. But the opposition of the peasantry to requisitioning was all the more fierce. What the peasant wanted, at
the end of the war, was not to seize the large estates but to
regain the liberty to dispose as he wished of the products of
his labour. At the time of the defeat he fumed against the
traditional powers which had been responsible for the war,
but very soon socialism came to seem the enemy against which
he had to defend himself, and the bourgeoisie, which upheld
the freedom of property, his natural ally. The peasantry, in
Germany, formed the mass basis of the bourgeois parties
which were being reconstituted.

But however important and essential this difference may
be it still does not suffice to explain the divergent course of the
revolutions in Russia and Germany. For in a highly industrial-
ized country such as Germany the behaviour of the peasantry
could not possibly have the same influence upon the course of
the revolution as in agrarian Russia. The different outcome
of the two revolutions can be explained also, and above all, by
the fact that the Russian Revolution broke out during the war,
while the German Revolution occurred after the war.

Since 1848 all the successful popular revolutions in Europe
were the result of a war; and they always took place in the
defeated countries, never in the victorious countries. Thus,
in 1870–1 it was France, not Germany; in 1905–6, Russia,
not Japan; in 1917–18, Russia, Germany, and Hungary, not
France or Britain; which were shaken by revolutions. After
1848 a popular revolution was never able to break out and
succeed except when military defeats had weakened discipline
in the army and had dissolved the repressive apparatus by
means of which the ruling classes keep the populace quiet.

It was this mass movement for peace at any price that put
the Bolsheviks in power. That is why Bolshevism was able to
recover so quickly from the effects of its defeat in July; every
month that the war and the disintegration of the economy

continued, and the mass opposition to the war increased, the Bolsheviks gained new mass support. For this reason they were able to attract the overwhelming majority of workers and to increase rapidly their influence among the soldiers. The troops no longer desired to fight for a government which continued the war. And similarly, the subsequent course of the war enabled the new Soviet government to maintain itself in power. It was the defeat of Germany which saved the Soviet government from the most dangerous kind of intervention, that of Prussian militarism, which was already established on Russian soil.

When the revolution broke out in Germany the war was already over. The German army was demobilized before Christmas 1918, and so there was lacking here from the outset the explosive revolutionary force of a mobilized revolutionary army, defeated on the field of battle, which played such a decisive role in the Russian Revolution. In Russia, the mass of the people, tired of war, and desiring peace at any price, joined the revolution; but in Germany, where the revolution occurred after the war, this weariness had a contrary effect. People wanted peace; to continue the revolution meant provoking a civil war and the intervention of the victorious powers, continuing under the red flag a war that had just been lost under the black-white-red flag. The Spartacists might say that the armies of the *Entente* would mutiny if they were made to intervene against the proletarian revolution in Germany, but who could be sure? The masses were too weary, needed peace too much after four years of war, were too repelled by the idea of any further bloodletting, to risk such an adventure.

Moreover, while the war in Russia produced an increasing disorganization of the economy, and fed the revolution, in Germany the economy was restored a few months after the end of the war. The demobilized soldiers and the workers discharged from the war factories found employment again. Their energies became concentrated upon wage demands and struggles over working conditions in the factories. Thus, in the consciousness of the masses themselves the high tide of the revolution of November was very quickly followed by an ebb tide. The Communist militants who called for a violent overthrow of bourgeois democracy were able to attract only a small minority of the German working class.

All the attempts to explain the different courses followed by the revolutions of 1917 and 1918 in terms of the qualities of the leaders and parties, their errors, weaknesses, illusions, and the presence or absence of revolutionary, committed socialist cadres, remain at a superficial level. They disregard the valuable lessons which Marx and Engels drew from the experience of the eighteenth- and nineteenth-century revolutions. It is undoubtedly true that Social Democracy, which had developed in the course of decades of struggle on the terrain of bourgeois democracy and for bourgeois democracy, and was impregnated with reformism by decades of reformist practice, could only seek to achieve, in the hour of revolution, what it had been fighting for during its long, peaceful evolution; namely, democracy and social legislation. But if, in the course of the revolution, the proletarian masses had become as revolutionary as they became in Russia, then Social Democracy would have been overwhelmed either by Spartacus, or by the left wing independents, or it would have had to adapt itself to the revolutionary spirit of the masses as did the Hungarian Social Democrats in March 1919. If, in Central Europe, the vast majority of the proletariat has continued to support Social Democracy, and if Social Democracy has kept the revolution within the limits of democracy, incapable of abolishing capitalist property relations and hence restoring bourgeois democracy and preparing the counter-revolution, this is not because there were no revolutionary cadres able and willing to lead the masses in an assault upon capitalism, but because the events themselves, the social conditions in which the revolution took place in Central Europe, confined the action of the masses within these limits.

OTTO BAUER, *Problems of the Austrian Revolution*[6]

Adler's action[7] was a turning point in the history of the labour movement. For the masses who had lived in hopeless and

[6] From *Die Österreichische Revolution* (1924), pp. 69–70, 132–9, 175–6, 179–84, 201. In this book Otto Bauer provided an extensive survey and analysis of the problems confronted by Austrian Social Democracy after the First World War. The excerpts translated are intended to illustrate the main points in his analysis. An English version of the book, considerably abridged, was published in 1925 and reprinted 1970. See Bibliography. [Eds.]

[7] On 24 October 1916 Friedrich Adler assassinated the Prime Minister, Count Stürgkh. [Eds.]

passive despair he became a hero who had offered his life to
avenge their sufferings. The influence of his act grew stronger
as its immediate success became apparent. The policy of
Koerber, who succeeded Stürgkh, relaxed the wartime absolutism and offered stronger opposition to Tisza's dictatorship in the Empire. A hope emerged that Parliament would be
recalled. A conference convened by the Social Democratic
Party and the trade unions on 5 November 1916 was able to
reveal at last the horrors of military despotism in the war
industries, and thereby provide a dramatic justification of
Adler's action. The March Revolution in Russia, a few weeks
later, revolutionized popular sentiment in Austria. The fear
of Russian Tsardom was now dispelled by enthusiasm for the
Russian Revolution. The Tsar had been resisted, but nobody
wanted to make war on the Revolution. The struggle for
democracy became linked with the struggle for peace. The
Central Powers now confronted democratic societies in the
East as well as in the West; their war had become nothing
more than a war of semi-feudal military monarchies against
democracy. The movement among the masses found expression in increasingly frequent strikes which militarism, with
all its coercive apparatus, was no longer able to prevent. The
decree of 18 March 1917, which revised the labour regulations
in the war industries, and relaxed wartime absolutism, was
the first capitulation by the authoritarian state to the popular
movement. On 18 and 19 May 1917 the trial of Friedrich
Adler took place. The outspoken revolutionary speech which
he was at last able to make produced a passionate response
among the masses, and its effect extended far beyond the
ranks of the working class. . . .

The proletarian revolution in Austria was confronted by
Entente imperialism. The *Entente* could cut off supplies of
food and coal, thus starving us out, occupy our territory with
its troops, or expose us to the attacks of neighbouring states.
Thus the power of the victors set very definite limits upon the
proletarian revolution in Austria.

In sharp contrast with this objective situation of the proletarian revolution were the subjective illusions with which
the revolution had filled large sections of the working class.
The war brought about a fundamental change in the position

and the mentality of the proletariat. It tore the workers away from the factories and work places.· In the trenches they suffered unspeakable things; their minds became filled with hatred of the oppressors and profiteers who had amassed money out of popular need at home while they looked death in the face every hour, and of the generals and officers who lived in luxury while they starved. . . . They absorbed eagerly the stories of returning soldiers who, as prisoners of war in Russia, had witnessed the first phase of the Russian Revolution; the phase of civil war, of bloody terror against officers, capitalists, and peasants, of expropriations, requisitions, and nationalization. The years in the trenches had dulled their habits of work and accustomed them to requisitions and plundering, fostering in them a belief in the efficacy of force. Now came the revolution, and their homecoming. But at home they found hunger, cold, and unemployment. The four years' accumulation of hatred and anger had to find an outlet. Now they would be revenged on those who had ill-treated them for four years, and demand that the revolution, which had expelled the Emperor, should pull down the powerful, the rich, and the guilty from their seats. Now they would see what the promised gratitude of the fatherland to its heroes amounted to, and as they met with no other response than privation and misery, they concluded that a few thousand resolute armed men, with one vigorous blow, could abolish the social order which had brought war, suffering, and misery upon them.

For four years military managers had been in command in the war industries. As labour discipline in the factories was based upon the military power, it dissolved when the latter collapsed. Industry lapsed into a state of chaos. Orders for war material ceased suddenly. The coal famine, the lack of raw materials, the breakdown of labour discipline, disinclination for work on the part of a working class exhausted by wartime overwork, weakened by hunger, and profoundly affected by the events of the revolution, were all so many obstacles to the adaptation of production to peacetime conditions. The factories were transformed into forums for debate. Industry was not able to absorb the workers who streamed out of the munition factories or returned home from the front. The number of unemployed increased every month, reaching its highest point in May 1919 when there were 186,030 unemployed, of whom 131,500 were in Vienna alone.

Wild excitement prevailed in the barracks of the *Volkswehr*,[8] which was conscious of being the chief support of the revolution. In the discussions in the soldiers' councils Social Democrats and Communists fought out their hardest battles. The *Volkswehr* thought that with weapons in its hands it could immediately effect the victory of the proletariat. Alongside the wildly excited homecomers, the despairing unemployed, and the militiamen filled with revolutionary romanticism, there were also disabled soldiers who wanted to avenge their personal injuries upon the social order that was responsible for them, emotionally disturbed women whose husbands had languished in war captivity for years, intellectuals and literary men of all kinds who, suddenly converted to socialism, were filled with the Utopian radicalism of the neophyte, Bolshevik agitators sent back from Russia. Every edition of the newspaper brought news of the struggles of the Spartacus League in Germany. Every speech announced the glory of the great Russian Revolution which, at one stroke, had abolished exploitation for ever. The masses, who had just seen the overthrow of the once powerful Empire, ignored the strength of *Entente* capitalism; they believed that the revolution would now wing its way to the victorious countries. 'Dictatorship of the proletariat', 'All power to the councils', were the cries that now resounded through the streets.

The workers' councils in Austria arose out of the January strike, and when the revolution came the new institution spread rapidly. The heightened consciousness of power, the awakened impulse to activity of the liberated masses, sought and found their initial field of action in this institution. Economic necessity gave a direction to this activity and the organization of a war economy provided ample means. The workers' councils joined the soldiers' councils and the peasants' councils, which were coming into existence, to form local and district economic commissions. They controlled the collection of the harvest and cattle rearing, as well as the

[8] People's militia. See also Biographical Note on Julius Deutsch, p. 289 below. [Eds.]

allocation of housing; they attempted to terrorize profiteers; and they prevented the export of food from their districts. As a rule they co-operated with the legal authorities; in theory, the authorities used the workers' councils as their organs of control; but in reality the councils dictated to the authorities, and at times, they acted independently and in opposition to the authorities.... In the first few months of the revolution the movement was elemental and unorganized, and there was not yet any integration of the workers' councils of the various districts. The movement was most widely spread in Upper Austria, where the workers' councils were instrumental in prohibiting external trade and protecting the extremely large stocks of wheat and cattle from the activities of the illicit traders of Vienna....

It was not only the urban and industrial workers who were revolutionized by the war. There was also a great upheaval among the peasants, but from the beginning this movement had an ambiguous character. The peasants too had returned home from the trenches filled with a hatred of war and militarism, bureaucracy and plutocracy. They too hailed the new-found freedom, the Republic, and the overthrow of militarism. . . .

It was a real democratic movement which at that time swept through the peasantry. But peasant democracy is not identical with proletarian democracy. In the mind of the peasant the new-found freedom, which he as well as the worker wanted to use, developed in a way that was diametrically opposed to the needs of the proletariat. During the war the enormous military requisitioning apparatus had weighed heavily upon the peasantry and had destroyed the most valuable property of the Alpine peasantry, their cattle. The peasants' hatred of this requisitioning system turned them into revolutionaries. The obligation to sell the products of their labour below the market price seemed to them a form of plunder which the revolution must abolish. Hence the freedom which the peasants expected from the revolution that had destroyed militarism was first and foremost freedom from the oppressive war administration.

But the revolution was bound to disappoint this expectation. In a time of dire need it could not dispense with the centralized system of requisitioning and distributing food. The provisioning of the towns and industrial centres, above all Vienna, could not have been secured without state regulation and control. The peasant saw that the revolution denied him what he understood by freedom, that the military requisition detachments had been replaced by workers' councils which enforced the delivery of supplies, hunted down illicit traders, and combated any infraction of the maximum price regulations. He saw in the proletariat the enemy who refused to allow him to dispose freely of the products of his labour, and he began to hate the proletariat as formerly he had hated militarism.

The hostile sentiments of the peasantry toward the proletariat were encouraged by the urban middle class of the Alpine provinces and by the priesthood. The urban trading class was a natural ally of the peasantry against the central system of regulating food distribution, and looked to the peasant masses for support against the proletariat. The priests reinforced and organized the peasant movement as the strongest bulwark against the proletarian revolution. Newspapers and sermons told the peasant that his corn, his cattle, and his timber were being requisitioned in order to allow a hundred thousand unemployed workers in Vienna to be kept in idleness by the State; that the central system of control which oppressed the peasant was maintained by an alliance between Jewish profiteers and Jewish labour leaders in the Government; that the revolution aimed at socializing his property and destroying his church.

The peasant proceeded to adopt an attitude of defiance, and put every obstacle in the way of delivering supplies. Peasants' councils struggled with workers' councils for control of the administrative machinery.... The peasant knew that he was stronger; he had plenty of food in his cupboard, and he could blockade the town. If it came to civil war, it was not the peasant but the worker who would starve. Moreover, he did not lack arms, for when the army had melted away the returning soldiers had either sold their rifles to the peasants or left them behind as booty....

Austria is divided into two areas almost equal in population. On one side is the great industrial district which comprises

Vienna and a quarter of the Wienerwald and Upper Styria; on the other side is the great agrarian region which includes all the other provinces. In the industrial district all real power was in the hands of the proletariat. In the agrarian region, where there are only a few towns and industrial centres of any size scattered through the countryside, the proletariat was not altogether powerless, but the peasantry formed the strongest power and could not be suppressed. It was impossible to govern the industrial district in opposition to the workers, but it was equally impossible to govern the great agrarian district in opposition to the peasants. The economic structure of the country therefore created a balance of power between the classes which could only have been abolished by force in a bloody civil war. Large sections of the proletariat were eager for such a civil war. The proletariat in Vienna, in Wiener-Neustadt, and in Donawitz, could not see beyond its powerful position in the industrial region. It was oblivious of the unshakeable power of the peasantry in the agrarian region, and equally blind to the menacing power of *Entente* imperialism externally. Consequently, it regarded the establishment of the dictatorship of the proletariat as a possibility.

But the establishment of such a dictatorship would have meant nothing less than suicide for the revolution. In the industrial region the proletariat could have set up its dictatorship without encountering insuperable opposition, but in the agrarian region the attempt would have failed. . . . The provinces would have answered the proclamation of a dictatorship by separating themselves from Vienna and breaking away from the state. The struggle against the counter-revolution in the provinces would then have led inevitably to a bloody civil war, and this would have provoked the intervention of the *Entente*. The *Entente* powers could not have tolerated the interruption of communications by civil war in a country which provided their passage from the Adriatic to Czechoslovakia and Poland, and they were determined not to allow the revolution to develop beyond the limits of democracy. Had the 'peace and order' which they desired been destroyed, they would have stopped the food trains and the coal trains and thus brought famine upon the whole industrial district; they would have given permission to the Czechs and the

Yugoslavs to march and thus have involved us in war; they would have caused the most important railway junctions and towns to be occupied by Italian troops and thus made an end of the revolution. The dictatorship of the proletariat would have ended with the dictatorship of foreign rulers.

Large sections of the proletariat did not realize these dangers, but it was the duty of Social Democracy to see them. Thus a dual task devolved upon Social Democracy; on one side, by taking advantage of the powerful revolutionary agitation among the masses and the severe shocks which the capitalist social order had suffered, to capture for the proletariat strong and permanent positions in the state and in the factories, in the barracks and in the schools; but on the other side, to prevent this revolutionary agitation from developing into civil war and an open collision with the superior forces of *Entente* imperialism, which would have opened the gates to famine, invasion, and counter-revolution. . . .

The conditions of disintegration into which capitalist production had fallen undermined belief in capitalism. In Russia the whole of industry had been nationalized and the great agrarian transformation completed in the course of the year 1918. In November 1918, the Socialization Commission began its work in Germany. In the stormy winter of 1918–19 the German Government continued to announce officially that socialization was 'on the march'. In the spring of 1919 the Hungarian Soviet Republic socialized the whole of industry. In an elemental and violent movement the Austrian workers also demanded the right of self-determination in industry. In isolated cases—such as the Donawitz Works of the *Alpine Montangesellschaft* on 7 April 1919—the workers deposed the managers and elected a committee to run the undertaking.

The faith of capitalist society in itself was undermined. During the war capitalist production had been organized in compulsory associations under the power of the state. Was it not now incumbent upon the working class to assume the heritage of the military power in order to develop on socialist lines the large organizational structures which had originally served war aims? The finances of the defeated states had fallen into a condition of decay which it did not seem possible to overcome by the ordinary measures of taxation. Was it not inevitable that the states should sequestrate a great part of accumulated private property to enable it to put its house in order? Even the bourgeois world perceived the advent of a 'new economic order', and University professors wrote treatises upon socialization as the task of the hour. In Vienna as in Berlin, in Leipzig as in Munich, they placed themselves at the disposal of the socialization commissions, elaborated socialization projects, and not infrequently taunted Social Democracy with its lack of ardour in tackling this great task. Within a few months a whole literature on socialization sprang up. It was the ideological reflection of the profound economic shock which the capitalist social order had suffered during the war and the revolution. Although very few of the numerous projects which competed with each other in the socialization literature of the first months of the revolution were achieved, the severe economic shock reflected in the socialization literature created practical needs, urgently demanding satisfaction, which actually transformed the capitalist mode of production in a fundamental way and introduced into it quite new elements, the nucleus of the socialist organization of the future. . . .

The working class had to utilize their predominant position in the Republic, for which they had to thank the revolution, in order to adapt the whole system of our social legislation to the new conditions. Thus the entire first year of the Republic was occupied with the fruitful labour of social legislation. Labour protection legislation was extended by prohibiting night work for women and young persons, by the regulation of child labour and domestic work, and by special laws concerning bakers, miners, and clerical workers, but however important this work of social reform might be, the mere extension of the inherited social legislation of a past age could not suffice to meet the pressing needs of the time. The workers agitated for the transformation of the whole mode of production. Socialization was the slogan of the day. But this slogan had an entirely different meaning for the workers than for the bureaucrats. For the latter, trained in the school of war mobilization, socialization meant the state organization and regulation of national activities. On the other hand, the worker did not want to be a living tool of the employer any longer, but to participate in the control of the industry in which he was engaged. In order to proceed with socialization upon these lines, it was necessary first of all to form the personnel of each undertaking into a community, to be equipped with proper organs which would participate in the control and direction of the enterprise. The working class everywhere agitated for this end.

In Russia the Bolsheviks, immediately after the October Revolution, had created works' councils as organs of 'labour control in the enterprises'. In Germany, workers' committees had come into existence during the war. In England the Whitley Committee of the Ministry of Reconstruction had drawn up a great project for the organization of industry, the basis of which was to be the works' councils. When the Socialization Commission was appointed in Austria after the February elections, and I was chosen as its president, the first task to which it addressed itself was the elaboration of a bill governing works' councils. After careful preparations, in which the trade unions took an active part, the bill was introduced in the National Assembly on 24 April and approved on 15 May 1919.

Apart from Soviet Russia, Austria was the first state to set up works' councils, which were not established in Germany until 1920, and in Czechoslovakia until 1921. In Austria we profited from the flood tide of the Central European revolution, when Soviet dictatorships prevailed in Budapest and in Munich, to impose the works' councils' law upon private enterprise. Hence legislation made greater inroads into the capitalist system than did the subsequent legislation in Germany and Czechoslovakia, which was passed when the tide of revolution was ebbing. Our law invested the works' councils with an unlimited right to defend the economic, social, and educational interests of workers and employees. The specific duties of works' councils were enumerated by way of illustration, but they were not confined to these particular activities. Thus the way in which the workers would be able to use the new institution depended upon their own strength and the efficiency of their works' council. . . .

The works' councils are still in their infancy. The revolution was able to establish them, but their development requires time and experience; only through a gradual development, a gradual self-education in the practice of works' council activity, will the workers be able to produce from their own ranks a staff of trained representatives able to take full advantage of the new institution. Only this self-education in and through the practice of works' councils will create the prerequisites for a socialist mode of production. The example of Russia, where the democratic organization of industry which was attempted immediately after the October Revolution soon gave way to bureaucratic state capitalism, demonstrates that only bureaucratic state socialism—which merely replaces the despotism of the employer by the despotism of the bureaucrat —is possible so long as the workers lack the capacity for self-government in the labour process. Democratic socialism, the socialism which the workers want and strive for, the socialism which achieves the right of self-determination in the labour process, is only possible when the workers are able to control production without disrupting it. As an instrument of proletarian self-government in the production process the works' councils constitute a preliminary stage of the socialist mode of production. Consequently, their creation and development is a more important preparation for a socialist system of society than any forcible act of expropriation, if the results of the latter are no more than state or municipal undertakings administered on bureaucratic lines....

In modern capitalist society, alongside political democracy, embodied in the democratic organization of the state and municipality, an industrial democracy is developing, which is embodied in the great democratically organized trade unions and co-operative societies of the workers, in the professional associations of employees and officials, and in peasant co-operative societies. Political democracy recognizes men only as citizens, disregarding the economic position, occupation, or social function of each citizen; it summons all citizens without distinction to the ballot box; it groups them according to geographical constituencies. Industrial democracy, on the other hand, groups men according to their occupations, their work-places, and the functions they exercise in the community; it organizes them, in terms of their social functions, into craft, professional, or industrial associations.... While

political democracy requires that the government should rule
in agreement with parliament, which is chosen by the electorate once every few years, functional democracy requires
that the government in each branch of its activity should remain in constant touch with the citizens directly affected by
this branch of government, organized according to their work
places or their social and economic function. A combination
of political and functional democracy was the essence of the
policy imposed on the Austrian government by the redistri-
bution of power which the revolution effected.

The bourgeoisie saw in this strong infusion of functional
democracy into the practice of government nothing more than
the activity of illegal subsidiary governments, or veiled Bolshevism. As a matter of fact it was something more than a
broadening of the democratic idea of government with the
consent of the governed. It meant the salvation of the country
from catastrophe, and was at the same time a potent means for
the self-education of the masses. It was a way of effecting a
complete revolution in the relation of the masses to the state,
of awakening the initiative and encouraging the most fruitful
kinds of spontaneous activity among the workers.

OTTO BAUER, *Fascism*[9]

The revolutions of 1918 were followed by the counter-revolution, which did not everywhere assume the particular traits of
Fascism. Democracy was replaced in Poland by the military
dictatorship of Pilsudski, and in Yugoslavia by a dynastic-
military absolutism of the old style. The 'Awakening Hungary' movement in the Hungarian counter-revolution of 1919,
and the terroristic groups which the Bulgarian government of
Zankoff despatched against the overthrown peasants' party
and against the workers, already resembled the Fascist storm
troops; but very soon in both countries power reverted to the
old, and old-fashioned, oligarchy. The new Fascist form of
despotism was victorious for the first time in Italy and in
Germany. Today, of course, it is the newly discovered form
of dictatorship of the capitalist class, which is now imitated
by counter-revolutionary governments of quite different
origins.

[9] From 'Der Faschismus', *Der Sozialistische Kampf* (1938), pp. 75–83. [Eds.]

Fascism is the product of three closely interconnected social processes. First, the war expelled masses of participants in the war from bourgeois life and turned them into *déclassés*. Unable to find their way back into the bourgeois styles of life and work, and clinging to the forms of life and the ideologies acquired during the war, they formed, after the war, the Fascist 'militias', the people's 'defence leagues', with their distinctive militaristic, anti-democratic, and nationalist ideologies. Second, the economic crises of the postwar period impoverished large masses of the lower middle class and peasantry. These pauperized and embittered masses seceded from the bourgeois-democratic parties to which they had previously given their allegiance, turned with disillusionment and hatred against democracy, through which they had previously represented their interests, and rallied around the militarist-nationalist 'militias' and 'defence leagues'. Third, the economic crises of the postwar period reduced the profits of the capitalist class. With its profits threatened the capitalist class sought to restore them by raising the level of exploitation. It wanted to break the resistance of the working class, and doubted whether it could do this under a democratic regime. It used the Fascist groups and people's militias created by the rebellious mass movements of the petty bourgeoisie and peasantry at first to intimidate the working class and force it on the defensive, and subsequently to destroy democracy. It supported the Fascists initially with money. Then it persuaded the state apparatus to deliver weapons to the Fascist militias and to ensure that Fascist acts of violence against the working class went unpunished. Finally, it persuaded the state apparatus to hand over power to the Fascists.

Let us now consider these three interconnected processes more closely. The nuclei of the Italian Fascist party were formed by the reserve officers demobilized after the war. For years, they had been in command; now they found no position in bourgeois life worthy of their self-reliance and ambition. Around them rallied *déclassés* from the ranks of the *Arditi*, the wartime storm troops, proud of their war records and their wounds, embittered because the fatherland for which they had bled could offer them no position, or none which satisfied their demands. They did not want to give up the habits acquired in war. They wanted to command and be commanded, to wear uniforms and to march. They began to create a private army. In Germany this stratum was even broader. The Versailles peace treaty had compelled Germany to dismiss a great number of its professional officers, and they constituted the leading stratum in the military *Freikorps* and the 'Defence Leagues' which began to be formed after the war. The political chaos of the postwar period gave the nascent Fascist militias the opportunity to consolidate themselves and to raise their prestige; in Italy through the Fiume adventure, and in Germany, through the struggles in the Baltic and Upper Silesia.

In these nuclei the original ideology of Fascism developed. Arising out of the war, it is above all militaristic, demanding discipline from the masses in response to the leader's power of command. It is sharply opposed to the right of self-determination of the masses, whose only vocation is that of disciplined obedience, and is consequently hostile to all forms of democracy. It despises the 'bourgeois', civilian desire for peace, comfort, and pleasure, and opposes to it a warlike, 'heroic' ideal of life. It is filled with the nationalism whipped up by the war. It seeks to arouse the masses against the liberal government in Italy which allowed itself to be cheated of the spoils of victory by its allies; against the republican government of Germany which submitted without dignity to the dictates of the victorious powers. It is typically petty bourgeois, directed against large capital and the proletariat at the same time; for the officer hates the racketeer and the war profiteer, and despises the proletarian. This anti-capitalism is of course only directed against the specific parasitical forms of capital during the period of war and inflation; the officer values war industry but hates the racketeer, so he is hostile to the 'profiteering', but not to the 'productive', capitalist. Its opposition is much more passionate to proletarian socialism, which in Italy fought vigorously against participation in the war, and for this reason grew stronger by leaps and bounds after the war. In Germany, socialism came to power as a result of defeat, and for this reason seemed to be the beneficiary of defeat and the agent of the victorious powers.

At a time when the power of socialism to attract the masses

is at its strongest, Fascism represents its own ideal as 'national socialism', and in these terms opposes proletarian socialism. More precisely, it is claimed that national socialism means, instead of the egoistic exploitation of the consequences of war by the proletariat, the subordination of all 'self-interest' to the 'common interest', of all economic and social forces to the task of national self-assertion against the external enemy. It associates its nationalism with anti-bourgeois modes of thought; the bourgeois democracy of the West is nothing but the dominance of the richest and most powerful capitalist classes; Italy, 'the great proletarian woman', is cheated of the spoils of victory by the English, French, and American capitalists; the German people are made to pay tribute to international Jewish high finance which conceals itself behind Western democracy and uses German democracy as its tool. It represents its fight against democracy to the masses as a fight against the class rule of the bourgeoisie, to the capitalists as a fight against the mob rule of the proletariat, to the nationalist intelligentsia as a fight for the co-ordination of all national forces against the external enemy.

But the military storm troops, who were the original champions of the Fascist ideology, could only acquire strength if they succeeded in bringing larger numbers of people to accept their leadership, and become their followers. The first social stratum to become imbued with the Fascist ideology which arose out of the war was the intelligentsia. In Italy and Germany parliamentary democracy was of recent date. In Italy, the parliamentary form of government was long-established, but parliament had only been elected on the basis of universal, equal suffrage since 1913. In Germany, universal and equal suffrage was long-established but the government had only been responsible to parliament since 1918. In both countries the intelligentsia was soon disillusioned by the new democracy, seeing in it, on one side, a camouflaged plutocracy, and on the other side, the rule of the mass as it is in capitalist society, a coarse, uneducated mass, inclining to violent activity in times of tumult. Itself impoverished by the devaluation of money and economic crises, the intelligentsia hated the proletarian *parvenus* who sat on the government bench. Without understanding, they opposed the struggles about social-political problems which, under the pressure of the masses, dominated public life. Above all the nationalism of the intelligentsia, whipped up by the war, set them in conflict with the young democracy.

The nationalist intelligentsia became the mediator between the Fascist storm troops and the mass of the petty bourgeoisie and peasantry. But it needed serious economic and social convulsions to detach the petty bourgeois and peasant masses from the historical bourgeois-democratic parties and lead them to Fascism. After the war, the economic and social development of the states which had taken part in it was at first dominated by inflation. With the rapid devaluation of money, the savings of the petty bourgeoisie dwindled, the working capital of the small merchants and master craftsmen was consumed, and large numbers became impoverished. At the same time the devaluation of money led to ever more extensive and more violent wage struggles, which again and again brought the transport system and public undertakings to a standstill. The petty bourgeois, who could not defend himself against devaluation, was embittered by the wage struggles between capital and labour which continually disturbed his peace. He regarded the wage increases obtained by the working class, which were a consequence of devaluation, as its cause. He resented the fact that some sections of the working class could continually obtain wage rises to compensate them for devaluation, while he was unable to increase his income to the same extent. With bitterness he saw his level of living fall below that of many sections of the working class, and the national income redistributed to his disadvantage. If he hated the inflation racketeers, he hated the rebellious working class even more.

In the year 1919 a wave of strikes, which wrested substantial concessions from both large and small entrepreneurs, swept over the whole of Italy. The peak of the strike wave was the armed occupation of factories in August 1920. The liberal government of Giolitti did not dare to employ state coercion against the rebellious mass movement, which affected both the industrial and the agricultural workers, and sought to appease the movement by negotiations, agreements, compromises, and concessions. Parliament, divided among feuding parties, could not form a stable and strong government, nor solve any of the burning economic questions except by laborious compromise negotiations, which meant that none were settled quickly or definitively. In consequence, large sections of the Italian petty bourgeoisie turned away from democracy, and began to believe that only the iron will of a leader could compel the proletariat to obedience, put an end to the fierce class struggles, which continually interrupted the peaceful course of economic life, and to the crippling party feuds, and restore the shattered economy.

In the early postwar years a Fascist populist movement had already emerged in Germany too, and it had become menacingly powerful by the time of the inflation. In 1923, when the French occupation of the Ruhr inflamed nationalist passions, the total collapse of the mark pauperized the mass of the people, and the populist defence leagues marched to the northern border of Bavaria, Germany was already in serious danger of falling into the hands of a popular Fascist movement. But at that time bourgeois democracy still resisted the Fascist assault. The struggle in the Ruhr War had shown how hopeless it was to resist the victorious powers. The German bourgeoisie and peasantry still needed the help of the Western powers, rich in capital, to stabilize the mark, to reach agreement about reparations, and above all to obtain substantial credits for the reconstruction of German enterprises. Hence they desired no nationalist Fascist adventures. After the stabilization of the mark, when German commodity prices rose rapidly and there was a massive influx of foreign credits, the populist flood quickly ebbed. During the period of prosperity Hitler's National Socialist Party was an insignificant splinter group. But as soon as the 1929 crisis began, populist Fascism re-emerged. Democracy could not protect the petty bourgeoisie and peasantry from impoverishment so they turned against democracy, and streamed into the ranks of National Socialists. . . .

But the Fascist movement became a mass movement of the petty bourgeoisie and peasantry, and attained power, only because the capitalist class decided to use it to crush the working class. In the early postwar period Italy carried out a genuine agrarian revolution. Vigorous movements of tenant farmers and fee farmers against the large landowners, of day labourers against the large landowners and tenants, transformed the Italian agrarian system. The *terzeria*, the large landowners' right to two-thirds of the tenant's produce, was abolished. The landowners were compelled to provide seeds and fertilizer, the creation of tenancies was made subject to joint commissions on which the tenants had parity. The day labourers of the Po valley enforced wage rises and the guarantee of a minimum number of days work each year. Large estates were occupied by force, and government had to sanction these forcible occupations by decree. Eventually the large landowners began to defend themselves, and in 1921 they appealed to the Fascist groups for help. When a landowner did this, heavily armed Fascists occupied the village, deposed the local council, established a new mayor, set the office of the union of day workers on fire, manhandled and drove away its leaders, and murdered any who resisted. Through these 'punitive expeditions' the power of the rural proletariat was broken. The example set by the large landowners was then followed by the urban bourgeoisie. Soon there were 'punitive expeditions' in the towns as well, the Fascists occupied the towns, forced the resignation of red mayors and local councils, destroyed trade union offices, drove out, manhandled and murdered the workers' representatives.

The capitalist class had discovered the means to resist the working class offensive, and to crush the working class. They did not yet think of handing over state power to the Fascists, but only wanted to use them in order to crush the working class. They placed large amounts of money at the Fascists' disposal, to enable them to maintain and arm the storm troops, who could be sent into action at any time against rebellious workers. They made sure that their state power supported the actions of the Fascists. Already in October 1920 the chief of the general staff, Badoglio, had instructed the divisional commanders to support the Fascist movement. Weapons went from the army's stores into the hands of the Fascists. When the Fascists undertook 'punitive expeditions' against the workers, the police only intervened on the pretext of preventing clashes, to seize the workers' weapons, and to imprison their leaders.

The cheap victories which Fascism was able to win thanks to such support from the state power attracted ever larger numbers of people to it. In the 'punitive expeditions' anyone who wore the black shirt could commit murder and arson, or rob, without fear of punishment, and this circumstance drove the whole *Lumpenproletariat* to the Fascists. The Fascist storm troops were clothed and paid out of the large subsidies paid by the capitalists and landowners, and this brought the unemployed into their ranks. Fascism was advancing rapidly and victoriously, and this attracted those people from all classes who are always on the side of the victors. The Fascist militia became the assembly point for the *déclassés* of all classes. But as a result of the help which it had received from the bourgeoisie Fascism became too strong to serve as a mere tool, and sought power itself. The choice facing the bourgeoisie was then either to repress by force the Fascist private army which it had financed and armed, and thereby unfetter the subdued proletariat, or to hand over the state power to this private army. In this situation the bourgeoisie left its own representatives in government and parliament in the lurch and preferred to hand over state power to the Fascists. The struggle between capital and labour, in the course of which the bourgeoisie had used the Fascist gangs, seemed to end when these gangs, having suppressed the proletariat, chased the representatives of the bourgeoisie too out of parliament and government, dissolved the bourgeois parties, and were able to set up their coercive rule over all classes. 'The struggle seems to end with all classes equally powerless and mute, yielding to the club' (Karl Marx, *The Eighteenth Brumaire of Louis Bonaparte*).

History repeated itself in Germany. Here too populist Fascism was supported by the bourgeoisie and the state power during the period of inflation. The Junkers welcomed to their estates the members of the *Freikorps* returning from the Baltic and Upper Silesia. Heavy industry subsidized the populist defence leagues, and the state formed from them the 'Black Reichswehr'. In 1923, the government exploited the mass sentiment resulting from the upsurge of the populist movement, and the weakness of the working class, intimidated and forced on to the defensive by Fascism, to launch its action against the workers' governments in Saxony and Thuringia, and to abrogate the eight-hour day.

But this alliance between capital and Fascism broke down after the end of the Ruhr conflict. When the German bourgeoisie, at this time, needed large foreign loans to support the re-established currency, and to meet its reparation payments, and large foreign credits for its banks and industrial enterprises in order to replace the circulating capital destroyed by inflation, and hence needed 'conciliatory policies', it withdrew its support from the populist movement. In the period of prosperity the German bourgeoisie supported the bourgeois-democratic parties. The People's Party took part in the democratic government, the German Nationalists associated themselves more closely with the democratic regime. Only after the onset of the 1929 crisis did the capitalists and Junkers again draw closer to Fascism. As the National Socialist movement, which had declined greatly during the period of prosperity, rapidly gained the support of the petty bourgeois and peasant masses impoverished by the crisis, the Junkers and heavy industry soon recognized it as a means of repressing the working class, limiting the influence of the workers' parties and the trade unions, and eliminating the obstacles which democratic institutions put in the way of capital's struggle to raise the level of exploitation and restore profits. . . .

Fascism often justifies itself to the bourgeoisie by claiming to have saved it from the proletarian revolution, from 'Bolshevism'. In its propaganda, indeed, Fascism liked to scare intellectuals, the petty bourgeoisie and peasants with the spectre of Bolshevism. But in reality Fascism did not triumph at a moment when the bourgeoisie was threatened with proletarian revolution. It triumphed when the proletariat had already been weakened for a long time and forced on to the defensive, when the revolutionary flood had already ebbed. The capitalist class and the large landowners did not surrender state power to the Fascist gangs in order to protect themselves against the threat of proletarian revolution, but with the object of depressing wages, destroying the social conquests of the working class, wrecking the trade unions and the political power of the working class. Its aim, therefore, was not to suppress revolutionary socialism, but to smash the achievements of reformist socialism. . . .

In bourgeois democracy the capitalist class rules, but it rules under the constant pressure of the working class. It is obliged to make ever wider concessions to the working class. The continual struggle of reformist socialism and the trade unions for higher wages, shorter working hours, the extension of social legislation and administration, does not of course damage capitalism in its period of expansion; on the contrary, it raises it to a higher technical, social, and cultural level. But in the grave economic crises which followed the World War the conquests of reformist socialism appear to the capitalist class as obstacles to the 'normal' process of production and circulation determined by changes in the rate of profit. It is determined to refuse any further concessions and to rescind those concessions already made to the working class. Democratic institutions prove a hindrance and so it turns against these institutions. The democratic legal order does not allow the state power to deploy the means of coercion against reformist socialists who carry on their struggle by legal means; hence the capitalist class makes use of the illegal, private means of coercion of the Fascist bands. . . .

The Fascist dictatorship arises, therefore, as the result of a unique balance of class forces. On one side stands a bourgeoisie which is master of the means of production and circulation, and of the state power. But the economic crisis has annihilated the profits of this bourgeoisie, and democratic institutions prevent it from coercing the proletariat to the extent that seems necessary in order to restore its profits. It is still too weak to attain its end by those cultural and ideological means which it uses to dominate the mass of voters in bourgeois democracy. Hampered by the democratic legal order, it is too weak to crush the proletariat by legal means, through the legal state apparatus. But it is strong enough to pay a lawless, illegal private army, to arm it, and to turn it loose upon the working class.

On the other side stands a working class led by reformist socialism and the trade unions. Reformism and the trade unions have become stronger than the bourgeoisie can tolerate. Their resistance to attempts to raise the rate of exploitation stands in the way of deflation. It can no longer be broken except by force. If reformist socialism is attacked by force precisely because of its strength, and the degree of its success, its resistance to the use of force, on the other hand, is too weak. Carrying on its activities in the arena of the existing bourgeois democracy, adhering to democracy as its sphere of struggle and the source of its strength, it appears to the petty bourgeois, peasant, and proletarian masses as part of the 'system', as a party which participates in and profits from bourgeois democracy, which is unable to protect them from the impoverishment resulting from the economic crisis. That is why reformist socialism cannot attract to itself the masses revolutionized by the crisis. They flock to its deadly enemy, Fascism.

The outcome of this balance of forces, or rather of the weakness of both classes, is the victory of Fascism, which crushes the working class in the service of the capitalists, but while paid by the capitalists grows so far beyond them that they themselves are obliged to make it the unlimited master over the whole people, and also over themselves. Just as the absolutism of the early capitalist epoch, from the sixteenth to the eighteenth century, developed on the basis of the balance of forces between the feudal nobility and the bourgeoisie, and the Bonapartism of the nineteenth century resulted from the temporary balance of forces between the bourgeoisie and the nobility on one side and between the proletariat and the bourgeoisie on the other, arising from the struggles of the 1848 Revolution, so the new Fascist absolutism is the consequence of a temporary equilibrium in which the bourgeoisie could not impose its will on the proletariat with the old legal methods, while the proletariat could not liberate itself from the domination of the bourgeoisie. Hence both classes succumbed to the dictatorship of the armed gangs, which the capitalist class had used against the proletariat until they themselves finally had to submit to their dictatorship.

In portraying bourgeois democracy I have given an account of the economic and ideological mechanism by means of which the capitalist class makes the voters, parties, and governments of bourgeois democracy serve its needs, its profits, and its will. This whole mechanism remains completely effective even under the Fascist dictatorship. The

development of the economy remains dependent on the rate
of profit, and the interests of profit-making disguise themselves as community interests. The state and the economy
continue to be dependent upon credit, and all the interests
of high finance disguise themselves as the interests of the
state and the economy. The high priests of property can
pursue their interests as if they were the interests of the mass
of small proprietors.

But while the capitalists and large landowners maintain
their class rule under the Fascist dictatorship, the checks and
balances which restrict their domination in a bourgeois democracy disappear. In a bourgeois democracy, the capitalist class
could only exercise its rule through the bourgeois mass parties
which were answerable to the bourgeoisie, the peasantry, and
the employees in elections, and had to canvass for votes, so
that they were obliged to take account of the interests, opinions, and moods of these groups. Under the Fascist dictatorship the capitalists and large landowners can influence the
dictators no less directly than in bourgeois democracy,
through their control of the economy, the state of business,
and public credit, whereas the mass of citizens and peasants
are reduced to silence and can no longer defend their interests,
as a result of the incorporation of their organizations and the
abolition of freedom of the press and of voting. . . .

In the period of its struggle for power Fascism based itself
precisely upon the petty bourgeois and peasant masses who
were impoverished by the economic crisis, revolutionized and
filled with anti-capitalist sentiments. But once in power it
came inevitably under the determining influence of the capitalist forces in society, and was bound therefore to suppress
the Utopian, petty bourgeois radicalism of its own followers.
In Italy, this occurred during the fierce struggles within the
Fascist party in 1923. In Rome the party split into two factions, while in Livorno and Bologna oppositional groups
attacked the party central offices. In many places there were
rebellions with the slogan of a 'second march on Rome'. The
dictators crushed these petty bourgeois rebellions by expelling
tens of thousands of blackshirts from the party, by prohibiting
all provincial congresses, and by replacing the leaders and
committees at the lower levels of the party. Between 1923 and

1925 the Fascist party was transformed into a pliable instrument of the state power, in which there was no longer any free discussion, free choice of leaders, or freedom to form one's own outlook. The petty bourgeoisie was completely deprived of power, and the dictatorship, under the influence of the large capitalists and landowners, now rules over the petty bourgeoisie and peasantry. The same process took place in Germany. Hitler crushed the petty bourgeois rebellion of the S.A., which demanded a 'second revolution', with the murders of 30 June 1934, changed the party into a mere instrument of dictatorial rule by proclaiming that 'the leader is the party', and thus broke the petty bourgeois resistance to capitalist dictatorship. In order to satisfy the petty bourgeois he gave full vent to his hatred of the Jews.

Bourgeois democracy secured for all citizens enjoyment of the rights of individual freedom, free elections of legislative bodies, and thereby control of public administration. Even though the bourgeoisie ruled, its rule was still limited by the influence of the mass of proletarian voters, and by the strength of proletarian organizations. Fascism annihilates all individual liberty, abolishes free elections, destroys the proletarian organizations; thus the working class is wholly deprived of its rights and power. Class rule restrained by democratic institutions is replaced by 'totalitarian' dictatorship, that is, by unrestricted class rule. The Fascist counter-revolution means therefore a transition from the class rule of the whole bourgeoisie, limited by democratic institutions, to the unrestricted dictatorship of the large capitalists and landowners.

The social order is stronger than the political constitution. The economic power of capital subordinates every state power so long as the commanding heights of the economy remain in its hands. Bourgeois democracy did not result from the intentions of the capitalists; it was achieved by the class struggles of the workers, the petty bourgeoisie, and the peasants against the capitalist class. None the less, once it was established it became a means of domination by the capitalist class. But it is precisely the struggles on the terrain of democracy which have raised capitalism to a higher technical, social, and cultural level, have changed the petty bourgeois parties which once fought against the capitalist class into its tools, have ended the revolutionary unrest in the working class, and have pacified it through reforms. So too the Fascist dictatorship was in no way desired by the capitalist class. A plebeian movement of rebellion, suffused with anti-capitalist sentiments, comprising *déclassés* from all classes, excluded from the bourgeois way of life by war and crises, was able to sweep along with it, in consequence of the economic and social convulsions of the postwar period, the impoverished, rebellious, anti-capitalist masses of the petty bourgeoisie and the peasantry. The capitalist class made use of this plebeian movement, but initially did not think of surrending power to it. Eventually it had to do so, not without reluctance and apprehension; but while this petty bourgeois rebellion destroyed democracy ... there emerged from it the unlimited dictatorship of large capital and the large landowners.

But if the capitalist class rules by means of the Fascist dictatorship, the ruling class is no more identical with the governing caste in this case than it was in the previous capitalist political regimes. In many countries during the era of the liberal state the ruling capitalist class left the business of parliament and the direction of government to the liberal sections of the landed and bureaucratic nobility: in England, to the Whigs; in Austria, to the 'landowners loyal to the constitution' and to the 'Josephine' bureaucracy; in Russia, to the Zemstvo liberals. In bourgeois democracy the bourgeoisie rules through the governing caste of professional politicians of the bourgeois mass parties. Under the Fascist dictatorship large capital and the large landowners exercise their own dictatorship by making use of the Fascist governing caste which has achieved power. As in the liberal and democratic state there may arise, in this case too, temporary strains, antagonisms, and conflicts between the ruling class and the governing caste. Such antagonisms, which are sometimes bitter in the early stages of the Fascist dictatorship, then become milder when Fascism has crushed the Utopian, petty bourgeois radicalism in its own ranks, constantly re-emerge. The 'managed economy', which emerged from the economic crisis and was further developed by Fascism, obliges the Fascist dictatorship continually to make economic decisions which damage the interests of now one, now another, section of the capitalist ruling class, and in this way set the Fascist governing caste in opposition to factions of the capitalist ruling class.

In the first phase of its development the Fascist dictatorship can, of course, rally not only the capitalist class, but also broad sections of the people. For the uniform, strong, and ruthless will of the dictatorship can accomplish things which democracy, disrupted by internal struggles, staggering from compromise to compromise, and ill-adapted to ruthless action against the resistance of special interests, cannot do. The officer spirit of the dictators imposes authority and discipline in the public service; and all Europe is enchanted because the trains in Italy arrive more punctually than they did. Ruthless confiscation intimidates the racketeer; the dictatorship can prevent currency from being transferred abroad, thus making the supply scarce in foreign markets and maintaining the exchange rate, even though its creation of the means for expanding employment and for rearmament is inflationary. The dictatorship, much less constrained than bourgeois democracy by the special interests of individual capitalist groups and by economic-political traditions and prejudices, is able to develop the 'managed economy' more rapidly and to retard the growth of unemployment by inflationary and super-protectionist economic policies. It depresses wages ruthlessly, reduces 'social overheads', and thus restores the level of profits. It forces the unemployed ruthlessly into compulsory labour, and hence can boast of great public works. Having grown out of a nationalistic–militaristic movement it represses all regional particularisms by force, and in this way re-establishes national unity, pursues aggressive foreign policies and measures of rearmament which alarm the democratic states and put them on the defensive; and its successes in this sphere increase its prestige.

In the course of its further development, however, the social basis of the Fascist dictatorship becomes narrower. By means of currency regulations it can maintain the rate of exchange abroad for a long period even though it has to devalue the currency internally by the inflationary creation of means for providing work and for rearmament; but the tension between the rate of exchange and purchasing power becomes an obstacle to exporting, and the internal devaluation through inflation becomes evident to the mass of the people in oppressively rising prices. Since it is militaristically and nationalistically oriented the dictatorship builds up the 'managed economy' as a preparation for a war economy, and this, besides imposing heavy sacrifices upon the mass of the people, also brings it into conflict with powerful capitalist interests. The high cost of rearmament burdens not only the people, but also capital, while the aggressive nationalist foreign policies plunge the country into difficult situations which threaten to end in war. The dictatorship's claim to a 'totalitarian' domination of the whole life of the nation, even its cultural life, comes into conflict with the traditions and ideologies of many strata of the bourgeoisie. Thus, large sections of the ruling capitalist class entered into opposition against the dictatorship of the governing Fascist caste. Only those sections of the capitalist class which most need and believe in violence, those for whom the violent suppression of the proletariat internally and a vigorous, warlike policy in foreign affairs, are worth every economic and intellectual sacrifice, continue to uphold the dictatorship, being at the same time its supporters and its masters. The dictatorship of capital through the ruling caste which resulted from the military–nationalistic movement of war veterans, contracts to a dictatorship of the warlike faction of the capitalist class.

The pacifist elements in the capitalist class—the consumer goods industry oriented to exports, which needs a peaceful exchange of commodities between nations, the merchants who are hampered by the war economy, the *rentier* class which fears a decline in share values in the event of war—are all pushed into the background. The warlike elements in the capitalist class, and above all the armaments industry and the landowning aristocracy who have close family links with the officer corps, gain the upper hand. Since capital exercises its dictatorship through the warlike caste of leaders which emerged from the nationalistic–militaristic movement, the warlike tendencies carry the day within the capitalist class. The aggressive, expansionist policies of the Fascist powers, directed against the balance of power resulting from the last war, disturbs all power relationships on the continent, creating mutual distrust between all states, initiating a new arms race, and threatening to end in a new war.

It is of course no accident that such a warlike dictatorship of capital had its first successes in Italy and Germany. In both countries this was affected by the particular national political situation; in Italy by the specific form which the class struggle assumed under the influence of the struggle for and against Italy's intervention in the war; and in Germany, as a consequence of military defeat. But once Fascism is victorious and has established its rule in these two great states, the model can be imitated in other states, under other conditions and without the same national political conditions being present. Fascism has shown the capitalist class of all countries that a resolute minority of daring mercenaries can deprive a whole people of its freedom, its democratic institutions, its autonomous associations, can totally crush the working class, and establish a capitalist–militarist dictatorship. This example provokes imitation, even where the pre-conditions for the victory of Fascism are not the same as in Italy and Germany, as the rise of the Fascist dictatorship in Austria illustrates.

Austria was far more seriously affected by defeat in the World War than was Germany. The vast empire collapsed, and what remained was a small country, politically powerless, and economically helpless. Its industry, deprived of its old markets, declined. Its bourgeoisie and its peasantry wavered between the hope of union with Germany and the hope of a restoration of the old Danubian monarchy. A Fascist movement arose here too; but from the beginning, it contained within itself the seeds of a division between German-national and Austrian-patriotic elements; between those whose ultimate goal was union with Germany, and those who aimed at a restoration of the Habsburg monarchy; between Fascist nationalism, subsidized by heavy industry, which was dominated by German capital, and the black and yellow reaction led by the landowning aristocracy. When National Socialism was victorious in Germany, it swept over a large part of the German–Austrian people too; and the old-Austrian, Habsburg, clerical separatism began to defend itself against the danger of being incorporated into the Third Reich. The German–Austrian bourgeoisie, torn apart by the old conflict between being German and being Austrian, could no longer maintain its rule by democratic means. Its Austrian-clerical faction would have had to seek an alliance with the working class in order to resist the onslaught of National Socialism on a democratic basis, and would have become a prisoner of the working class. That was the least of their desires at the moment when Hitler's victory over the German workers strengthened their desire to break the power of the working class in Austria as well. So the clerical, Austrian-patriotic faction of the German–Austrian bourgeoisie, hostile to union with Germany, resolved to use the state power to establish a dictatorship which was intended to suppress by force German-nationalist Fascism and the working class at the same time. On the surface it imitated Fascist methods, adopted Fascist ideology, and linked it with Catholic clericalism. In reality, however, its 'Fatherland Front' did not arise from a popular mass movement, as did the Fascist party in Italy and the National Socialist Party in Germany, but was invented and established by the government, and was imposed on the mass of the people by the coercive power of the state. In this case Fascism is not the natural product of grass roots movements and class struggles, but an artefact which the constitutional state power has imposed on the people.

The development of military technology has greatly strengthened the state power against the mass of the people. Equipped with machine guns, cannons, tanks, armoured vehicles, aircraft, and poison gas, the state can crush every people and deprive it of its liberties and democratic institutions. The development of the 'managed economy' greatly extends the power of the state over all economic enterprises and hence over all those employed in them; and this power can become, and has become, a means of political domination. Modern technology, above all in radio and films, puts into the hands of the state an effective monopoly in the means of influencing the minds of the people. Fascism has transformed all the techniques of mass organization and mass demonstrations, which the political parties had developed on a democratic basis, especially in children's and youth organizations, the political utilization of sport, the power of suggestion of mass parades, from instruments of popular struggle into means of dominating the people. The capitalist class, controlling all these means of military force, of economic power, and of the domination of the minds of the masses, can everywhere use the state power to develop rapidly and vigorously the beginnings of Fascist movements, which are formed everywhere under the impression of the German and Italian example. Thus the constitutional state power, imitating the methods of Italian and German Fascism, established a dictatorship in Austria and in the Baltic countries; and in all capitalist countries Fascist leagues are given the opportunity to ally themselves with the state power and to come to power by this means....

The great wave of Fascism which swept over Europe in the wake of the economic crisis reached its peak in the years 1933 and 1934. Following the triumph of Fascism in Germany, Austria, and the Baltic countries, the Fascist movements became stronger in all the democratic states, but with the economic recovery in 1934 and 1935 these movements failed to develop. Where the economic situation grew noticeably better, as in Great Britain, the Scandinavian countries, and Belgium, the Fascist wave soon ebbed. Only in France, which was gripped by the economic crisis later than other countries, and where the bourgeoisie combated the crisis with deflationary measures later than elsewhere, did Fascism remain a real threat to democracy. But for that reason it continued to be dangerous for all the Continental democracies, for if it triumphed in France few of these other democracies would be able to resist it. Even if the Fascist threat should disappear in the democratic countries as the world economic crisis is overcome, there will be new waves of Fascism when the economic recovery encounters setbacks, and when great struggles, the dangers of war, and war itself convulse capitalist society anew. If the threat to profits arising from the world economic crisis was enough to throw the bourgeoisie into the arms of Fascism, it is more likely than ever to seek refuge in dictatorship when its property and its whole social order is threatened.

These experiences demolish the illusion of reformist socialism that the working class can peacefully and gradually fill the democratic forms with a socialist content, simply by utilizing democratic institutions, without any revolutionary leap;

that the capitalist social order can evolve into a socialist one. The working class has learnt from experience that bitter class conflict destroys democracy and replaces it with a Fascist dictatorship of capital, and it must recognize that the complete and lasting freedom of the people will only be ensured when classes themselves, and with them the class conflicts of the capitalist social order, have been abolished. If the working class had hoped to achieve a socialist order of society by utilizing democracy, it must now recognize that it has first to fight for its own dominance and to build up a socialist social order before a complete and lasting democracy will be possible.

V. Democracy and Dictatorship

KARL RENNER, *Democracy and the Council System*[1]

The transformation of economic life and the associated revolution in ideas as a result of the war, has called forth a movement in all strata of society which poses afresh the relation between the state and the economy, between politics and economics. This relation has always preoccupied the various schools of socialist thought, but today it affects in a direct and practical way even the circles of the employers and all the bourgeois sections of the population. In the course of the war the state has penetrated more deeply than ever before into the economic sphere, which is, according to the bourgeois way of thinking, the realm of private property and private contractual relations. It seems almost a reaction against this when it is proposed to supersede, or at least restrict, politics by economics, to subordinate the state and its traditional authoritarian organs to the economy with its occupational groups and classes. The dynastic authoritarian state had scarcely been abolished by the revolution, and replaced by the democratic republic, when we were confronted with the question that had already been posed in the West: should we have democracy or a council system? Economic democracy, admittedly conceived in different ways by different groups, was supposed to take over from purely political democracy.

My object today is to examine this movement in order to arrive at some inductive generalizations. I should make clear from the outset that I do not mean by the council system (as is often meant by public opinion) simply the Russian dictatorship of workers', peasants', and soldiers' councils. For the council system does not necessarily involve dictatorship,[2] nor

---

[1] From 'Demokratie und Rätesystem', *Der Kampf*, xiv (1921), pp. 54–67. This essay was given originally as a lecture to the Socialist Society for Law and Political Science on 10 December 1920. [Eds.]

[2] The question of dictatorship is deliberately excluded from consideration here.

is it confined to a single group. The Russian councils are only
a particular, limiting case of the phenomenon. I understand
by the council system, from the legal aspect,[3] the assignment
of political functions or political significance tø economic
groups, that is, to collectivities which are formed by the common interests of an occupation, a status group, or a class, as
permanent, voluntary organizations with political functions
and authority. The phenomenon we are studying exists
wherever such a group, and the 'council' which it establishes,
assumes the functions of a legislative, administrative, or judi-
cial body; and wherever, under certain conditions, a system of
such councils takes over whole branches of state activity,
either through a Congress of Councils assuming the functions
of a parliament, or through a universal councils' organization
being called upon to take over the whole public authority.
Those bodies which call themselves councils, but which deliberately place themselves outside the state sphere, and
oppose becoming involved in legislation, are political party
organizations and not councils in our sense.[4]

Medieval law recognized many kinds of corporation of a
purely economic origin and economic nature which assumed
some part of public authority. The manorial lords acquired
the public power inherited from antiquity and transformed
it into the feudal state; the guilds gradually took control of
the cities and established them as republics. The phenomenon
we are investigating is very ancient. It appeared to have been
completely destroyed; first through force by princely absolutism and subsequently through the democratic legal order
of the republic which established a powerful unified state
based upon the whole body of free and equal citizens, without
any intermediate associations. Thus the concept of democracy
appeared to be confined to the state and its institutions, and
not to be applicable to economic life. On the contrary, economic life was regarded as a sphere in which entrepreneur and
worker, creditor and debtor, owner and non-owner, confront
each other, and there is no room for democratic institutions.

[3] This concentration upon the legal aspect was determined by the interests of the
society to which this address was delivered.

[4] Thus the Austrian workers' council organization, in its present form, does not
come within the terms of our definition of the council system.

Precisely for this reason, the democratic state power seemed to be instituted in order to contain these conflicts and to provide conditions of equality for them through the legal systems and the courts. In the traditional view there appeared to be a conceptual opposition between state and economy; but during the war we witnessed a powerful incursion by the state into the economy, and a no less vigorous penetration of the state by the economy. We can characterize the latter, in accordance with the banner that it generally flaunted, as the politics of the council movement.

The application of the concept of democracy, previously limited to political life, in the investigation and explanation of economic structures, is surely due to Sidney and Beatrice Webb. The Webbs investigated for the first time, from a juridical, constitutional standpoint, the powerful English trade unions and consumer co-operatives, which developed independently of the state and in conflict with it. They discovered that in the course of a century or a century and a half there had developed on a purely economic basis two powerful organizations with all the characteristics of democracy similar to those in the state. They were organizations with a mass electorate, regulating and controlling organs, officials, their own finances, and so on. The Webbs showed that in these organizations the most difficult administrative and constitutional problems were posed by simple workers, and were solved in a purely empirical way. A person living in continental Europe has no adequate idea of the scope and power of these organizations. The British co-operative movement today embraces about a third of all households in the country, and its budget, its turn-over, and the number of its officials far exceed those of a small state. The English Co-operative Wholesale Society has a merchant fleet, which German Austria does not have; and its capital reserve is several times larger than the credits we are seeking from the *Entente*. Of a different nature, but no less powerful, are the English trade unions. The Webbs discovered economic democracy, and once our eyes were opened we began to notice many related phenomena.

In their most recent book (*A Constitution for the Socialist Commonwealth of Great Britain*) the Webbs provide a general survey of these democratic organizations. They distinguish between 'democracies of consumers' and 'democracies of producers' using these terms in the broadest sense to refer to all receivers and producers of goods and services. Besides the co-operative union already mentioned, which has a membership of three to four million out of the ten million families in England, there is also included in the consumers' democracies the extended network of Friendly Societies (with approximately six to seven million members) which provides sickness and death benefits, and other welfare services, that are provided to some extent in Austria by the state and its agencies. In addition, there is the great association of workers' clubs, with more than half a million members, which buys or rents property, builds workers' houses and maintains eating places, rest and convalescent homes, reading rooms and lending libraries. There are also numerous building co-operatives and a great variety of organizations for economic aid.

The agencies of local administration—the municipalities, districts, and counties—compete with the voluntary consumers' democracies. In England they have been completely democratic for a generation, although they are based upon obligatory membership; and since municipal socialism has become the directing idea of local administration in the last two decades, the municipalities appear to practical Englishmen, who do not make a conceptual and practical distinction between state and society as we do, to be in many respects also organizations concerned with the consumption of goods and services. For aside from their authoritarian state functions, which have receded both practically and financially more and more into the background, they provide members of the community with goods, albeit of a particular kind (gas, electricity, water, houses, etc.) and services (tramways, hospital care, convalescent homes) and not infrequently since the war, also food, in much the same way as the consumers' associations. As democracy is practised in the one case just as it is in the other, the distinction between them becomes blurred. That voluntary members pay their dues, or that obligatory members pay taxes, is unimportant compared with the fact that in both cases all adults vote, and only obey representatives whom they control. The only important question for discussion in the end is whether, for particular commodi-

ties and services, the citizen in town or country is more effectively and expediently provided for by the free co-operative of
consumers' associations or by the obligatory co-operative. It
should be added that the old consumers' associations are not
limited to providing food, convalescent homes, and hospitals,
but also maintain schools and medical care for mothers and
children. At this stage of political and social development,
therefore, the question naturally arises: should we have a
voluntary, purely economic democracy, or an obligatory political democracy, the economy or the state? Which is better?

The producers' democracies are contrasted with the
organization of consumption (in the wider sense) and for the
Webbs it is the worker, and not the capitalist, who is the
producer. The oldest forms of this type are the medieval
guilds, and following these the workers' producer co-operatives. Many investigators have asked why such organizations
have not acquired a greater significance. In all cases the trade
unions have overshadowed them. In England today the unions
embrace half or more of the whole employed population. The
older trade-unionism involved only the skilled workers, but
more recently it has embraced the unskilled workers as well,
and in the most recent postwar development it has begun to
affect the 'intellectual' workers, perhaps more profoundly and
vigorously than in any other country. The trade union movement of the 'brain worker' has begun to impinge upon the old
feudal style corporations of the liberal professions, but it still
rejects a general amalgamation or a common policy. The
Webbs add to these democracies of production another type,
to which they attach great significance, namely the 'Subject
Associations' of the liberal professions and of clerical workers,
which strive to improve professional competence and to
extend professional knowledge. We have similar but not
identical associations here; for whereas our brain workers are
generally regular employees of the state, the municipalities, or
large and small enterprises, and thus count as socially dependent workers, in England they are as a rule independent and
confine themselves to providing their services to various offices
and enterprises for a stipulated price from case to case, or for
a remuneration which is called a 'fee'. This explains several
conspicuous features of English society: first that the state

can manage with very few employees; second, that there are liberal professions there, which are unknown here; and finally, that there is a broad intellectual middle class, made up of genuine liberal professions which possess a high degree of economic and cultural independence and occupy a social position between entrepreneurs and workers. England is a non-bureaucratic country. In addition to the voluntary organizations of producers there are also compulsory organizations, though these are insignificant in England. In the German world the state has preferred to set up such compulsory organizations, in order to make them serve political ends; and so we have obligatory trade co-operatives, the German guilds, the chambers of the liberal professions, of commerce, etc.

With regard to the existing producers' and consumers' democracies, either voluntary or compulsory, there now arises the question whether, and in what way, they should stand in opposition to the state or be incorporated in it. Even in England this question has aroused revolutionary passions, and already during the war the state power found itself compelled to concede to the miners and to the workers in war industries, factory councils, district commissions on which they had parity, etc. which were endowed with some executive authority; and on the other side to draw in the employers' associations. It is beyond my scope here to discuss all the details of this movement, or the question of socialization with which it is closely connected. For socialization belongs in this sphere; it does not mean mere state-ization or nationalization, but at least to some extent transfer of enterprises to the control of councils of consumers and producers. I shall confine myself to expounding the Webbs' main proposal.

The Webbs and their school see as the decisive step toward a renewal of economic and social life the institution of a second, so-called social parliament. The House of Lords is to be abolished, the present House of Commons will be restricted to purely political affairs, and alongside the so-called 'political' parliament, a 'social parliament' is to be established as its twin brother with equal rights. The political parliament, elected on the basis of universal adult suffrage in territorial constituencies, will be responsible for foreign policy, colonial

administration, public order, the courts, and the protection
of personal freedom (the latter also against the second parliament). The affairs of this parliament will be conducted as at
present by a committee of the parliamentary majority according to the principle of cabinet government.

The social parliament, by contrast, will direct all economic
and social legislation and administration quite independently
of the first parliament. It will not be constituted, however, on
the basis of indirect voting or nomination by the economic
and social democracies mentioned earlier, but in the same
way as the first parliament by popular vote in territorial electoral districts, though these will not coincide with the political
districts. Any representation of particular strata or occupational groups will be completely and explicitly excluded. In
this second parliament, however, executive power will not be
entrusted to a cabinet, but as in the case of local and regional
administration, to a system of permanent committees and
their presidents. All the rights of the British crown over property and taxation, mines, water-power, etc. in short all sources
of national prosperity, will be transferred to this social parliament. The administration of the Treasury would be assigned
to one of these committees.

This second parliament would act independently of the
first, though of course there would be contact between them
in particular cases. When economic legislation required civil
or criminal sanctions the social parliament would seek the
support of the political one; when the political parliament
made a demand upon economic resources (for the army or
war) it would ask for the agreement of the social parliament.
This would be necessary above all for its budget. If an agreement could not be reached through meetings, the decision
would be made by a vote in a combined sitting of the two
parliaments. The courts would decide the respective competence of each parliament in cases of dispute. In the Webbs'
opinion, the system would not be more cumbersome than the
present two-chamber system. The social parliament would
have the task of organizing the economy, carrying out progressive socialization and giving the state a more economic
character. Above all it would have to incorporate the economic
democracies organically into the state economy.

One may be tempted to compare the Webbs' system with German state socialism. That would be misleading in one respect, for the Webbs do not recognize any state power as a metaphysical power dominating the citizens. On the other hand, their conception of a social parliament on the basis of territorial votes in homogeneous electoral bodies does have the unmistakable character of state democracy. The voter does not vote as a consumer or producer, or as a member of an occupation, etc. in diverse representative bodies, but as a citizen of the state in the economic parliament. Even if the social parliament has the duty of developing the voluntary democracies, it is also supposed to organize and unify them. The economy does not break up the state; on the contrary, the state organizes the economy in a democratic form.

What is called Guild Socialism—a social orientation in the Anglo-Saxon world, for which one of its best-known representatives, G. D. H. Cole, has produced a systematic theory—goes a step further. Cole's most recent book, *Social Theory*, aims to make the sovereign, omnicompetent state unnecessary. The omnipotent state itself, as a democratic state, is an 'agent of tyranny', since the vastness of its ends and means renders not only the activities, but also the ends, of all other human organizations insignificant. Consequently, the state has to be abolished! From the outset Cole regards the state as only one of many variable forms of human organization, one group in the long series of other groups, such as the trade unions, churches, nations and so on. None of these groups derives its validity or its strength from the state. Most of them are more ancient and geographically more extensive than the state. None of these groups can be genuinely free, so long as the state can set the limits within which their lives are lived.

Guild socialism sets in place of the state a system of co-ordinated self-governing bodies, through which in the last analysis the necessary social synthesis is achieved. Cole's objective is freedom, and he finds it in the power of the group, in its capacity to carry out the task assigned to it. Cole also starts from democracy, but he rejects the view that democracy is one and indivisible; the conception derived from the French

Revolution which opposes the one indivisible state to the individual—the 'Ego' of philosophy—likewise conceived as integrated and indivisible.

It is impossible to represent human beings as selves or centres of consciousness; it is quite possible to represent, though with an inevitable element of distortion which must always be recognized, so much of human beings as they themselves put into associated effort for a specific purpose. [True representation therefore like true association is always specific and functional, and never general and inclusive.] What is represented is never man, the individual, but always certain purposes common to groups of individuals.[5]

To express this in a different way: the individual lives in a multitude of associations, each of which embraces only a particular side of man and serves only specific goals. Only particular functions of the individual are socialized. Thus the state as a universal exclusive community with fundamentally infinite goals, the sovereign state, which is also absolute with respect to the individual (for example, the Soviet state), is rejected. Cole asserts the essential equality of the state association with all other groups, hence with trade unions, churches, nations, etc. He rejects the parliamentary form of government on the grounds that it represents a delegation to an all-embracing power, which therefore destroys all true representation. He conceives life as divided into its various functions (consumption, production, beliefs), and each of these functions provided with a specific system of representation and self-government. He visualizes a supreme co-ordination of these self-governing bodies in the form of a 'Joint Congress', in which all the particular governments and specific goals would be reconciled. In Cole's eyes the state is that form of association in which men come together on the basis of identity rather than difference. In the democratic state men are conceived essentially as citizens, hence as identical; but the state makes use of their specialized functions, as engineers, miners, or doctors, in order to carry out its tasks, as it

---

[5] Cited from the original English text: G. D. H. Cole, *Social Theory* (1920), pp. 105–6. The sentence in square brackets was omitted by Renner. [Eds.]

were, under cover. The state as a territorial community, as a group, would perhaps have to restrict itself to the tasks of defence, justice, and education, while leaving everything else to the democracies outside the state.

It is interesting to note that the Webbs too reject the one indivisible democracy, and put in its place a system which derives from four human functions. Two of these are the functions of consumer and producer, but the Webbs demonstrate that even when all specific functions have been taken into account there remains always one common function, that of the citizen. Cole, however, thinks that the state always represents the citizen only as a consumer, as a person who claims and receives goods and services, whereas the guilds represent him above all as a producer. For example, the state devotes itself to seeing that New York gets its coal, but its authority does not regulate the life of the miner. If the state assumed the task of ordering and adjusting all these special interests, this would presuppose and bring about an intolerable state supremacy, which would destroy liberty. The central decision-making power should not, therefore, belong to the state, or to the state alone, but to a congress in which the guild councils would be represented, and in which the state itself would be only one element.

At first glance it may seem that this system of guild councils—even if we disregard our councils of citizens and estates —embodies the conservative view concerning the representation of the professional classes, and also the arguments of church propaganda, hostile to the state. But the guild socialists can no more be regarded as disciples of the medieval theory of professional corporations than the Webbs can be taken for state socialists. They are democrats through and through, adherents of the workers' movement, and above all admirers of the trade unions. Their theory is rather the philosophical reflection of the vigorous development of the workers' movement, and of the new legal institutions which emerged in England during and after the war. The workers have created within the framework of this state, alongside the trade unions and co-operatives, the independent or collateral bodies already mentioned which, sustained by the economic domination of production by the working class, were able to compete with the territorial associations of the state, the municipalities and counties, and perhaps even parliament.

State socialism and the idea of the representation of occupational strata are poor surrogates for the ideas which at present animate the world of Western democracy. One major difference is as follows: in England, thanks to local administration and the parliamentary regime, it has long since become self-evident that the elected authorities are not mere bloodless lawgiving bodies but themselves carry on the administration; the lower house as parliament through the Cabinet (the committee of the ruling majority), and the county and city councils through their committees. According to our traditional conceptions of the authoritarian state, administration appears to be a monopoly of the throne and the bureaucracy, and so there remains for the economic and cultural activity of our corporations in the state sphere only a more or less remote 'participation', which usually amounts to no more than an advisory role for appointed or elected representatives of the 'guilds'. Since these guilds themselves have no significant influence, the legislature could all the more easily decide to confer other privileges upon them. Hence the natural impulse to form associations was extremely weak, so long as the interest groups could undertake serious activities in their own field. Thus the law had to assist and was obliged, from the outset, to create the guilds as compulsory co-operatives, with the advantage that they were formed by an arbitrary rather than a natural bond and could be patriotically influenced to support the authoritarian state. The obligatory commercial co-operatives in Austria provide a typical example of these tendencies; their economic achievements are virtually nil, and their main function has consisted in making available election offices for conservative parties.

The chambers of trade and commerce, which can now look back on more than half a century of useful activity, did prove to be of some value; but they too are mainly consultative, not administrative bodies, and the new voluntary organizations of trade and industry have for some time been undermining their worth. The industrialists, the more valuable and combative section of the bourgeoisie, have equipped themselves with a whole network of guild organizations, in two different directions; on one side, associations of interest groups; and on the other side, the so-called employers' associations. The latter, as coalitions of entrepreneurs for dealing with matters concerning workers and employees, together with the trade unions, created the basis for the new social rights of collective bargaining and arbitration boards which were gained during the war and consolidated by the revolution. In this way, they removed, or at least reduced, one part of the state's social responsibilities. The chambers of labour are the most recent creation of the compulsory organizing activity of the state. Since these chambers have to implement the legislation of the factory councils, and to direct both the cultural and economic aspects of their work, they have a real administrative task, which makes them more important than the chambers of trade which, precisely because of their mixed and arbitrary composition, are unlikely to bring any solid benefits either to industry, to trade, or to business.

As we have seen, the Webbs' proposal aimed to provide the voluntary economic democracies with an overall democratic co-ordination through the social parliament. It is difficult to foresee whether this proposal has any prospect of realization, and in any case it harbours many difficulties and uncertainties; nevertheless, it springs wholly from the spirit of English democracy. In Germany the development of law has provided a substitute for it, which has already been achieved in the Reich Economic Council. This Economic Council, which was provisionally introduced by the decree of May 1920, had its origins in the council movement. The struggle over the workers' councils and their claims to power, over their attitude of opposition to the state or their incorporation into the constitution, is an aspect of the German Revolution. In the peasantry and in some sections of the bourgeoisie the idea of councils was not totally rejected, so long as all the so-called 'professional strata', and of course the employers and workers, were represented in the councils; it was along this path that the compromise embodied in Article 165 of the constitution was eventually reached. . . .

The form taken by the council idea in Russia diverges considerably from the practical forms it has assumed in Germany and England, and just as greatly from the intellectual conceptions of Cole and the Webbs. Nevertheless, there is one feature that underlies all these intellectual and political movements; namely, the assault by economic classes, occupations, and associations upon the state. The same driving force has produced here mere precursors, while there it has overshot the goal and has transformed itself into the state. Everywhere this idea comes into conflict with the traditional idea of democracy shaped by the French Revolution. The movement is in midcourse and a definitive judgement would be premature at this stage. Nevertheless, some conclusions can be formulated.

1. The conception of a uniform, indivisible, purely political democracy is untenable. On the basis of an advanced bourgeois political system a series of voluntary economic democracies, such as the trade unions and the co-operatives, have arisen; and their practical value, their indestructible life force, and their social significance for the masses are simply incontestable. Constitutional law can no longer simply ignore them, as it has done on the continent.

2. With regard to political democracy the way of thinking which opposes the sovereign personality of the state to the indivisible Ego of the citizen also seems to me untenable. Obviously the individual cannot be represented simply as a philosophical centre of consciousness. It is rather the case that the particular social functions of man are socialized by distinct organizations; and the state is only one social group among many others. To this extent Guild socialism is certainly right.

3. However, the state, as a particular group, does seem to me to be distinguished from all others, since its function is precisely to hold together and accommodate the multiplicity of conflicting groups. Cole himself does not contest this unifying role, as his Joint Congress shows. If all groups are differentiated according to their various functions, then it is just the state which has the role of integrating them. This raises the question, both in theory and practice, whether this integration begins at a level above the groups, as it does for Cole, and in the case of the National Economic Council, or whether it begins in the citizen himself, as the Webbs' idea of a social parliament suggests.

4. It is precisely at this point that the profound distinction between economic and political democracy is revealed. Political democracy sets itself the task of establishing all the various groups on a basis of absolute legal equality and freedom, and compelling them, by the technique of voting, to measure their real power and their moral force of attraction before the whole people, so that eventually they can reach a compromise among themselves which can be passed as a law for everyone. The role of political democracy is to reveal and set free all existing oppositions, but also to harmonize them, and to effect this accommodation through the law and the courts. That is why it is certainly the best instrument for social peace, replacing club-law and the ordeal of civil war by the parliamentary process and the judgement of the majority. But despite its many affinities with economic democracy, political democracy proves to be fundamentally different. The economic democracies rest upon *identity* of interests, and the election contest over representation only decides how correctly these interests have been interpreted. Political democracy presupposes conflicts of interest which can only be settled by the victory of one interest and the defeat of another. Hence, there necessarily stands behind political democracy the use of force, an organized public power, and coercive action.

5. It follows from this that all democratic safeguards collapse when one group confronts another, and neither can or will submit, when civil war is desired; and this is then always a struggle to possess the means of coercion, the real power of execution.

6. That group which possesses or gains the real power, will then form its own state. History shows that churches, orders, particular kin groups, trading companies, estates, like various bourgeois groups with their limited franchise, have formed their own states, in the pursuit of their particular interests. It is not excluded, therefore, that here and there states will again arise from estates or classes in the future. For example, in Hungary within a period of a few months the attempt to establish a working class state was followed by a state constituted by the officers' caste, and this again by an attempt to create a bourgeois constitutional state.

Approving or dissenting value judgements on such structures do not of course affect their existence. But the experiences the world has had with democracy do seem to show that
it guarantees unlimited opportunities for continued development at the least possible cost. The attractions of the dictatorship of the councils have therefore affected most strongly, on
one side the oldest autocracies, and on the other side the most
immature democracies, whereas they have made little impression so far on the old democracies. In the latter countries the
working masses seem to be quite convinced that political
democracy is bound to bring them the fulfilment of their
highest ideals without the gruesome game of chance of a civil
war. This conviction has undoubtedly received powerful support from the fact that in the economic democracies which
they themselves have set up, they possess such valuable instruments of defence against coercion, and of positive power
over the economy and the state, that they do not want to set
them at risk for the sake of an experiment. It is the tested
successes of economic democracy which gives them faith in
the value of political democracy. The working class of Eastern
Europe was deprived by the autocracy of any opportunity to
test democracy and to acquire confidence in it. Under the
gallows regime of Stolypin confidence in the law could not
mature, but only a belief in violence.

OTTO BAUER, *The Dictatorship of the Proletariat*[6]

The dictatorship of the proletariat has become something
entirely different from what was originally conceived by those
who established it. It is not the dictatorship of freely elected
Soviets. It is not the 'superior form of democracy' that Lenin
imagined, without a bureaucracy, or police, or a standing
army. It is not the free self-determination of the working
masses exercising their rule over the exploiting classes. It has
become the dictatorship of an all-powerful party bureaucracy
which stifles all freedom of speech and action even in the party
itself, and it dominates the people by means of the powerful
apparatus of the state and economic bureaucracy, the police,
and the army. This development was inevitable. Only this
bureaucratic dictatorship was able to accomplish the social

---

[6] From *Zwischen zwei Weltkriegen?* (1936), pp. 163–7. [Eds.]

revolution, but at a certain stage of development which Soviet society is rapidly approaching, this bureaucratic dictatorship will become an obstacle to further development.

The evolution of the dictatorship has established the bureaucracy of the party, the state and the economy as the master of the Soviet people. To be sure, this bureaucracy is in touch with the people and seeks their support, but it also exercises an absolute power over them. It seeks to obtain the consent of the governed to its decisions, but its power enables it to break by force any opposition to these decisions when it does not win consent. It co-operates with the mass of the people, but it is not subject to their power of decision.

Furthermore, the U.S.S.R. has been obliged to introduce considerable inequalities of income in all strata of the population—workers, clerical workers, peasants, and officials. It has been necessary to pay higher wages for more intensive, more skilled, or qualitatively superior work, in order to stimulate the growth of production. A privileged stratum of 'notables' has emerged in all classes, which enjoys, because of its particularly meritorious work, high incomes, great social consideration, and all kinds of privileges. The industrial bureaucracy is recruited from this stratum, whose children get priority in access to secondary education. It has particularly close links with the ruling party and with the bureaucratic state apparatus.

This development, though inevitable in itself, poses a grave danger: namely that a bureaucratic domination will become consolidated, not subject to popular control, and which, in close association with the 'notables' in all strata and relying upon them, might become the more or less permanent master of the mass of workers and peasants, controlling their means of production and disposing over the product of their labour. In this case it would not be a socialist society, but some kind of technocracy, the power of engineers, of economic managers, and of bureaucrats, that would emerge from the revolutionary process.

Such a danger can only be averted by the democratization of the Soviet constitution and of the basic relationships in Soviet enterprises. Only when the bureaucracy is subordinated to the decisions and control of the labouring masses themselves, when the incomes and privileges of the 'notables' are regulated by the mass of the unprivileged, will the working people as a whole become masters of the bureaucracy, of the state, of the factories, the instruments of labour, and the products of their labour. Only in this way can a socialist society be attained.

It is certainly not possible to pass abruptly from the Soviet dictatorship to democracy. The repercussions of the immense and violent revolutionary changes are still vividly present in the minds of millions of people, and a sudden transition to democracy would run the risk of unleashing social forces that would threaten the achievements of the revolution, bought at such great cost. But a gradual democratization of the Soviet constitution becomes possible to the extent that the growth of productivity permits a rise in the level of living, both urban and rural, that greater agricultural productivity can overcome the violent struggle for food supplies between town and country, that the mass of people begin to see in the property relations and organization of production resulting from the revolution a conquest which they are determined to maintain and develop as an indispensable condition for achieving the higher economic and cultural level to which they aspire. This democratization becomes necessary as the Soviet individual, rapidly raising his cultural level, gains a self-awareness and self-confidence which dispose him not to conform any longer to bureaucratic absolutism but to demand personal liberty, intellectual freedom, and the right to self-determination and self-administration. There are undoubtedly many obstacles in the way of a democratization of the Soviet system. No bureaucracy renounces joyfully the uncontrolled power to which it has become accustomed. The difficulties of democratization will be increased if the U.S.S.R. is threatened by war. But eventually democratization will have to become a reality if the revolution is to attain its end of establishing a genuine socialist form of society.

VI. The Development of Capitalism, Social Classes, and Class Conflict

RUDOLF HILFERDING, *The Capitalist Monopolies and the Banks*[1]

The development of capitalist industry produces concentration of banking, and this concentrated banking system is itself an important force in attaining the highest stage of capitalist concentration in cartels and trusts. How do the latter then react upon the banking system? The cartel or trust is an enterprise of very great financial capacity. In the relations of mutual dependence between capitalist enterprises it is the amount of capital that principally decides which enterprise shall become dependent upon the other. From the outset, the effect of advanced cartelization is that the banks also amalgamate and expand in order not to become dependent upon the cartel or trust. In this way cartelization itself requires the amalgamation of the banks, and conversely, amalgamation of the banks requires cartelization. For example, a number of banks have an interest in the amalgamation of steel concerns, and they work together to bring about this amalgamation even against the will of individual manufacturers.

Conversely, a community of interests brought about in the first place by manufacturers can have the consequence that two previously competing banks develop common interests and proceed to act in concert in a particular sphere. In a similar fashion, industrial combinations may influence the expansion of the industrial activities of a bank, which was perhaps previously concerned only with the raw materials sector of an industry, and is now obliged to extend its activities to the processing sector as well.

The cartel itself presupposes a large bank which is in a position to provide, on a regular basis, the vast credits needed

[1] From *Das Finanzkapital* (1910), chap. 14. [Eds.]

for current payments and productive investment in a whole industrial sector. But the cartel also brings about a still closer relationship between banking and industry. When competition in an industry is eliminated there is, first of all, an increase in the rate of profit, which plays an important role. When the elimination of competition is achieved by a merger, a new undertaking is created which can count upon higher profits, and these profits can be capitalized and provide additional gains for those who established the undertaking.[2] With the development of trusts this process becomes important in two respects. First, its realization constitutes a very important motive for the banks to encourage monopolization; and second, a part of the initial profits of the merger can be used to induce reluctant but significant producers to sell their factories, by offering a higher purchase price, thus facilitating the establishment of the cartel. This can perhaps be expressed in the following way: the cartel exerts a demand on the enterprises in a particular branch of industry; this demand increases to a certain degree the price of the enterprises[3] and this higher price is then paid in part out of the initial profits.

Cartelization also means greater security and uniformity in the earnings of the cartelized enterprises. The dangers of competition, which often threatened the existence of the individual enterprise, are eliminated and this leads to an increase in the share prices of these enterprises, which involves further capital gains when new shares are issued. Furthermore, the security of the capital invested in these enterprises is significantly increased. This permits a further expansion of industrial credit by the banks, which can then acquire a larger share in industrial profits. As a result of cartelization, therefore, the relations between the banks and industry become still closer, and at the same time the banks acquire an increasing control over the capital invested in industry.

We have seen that in the early stages of capitalist production, the money available to the banks is derived from two sources: on one side, from the resources of the non-productive

---

[2] In a long footnote, omitted here, Hilferding illustrates this process in the case of the American Sugar Trust created in 1887. [Eds.]

[3] We are concerned here with the 'price of capital', which is equivalent to the capitalized profit.

classes, and on the other side, from the capital reserves of industrial and commercial capitalists. We have also seen how credit develops in such a way as to place at the disposal of industry not only the whole capital reserves of the capitalist class but also the major part of the funds of the non-productive classes. In other words, present-day industry is carried on with an amount of capital far exceeding that which is owned by the industrial capitalists. With the development of capitalism there is also a continual increase in the amount of money which the non-productive classes place at the disposal of the banks, who in turn convey it to the industrialists. The control of these funds which are indispensable to industry rests with the banks and consequently, with the development of capitalism and of the machinery of credit, the dependence of industry upon the banks increases. On the other side, the banks can only attract the funds of the non-productive classes, and retain their continually growing capital over the long term, by paying interest on them. They could do this in the past, so long as the volume of money was not too great, by employing it in the form of credits for speculation and trade. With the increase in the available funds on one side, and the diminishing importance of speculation and trade on the other, they were bound to be transformed more and more into industrial capital. Without the continuous expansion of credit for production, the availability of funds for deposit would have declined long ago, as would the rate of interest on bank deposits. In fact, this is to some extent the case in England, where the deposit banks only furnish credit for commerce, and consequently the rate of interest on deposits is minimal. Hence deposits are continually withdrawn for investment in industry by the purchase of shares, and in this case the public does directly what is done by the banks where industry and the deposit banks are closely linked. For the public the result is the same, because in neither case does it receive any of the initial profits from the merger, but so far as industry is concerned it involves less dependence on bank capital in England as compared with Germany.

The dependence of industry on the banks is therefore a consequence of property relationships. An ever-increasing part of the capital of industry does not belong to the industrialists who use it. They are able to dispose over capital only through the banks, which represent the owners. On the other side, the banks have to invest an ever-increasing part of their capital in industry, and in this way they become to a greater and greater extent industrial capitalists. I call bank capital, that is, capital in money form which is actually transformed in this way into industrial capital, finance capital. So far as its owners are concerned, it always retains the money form; it is invested by them in the form of money capital, interest-bearing capital, and can always be withdrawn by them as money capital. But in reality the greater part of the capital so invested with the banks is transformed into industrial, productive capital (means of production and labour power) and is invested in the productive process. An ever increasing proportion of the capital used in industry is finance capital, capital at the disposition of the banks which is used by the industrialists.

Finance capital develops with the development of the joint-stock company and reaches its peak with the monopolization of industry. Industrial earnings acquire a more secure and regular character, and so the possibilities for investing banking capital in industry are extended. But the bank disposes of banking capital, and the owners of the majority of the shares in the bank dominate the bank. It is clear that with the increasing concentration of property, the owners of the fictitious capital which gives power over the banks, and the owners of the capital which gives power over industry, become increasingly the same people. As we have seen, this is all the more so as the large banks increasingly acquire the power to dipose over fictitious capital.

We have seen how industry becomes increasingly dependent upon banking capital, but this does not mean that the magnates of industry also become dependent on banking magnates. As capital itself at the highest stage of its development becomes finance capital, so the magnate of capital, the finance capitalist, increasingly concentrates his control over the whole national capital by means of his domination of bank-capital. Personal connections also play an important role here.

With cartelization and trustification finance capital attains its greatest power while merchant capital experiences its deepest degradation. A cycle in the development of capitalism is completed. At the outset of capitalist production money capital, in the form of usurers' and merchants' capital, plays a significant role in the accumulation of capital as well as in the transformation of handicraft production into capitalism. But there then arises a resistance of 'productive' capital, i.e. of the profit-earning capitalists—that is, of commerce and industry, against the interest-earning capitalists. Usurer's capital becomes subordinated to industrial capital. As money-trading capital it performs the functions of money which industry and commerce would otherwise have had to carry out themselves in the process of transformation of their commodities. As banking capital it arranges credit operations among the productive capitalists. The mobilization of capital and the continual expansion of credit gradually brings about a complete change in the position of the money capitalists. The power of the banks increases and they become founders and eventually rulers of industry, whose profits they seize for themselves as finance capital, just as formerly the old usurers seized, in the form of 'interest', the produce of the peasants and the ground rent of the lord of the manor. The Hegelians spoke of the negation of the negation: banking capital was the negation of usurer's capital and is itself negated by finance capital. The latter is the synthesis of usurer's and banking capital, and it appropriates to itself the fruits of social production at an infinitely higher stage of economic development.

The development of commercial capital, however, is quite different. The development of industry gradually excluded it from the ruling position over production which it had occupied during the period of manufacture. This decline is definitive, and the development of finance capital reduces the significance of trade both absolutely and relatively, transforming the once proud merchant into a mere agent of industry which is monopolized by finance capital.

OTTO BAUER, *The World View of Organized Capitalism*[4]

The defeat of the revolution of 1848 was a defeat for the generation of the German bourgeoisie educated by idealist philosophy. Bayonets had triumphed over the Idea, and the

---

[4] From *Das Weltbild des Kapitalismus* (1924), pp. 50–9. [Eds.]

bourgeoisie turned aside in disillusionment from idealism. As it became involved in the economic activities stimulated by the boom of the 1850s, the attention of its thinkers became focused upon the natural sciences. Rejoicing in the free competition which was eventually achieved in the aftermath of the revolution, it projected free competition upon the universe. Natural-scientific materialism attached itself to liberalism.

But German liberalism was defeated on the battlefields of 1866 and 1871. Under the powerful impact of Bismarck's victories the German bourgeoisie threw itself into the arms of the militaristic authoritarian state of the Junkers. Political liberalism was abandoned after 1871, economic liberalism after Bismarck's policy reorientation of 1878. Protective duties, policies favouring the middle class, land reform—these were the slogans that prevailed after 1878. The belief in free competition was shattered. The historical school and 'professorial socialism' overcame the doctrines of *laissez-faire*. Political economists and historians brought up the new generation to believe in the creative power of the state. With the decline of liberalism, materialism also began to lose ground. The bourgeois, who had made his peace with the state, had to make it with the church as well. He did this all the more gladly because the spiritual power of the church proved to be an extremely solid barrier against the rising labour movement. But new opposition to materialism arose from anti-capitalist as well as capitalist circles. The more effectively 'professorial socialism'—representing the authoritarian state in opposition to *laissez-faire*, the anti-capitalistically-minded agricultural producers in a period of agrarian crisis and rapid growth of rural indebtedness, and the petty bourgeoisie threatened by the victorious march of large-scale enterprise—opposed capitalist liberalism, the more strongly did it shake the world view of liberalism. The age was seeking a new world view in place of materialism. In 1881, three years after Bismarck forsook economic liberalism, the centenary celebration of the *Critique of Pure Reason* showed the growing strength of neo-Kantianism, which attempted to satisfy this need.

In the framework of the tariff system created by Bismarck there developed a new, *organized* capitalism, which replaced the older individualistic capitalism. Cartels, agricultural cooperatives, and trade unions organized the market. The slogan of the age was no longer free competition, but organization. State legislation and administration regulated with increasing vigour economic and social life; the dominant belief of the age was no longer the free play of forces but the direct utilization of political power for economic ends, both internally and externally. As organized collectivist capitalism developed with the growing strength of finance capital, the development of cartels, and imperialist policies, so bourgeois individualism declined. The bourgeois now regarded himself above all as a member of an organization and a citizen of the state; his highest values were no longer individual freedom, but loyalty to the state and the organization.

His view of nature was bound to change along with this change in his conceptions of society. In the first place his notion of the task of natural science changed. While the bourgeoisie was still combating feudalism and absolutism it fought for a world view which would replace the world of ideas of the feudal age. All the great achievements of natural scientific research from Copernicus to Darwin provided weapons against the ideas of the past. But now everything had changed. The bourgeoisie, having become the ruling class, no longer sought in natural science a means of satisfying its need for a world view, but looked for discoveries which were of immediate technical use and would help to perfect its methods of production. The sceptical positivism of Mach, Poincaré, or James teaches us to regard natural science in a new light. Our knowledge is simply a tool in the struggle for existence; it cannot investigate the nature of things, but only assemble and order experiences for practical ends. The hypotheses from which natural science deduces its experimentally testable natural laws were, for the earlier bourgeois thinkers, a way of satisfying their desire for a world-view, foundation stones for a conception of the world which they opposed to that of the feudal age; but for the positivists of our time, they are unimportant in themselves, and simply an aid to ordering and connecting the facts of experience mathematically. Copernicus's achievement was for the earlier bourgeoisie a revolutionary act against the ruling powers of the church; for the relativism of our time, it is merely an exchange of co-ordinate systems, the Copernican for the Ptolemaic, the former being preferred only because it makes calculation easier.

With this transformation in the conception of natural science as a whole, in the first instance the conception of natural laws changed. When the unlimited power of kings was the source of all law, deism regarded its god as the legislator for nature. When, in the republic, the people subjected to laws became the legislators, pantheism regarded the world subjected to the laws of nature as identical with the divine lawgiver. When the bourgeoisie proclaimed the immutable moral nature of man to be the source of all right, it looked for the source of natural laws in the unchanging capacity of man for knowledge. When the historical school of law conceived law as the emanation of the organically developing spirit of the people, natural laws also became stages of development in the dialectical movement of the world spirit. But our age has created another concept of law. When we speak of the laws of society, we are not thinking of the immutable rights of men and citizens which are themselves grounded in the moral development of man, nor of the great historical systems of law in which the stages of development of the spirit of the people are embodied, but of the daily legislative activity of our parliament, which today regulates protection against foot-and-mouth disease, tomorrow speculation on the stock exchange. In our age, the law is an instrument that is applied every day to economic ends. This concept of law is carried over to the laws of nature, which likewise become means to economic ends.

Our knowledge is only a means for our work and we try to shape it as purposefully, simply, and economically as possible. To this end, we subsume under one rule as many individual items of knowledge as possible, and then call such rules laws of nature. The law of nature is not a law given to the world by a god, nor a law dictated by our fixed capacity for knowledge of nature, nor a determination of the world spirit, but only a modest means used by man to order his experiences in the most simple, purposeful, and economical manner. No longer do the laws of nature provide us with knowledge of the essential characteristics of the world; they are simply a means to the more purposeful organization of our knowledge, which itself is only a means to the more effective organization of our work.

The mechanistic conception of nature sought to reduce all natural phenomena to laws of motion. For this conception the motion of particles was the essential element of the world, and light, heat, and electricity were only the sensations aroused in our consciousness by these motions through the sense organs. This idea has no meaning in the new conception. What we experience is only sensations; if we represent the experienced natural processes as phenomena of the movements of particles, we do this only in order to classify them in the simplest possible manner. This procedure is only justified in so far as it allows us to classify the phenomena of our experience more simply, more economically, than would be possible without using them.

In the period of manufacture, all human labour was a movement of materials through human force; if one wanted to make natural processes comprehensible by analogy with human labour, one was bound to think of them as the movement of materials by force. Even the introduction of machines did not change this situation, for the machine only took over the movements which the human hand and foot had previously had to carry out. The factory age, therefore, conceived the world by analogy with its work, and regarded it as a mechanical system. In our own time, industry based on machines is increasingly unimportant compared with the transformation industries; the steel, chemical, and electrical industries now stand in the forefront of our concerns. Besides the progress of these industries our main interest lies in the technical transformation of agriculture; the cultivation of plants, the effects of artificial fertilizers, the activity of soil bacteria, interest us today in the way that the spinning machine interested men a hundred years ago.

Thus our concept of labour has changed significantly: 'labour' comes to mean the chemical or electrical process that goes on in the basic technological system, and this process is merely initiated by the worker who sets it in motion by moving a lever or pressing a key. Production is the feeding of plants; the day labourer who spreads fertilizer is only a condition of production. Hence we no longer see the essence of human labour in mechanical movement, but in chemical, electrical, and physiological processes which are simply released by human mechanical movements. If we want to conceive world processes in terms of our labour, we can no longer reduce natural phenomena to movements of materials by force; chemical or electrical energy is now no less intelligible than mechanical labour. Along with the mechanical view atomism has also been abandoned. The thought of the age in which feudal corporations of domination and co-operation were destroyed by absolutism, and the latter in turn by liberalism, was concerned with the opposition between the individual and the collectivity, between the state and the citizen, between the universe and the atom, between God and creation. As in society, so in thought the collective totality and individual autonomy, universalism and individualism, combated each other. The period of transition from individualistic to organized capitalism overcomes both individualism and universalism.

The autonomy of the individual is destroyed. The individual person develops and is effective only in the various organizations to which he belongs. Today personalities can develop only in organizational activity and function only through organizations; they must serve the organization if they are to function in it. The individual is a product and instrument of the organization, just as the organization is a product and instrument of individuals. As the unorganized individual vanishes so does his theoretical reflection, the atom. For the modern natural scientist the atom is only an aid to thought, which can be used when it makes possible a simple representation of experience; it is no longer a real essence. The atom is dissolved into a planetary system of electrons, but the scientist thinks of this system too as only a practical aid to thought, not as a real essence.

Universalism also disappears with individualism. The present-day state is only one of many organizations, its legislation determined by the power of the organizations which influence it, its government a resultant of the strength of the parties contending for power. It is not a universal which stands above individuals, but the outcome of the play of forces among individuals. And with the disappearance of the state regarded as standing above society, there also disappear its various reflections; the lawgiving God of deism, Kant's lawgiving reason of the human species, and Hegel's world spirit.

Individualism and universalism are dissolved. The modern image of the world contains nothing but complexes of elements, observational bundles constituted by changing observations which sometimes connect and at other times are dissociated, which are never sharply separated from one another, but always interpenetrate. Nowhere are individuals sharply marked off from each other, but neither is there a planned and organized whole; it is like Impressionist painting which avoids all sharp contours, allows all lines to merge with each other and all shades of colour to interpenetrate. It is the world image of a period in which the old conflict between individualism and universalism has been transcended in a praxis in which the individual is no longer sovereign but is the creation and instrument of organizations, while the organization is not yet the well-articulated embodiment of the totality but is simply an instrument for individuals, not yet a socialist community, but a joint-stock company or cartel, a co-operative or trade union. It is the world image of a period in which the great traditional questions of the rights of personality and humanity, of the nature of the world and God, no longer have any significance; in which politics is carried on only by economic interest groups; in which science seeks only to classify in the most economical way what we experience, and art seeks only to reproduce what we observe.

The opposition between causality and teleology disappears along with that between individualism and universalism. The mechanistic conception of nature only recognized causal connections between phenomena. The desire for a pure causal science, which Hegel introduced into history, was satisfied in that sphere by Marx's conception of history. But his conception also served the aims of socialism and it was against this that the reaction of teleology was first directed. In the struggle against Marxism the neo-Kantians (Stammler, Windelband, and Rickert) restricted the scope of causality to the natural sciences; in dealing with history and society science has to employ the categories of means and ends, not cause and effect.

But then teleology ventured to approach natural science again. The causal laws of nature are just means to attain our ends; causality itself is teleologically grounded. Causal laws provide no explanation of the essence of things, only an economical description of our experiences; they cannot show us how a prime cause produces a phenomenon, but only how one phenomenon follows or accompanies another. The concept of causality is therefore thought of again in the manner of Hume; it is only justified biologically, by its practical usefulness. Consequently, its claims only extend as far as its serviceability. Where classification in terms of means and ends facilitates a simpler description of processes than one in terms of cause and effect, the former is to be preferred. For the modern state it is just a matter of expediency whether it should leave the satisfaction of a social need to the 'free play of forces' or provide for it by planned legislation and administration; so too for modern science it is a matter of expediency whether it is to represent a phenomenon by analogy with free competition, as the effect of a mechanism, or by analogy with planned activity as the outcome of goal-directed aspirations. Teleology found an opening particularly in biology; disappointed in Darwin, many adopted Lamarckian views again. Since the bourgeoisie is no longer fighting against theology, it also no longer fears teleology.

Finally, opinions about the mathematical methods of science also change, and here too the change occurs first in the sphere of the social sciences. On the model of mathematical natural science, and following closely its method, the physiocrats, the classical economists, and Marx, created mathematical theories of political economy. In Germany there now emerged for the first time a need for an economic science which could challenge both classical liberalism and Marxist socialism. The historical school rejected the mathematical procedure on which the liberal and socialist theories were founded, and argued that the task of political economy was not to represent individual incomes as quanta of social labour, but to portray economic phenomena in their qualitative diversity and describe their divergent development. The discursive-mathematical school of political economy was confronted by the descriptive historical. It was only later that the question of the validity of mathematical methods in natural science was raised. In this case, of course, nobody dared to propose that the discursive-mathematical method should simply be replaced by a representation of the concrete contents of experience, or that a history of nature should be substituted for natural science. Nevertheless, here also men learned not to overrate what mathematical methods can achieve. The dissolution of qualities into quantities no longer leads, as with Locke and the materialists, to the perception of the primary, uniquely real properties of bodies; it is only a means which our understanding employs in order to describe in the most economical way the world of material bodies, which is always qualitatively determined, and thus dominate it more effectively. For the new theory of knowledge, mathematics means something quite different from Descartes's system of innate ideas, from Locke's understanding of the primary, uniquely real properties of bodies, and from Kant's law-governed human reason; it is simply an appropriate means which man has invented to serve his technical aims.

This more modest evaluation of the mathematical method culminates in the need for an image of the world which no longer reduces it to quantities, but represents it in a qualitative form. For the idle rich who enjoy themselves without working, for the creative artist or scholar to whom work is not simply an acquisitive activity, for the religious person who repeatedly asks himself what it profits a man to acquire all the treasures of the world and at the same time lose his own soul, for the ethical or aesthetic socialist who turns away in disgust from the world of commerce—for all of these the world of goods comprises use values, not exchange values, and society is constituted by persons, not by economic subjects or citizens of the state. They regard with disdain or pity working humanity, which turns everything into sums of money; hence they are never content with the world image of the mathematical natural sciences which itself, as a mere means to economic ends, reduces the whole world to quanta of values—masses or amounts of energy on the model of the capitalist money economy. They were the bearers of the idealist current of thought, in opposition to materialism, which as the philosophy of the idle, of intellectuals and artists, was never completely overcome even in the period of materialism's greatest triumph. Today this counter-current is growing stronger. First, because the social stratum whose needs it expresses is more antagonistic than ever to the economic system which has undermined, through devaluation of the currency, the basis of its *rentier* existence. Second, because the dissolution of the mechanistic conception of nature makes possible the satisfaction of the need for a non-discursive image of the world without contradicting mathematical natural science; for if the latter is just a useful means to technical ends everyone is at liberty to create for himself a different world image for other ends.

Thus the whole mechanistic conception of nature, and all the philosophical systems based upon it, has been dissolved in modern positivism and relativism. But the self-dissolution of the classical world view of capitalism has been completed only within the limits of bourgeois thought. The task of freeing modern epistemology from these limitations has still to be accomplished.

MAX ADLER, *Metamorphosis of the Working Class*[5]

A buoyant mood now prevails among the opponents of Marxism. They exult over its collapse because, following the suppression of the Italian proletariat ten years ago, the German working class—the strongest in Europe—has also been crushed. All those who attach importance only to the surface of things—and this has always included most of the opponents of Marxism—are now announcing the end of Marxism. But one must distinguish, as did Friedrich Engels, between Marxism as a theory and Marxism as a movement. What is described today as the crisis, or even the collapse, of Marxism does not affect Marxism as a theory but only as a movement. Marxist theory has remained untouched by this whole crisis and defeat; indeed it is Marxism which not only enables us to understand correctly for the first time the catastrophe that has befallen the German workers' movement, but also to prevent it happening elsewhere and to prepare the means for recovering from it in Germany.

[5] From 'Wandlung der Arbeiterklasse?', *Der Kampf*, xxvi (1933), pp. 367–82, 406–14. [Eds.]

Considered in this light, it is immediately apparent that the collapse of the German movement did not occur because it was Marxist, but because it was not Marxist enough. If we pursue this idea further, it also becomes clear that the inadequate hold that Marxism still has upon the masses is the cause of the present weakness of the working class in all other countries too. This is demonstrated in a striking manner by the division of the socialist workers' movement, not only into the two camps of the Second and Third Internationals, but within the former into the reformist and the consistently Marxist orientations. Thus the proletariat as a whole still faces the task of grasping the real meaning of the Marxist critique of society, and so attaining that unity and resoluteness of political *action* which corresponds with the unity and comprehensiveness of Marxist *theory*. At the same time the spread of Marxist theory, with its unmasking of the illusions and deceptions of Fascism, and its ideal of social development, is the most effective means of reaching the white collar workers and so ultimately uniting the whole proletariat.

Marxism is far from having come to an end; on the contrary it is at the beginning of a new historical epoch, that of its mass currency in the world proletariat. Hence, it faces a really decisive turning point in the world. Only now does the Marxist spirit begin to take on flesh in the self-revolutionizing thought and will of the world proletariat. The terrible fate of German social democracy and of the German trade union movement will do more to awaken the mass of the people in all countries to Marxism than the most powerful educational work in books and lectures could achieve.

But the urgent question is then posed: why was such a terrible lesson necessary? How can one explain the fact that precisely in a country where the workers' movement was led by a large and highly developed proletariat, with many years of training in political and trade union work, it has shown such a feeble Marxist spirit and lack of revolutionary ardour? More generally, how has it come about that despite the progressive development of capitalism, of large-scale industry, and of the proletariat, the development of the latter's revolutionary strength has not been correspondingly stronger outside Germany as well? At the very moment of the world crisis of capitalism, and of an intensified attack by the forces of the capitalist class, the resistance of the proletariat has not increased in response, not to speak of its ability to take the offensive and use the capitalist crisis to put an end to capitalism! This leads to an observation which has already been made occasionally by various Marxist observers and now needs to be more thoroughly examined. This is the increasingly obvious fact that the development of the past decade has produced changes in the proletariat itself, eliminating its unified character, and thus gradually transforming its role and its revolutionary commitment to the class struggle into something essentially different from what they were taken to be in Marx's analysis.

There really does seem to be a point here where Marx's predictions have not been confirmed. In every other respect, the present political and economic world situation is a brilliant confirmation of Marxist theory. The objections of the revisionists and the bourgeois critics to the correctness of Marx's analysis of society have long since been abandoned. Everything that Marx said about the inevitability and the intensification of economic class antagonisms, about the increasing misery of the workers, about the displacement of human labour by machines, about the tendency of all states to become divided into two great opposing interest groups, has been literally fulfilled in the political sphere by Fascism, and in the economic sphere by the world crisis and mass unemployment. Only in one respect is there a notable deviation from the course of development that Marx delineated. With the development of the capitalist mode of production, according to Marx, the proletariat does not only increase in numbers but revolutionizes itself, so to speak, as a matter of course; hence for Marx it was unquestionable that the growing contradictions of capitalism would be accompanied by an even greater revolutionary indignation and strength of purpose. This is the ground for his conviction of the irresistibility of the socialist idea as a result of economic development. Already in the *Communist Manifesto* we read in a well-known passage:

. . . the condition for capital is wage labour. Wage labour rests exclusively on competition between the labourers. The advance of industry, whose involuntary promoter is the bourgeoisie, replaces the isolation of the labourers, due to competition, by their revolutionary combination, due to association. The development of modern industry, therefore, cuts from under its feet the very foundation on which the bourgeoisie produces and appropriates products. What the bourgeoisie therefore produces, above all, are its own gravediggers. Its fall and the victory of the proletariat are equally inevitable.

Similarly Marx wrote in another well-known passage, in volume I of *Capital*:

Along with the constantly diminishing number of the magnates of capital, who usurp and monopolize all the advantages of this process of transformation, grows the mass of misery, oppression, slavery, degradation, and exploitation; but with this too grows the revolt of the working class, a class always increasing in numbers, and disciplined, united, organized by the mechanism of the process of capitalist production itself. The monopoly of capital becomes a fetter upon the mode of production, which has sprung up and flourished along with, and under it.... The knell of capitalist private property sounds. The expropriators are expropriated.

The actual development of the proletariat up to the present time has not contradicted this view. Here also Marx's prophecy has been borne out in two respects. First, it is true that the numbers of the proletariat have increased, and that it has become increasingly organized. Indeed this organization has attained an extent and diversity that Marx and Engels could not have visualized. Besides the political and trade union organization which was their principal aim, there have emerged co-operatives, and in particular, a network of cultural associations, educational, sport, and training organizations which incorporate almost all the activities of all sections and age groups of the proletariat in an organizational apparatus. Second, Marx's prediction of the increasing misery, oppression, and degradation of large sections of the working class has come true. What is lacking is the growth of revolutionary indignation in the working class, the consolidation of all its energies in that irresistible revolutionary force which Marx always regarded as the historical function of the proletariat.

It is certainly true, as Marx wrote in the passage from *Capital*, part of which was quoted above, that: 'Centralization of the means of production and the socialization of labour at last reach a point where they become incompatible with their capitalist integument.' But when Marx continues: 'This integument is burst asunder', we have to recognize that this explosion which should have been the accomplishment of the revolutionary working class, for which it is today economically ripe and over-ripe, has not followed. Instead, at this historical moment when the expropriators could be expropriated the working class itself has been burst asunder. By its loss of unity and striking power, its lack of direction and its weakness in its most powerful section, the German working class, it has dug its own grave instead of being the gravedigger of capitalism. What is the source of this terrible contradiction of the course of proletarian development outlined by Marx? Here an important factor is the differentiation within the proletariat mentioned earlier, which has existed for decades at the upper levels, but has also become especially marked at the lower levels since the world crisis and its long-term unemployment. Its disastrous effects must be taken more fully into account in the theory and practice of the Marxist working-class movement than has been the case so far.

The historical role of the proletariat, as depicted by Marx, is to be, on the basis of economic necessity, the pioneer of a new socialist order of society, and consequently the bearer of a social revolution. This historical mission depends upon the *class character* of the proletariat which, in the Marxist sense, is above all economic. A class is a specific group of men, within a social collectivity, which has arisen through the production process itself; its members occupy a similar position in the process of production, have the same relation to the means of production and the profits of production, and ultimately acquire a corresponding consciousness. The proletariat is the group of productively active men within capitalist society who are at the same time separated from the means of production. That is why all its members are restricted to the amount of provisions (understanding this word in its widest sense) which the owners of the means of production allow it, which they need to be allowed for the continuation of the capitalist process of production. That is why Marx already defines the proletariat in the *Communist Manifesto* as '. . . a class of labourers, who live only so long as they find work, and who find work only so long as their labour increases capital'. Similarly, in *Capital*, he writes:

Our 'proletarian' is, economically considered, nothing other than the wage worker who produces and increases 'capital', and is thrown into the street as soon as he becomes superfluous for the needs of expansion of 'Monsieur Capital' (to use Pecqueur's impersonation).

This economic structure of the proletariat means for all its members the same oppressed life-situation, and consequently the formation of a uniform cultural outlook. In this life-situation the most oppressive feature is the lack of any prospect of improvement within the existing capitalist society. It is this feature of hopelessness which Lassalle expressed very effectively, from an agitational point of view, in his slogan of the 'iron law of wages'. As everyone knows, this means that the working class cannot hope ever to raise its level of living significantly above what is essential for the maintenance and reproduction of its labour power. Although Marx (in his *Critique of the Gotha Programme*) objected so strongly to Lassalle's slogan, his critique has nevertheless been widely misunderstood; sometimes by assuming that he considered the 'iron law' too pessimistic. In reality Marx never contested the fact that Lassalle asserted, and he criticized Lassalle's argument only because he thought that the 'iron law of wages' was founded upon a biological, Malthusian kind of argument. In this respect, incidentally, he did Lassalle an injustice, as he did on many other points. Marx does not question the 'iron law of wages' as being too strong, but expresses himself even more strongly. In the *Critique of the Gotha Programme* he says that:

the wage worker is only permitted to work for his own life, that is, to live, in so far as he also works a certain amount of time for the capitalist (and hence also for others who share in the surplus value). The whole capitalist system therefore turns upon in-creasing the amount of this free labour, by extending the working day, developing productivity, in other words, increasing the intensity of work. The system of wage labour is a system of slavery, and one which becomes all the more oppressive as the social forces of production develop, whether the worker is better or worse paid.

Marx, of course, never denied (nor did Lassalle) that the level of living could rise. This follows from the fact that Marx showed the socially necessary labour time for the production of labour power to be a historical quantity which depends on general cultural conditions, and on particular traditional ways of life, as well as on the victories of the working class. Nevertheless, he always emphasized that the tendency of the capitalist mode of production is to restrict the proletariat to a level of living compatible with increasing profit. This is all the more oppressive in relation to the continuous rise in the productivity of labour and the luxury which it makes possible for the possessing class.

As he wrote in *Wage-Labour and Capital*:

Thus, although the consumption of the worker has risen, the social satisfaction it affords has fallen in comparison with the augmented consumption of the capitalists, inaccessible to the worker, in comparison with the state of development of society as a whole.

The situation of the proletariat is therefore characterized by a level of living which is lower in relative terms and tends toward the lowest level of existence possible. Precisely because this relative minimum of existence cannot be exceeded, despite a progressive improvement in absolute terms, the feeling of being without any hope or prospect of attaining a really human cultural existence becomes all the more palpable in the proletariat. For nothing makes anyone feel the disadvantages of his own position more keenly than the contrast with the freer and happier lives of others. This is all the more so if his own situation is known to be undeserved, as is the more favoured situation of others, which was only made possible by his own misery and work. Then his unfortunate destiny changes into a pariah's fate. Another feature of the proletarian condition is the feeling of insecurity itself, even where the proletariat has attained a tolerable existence. This is an essential characteristic of the proletariat. It is determined by the economic fact of the industrial reserve army (unemployment) which is a necessary product of the capitalist process of production. It brings into the life of the proletariat the continual danger of unemployment, the terrible awareness of a hand-to-mouth existence, and above all the anxiety about how to survive in the event of a lengthy illness or incapacity for work due to age. Unemployment on one side and pauperization on the other are the dark shadows which make the fate of the working class still more sombre.

Already in Marx's work, therefore, the concept of the proletariat displays a certain differentiation. The workers in the production process form its main body, the industrial reserve army of the unemployed constitutes a second layer, and beneath these two, like a grimy sediment, are to be found the paupers, those who are totally excluded from production by illness, incapacity, or age, and also by every kind of crime or degeneracy, and who form the lumpenproletariat. This differentiation, however, is not sufficient to destroy the unified character of the proletariat. In the first place the lumpenproletariat, 'this passive putrefaction of the lowest layers of the old society', in relation to Marx's view of the actual configuration of the proletariat, represented an insignificant exception, a remnant of the decayed earlier forms of production. Consequently, he could regard this stratum, the lumpenproletariat, as one that would become less and less significant with the further development of large-scale industrial production. So far as the reserve army is concerned, it is true that Marx reckoned with its continuing growth. But he regarded unemployment as a phenomenon which, until the final crisis of the capitalist system, would have only a limited and fluctuating importance. In the disastrous cycle of crises and subsequent periods of recovery, it would sometimes increase, sometimes diminish again, and in terms of the numbers involved, as well as its duration in the life of each worker, would constitute an exception compared with his working activity. The emergence of mass unemployment, which Marx envisaged as a climax of the economic conflicts which he outlined, was equivalent, in his view, to the abolition of wage labour itself through the inner contradiction of capitalism, equivalent, that is, to the social revolution.

Quite a different picture is revealed by the present class

structure of the proletariat, as it has developed with particular rapidity under the unfavourable influence of the world crisis of capitalism, having long ago taken a new direction under more auspicious circumstances. This corresponds, certainly, in many respects with the misgivings that Marx, and especially Engels, had already expressed, but in the main it represents a new phenomenon. It consists essentially in the fact that the present-day proletariat is riddled with such economic conflicts—and an associated profound ideological alienation of various sections of the proletariat from each other—that it is doubtful whether we can speak of a single class. In the present structure of the proletariat the following strata can be distinguished: the great army of workers and employees whose conditions of life are proletarian; above them a stratum of those who enjoy a 'superior position in life'; and alongside them an army of employees of the party, trade unions, co-operatives, and friendly societies, whose numbers were still growing rapidly until quite recently. Beneath these strata are the unemployed, increasing in numbers, both absolutely and relatively, and finally, once again, the real lumpenproletariat. Thus, in the apparently unified class of the proletariat, we have five different strata which, in their social-psychological development, have eventually given rise to three basic orientations that have led, and still lead, to great and dangerous conflicts. These three orientations are those of the so-called labour aristocracy and bureaucracy, of the proletarians who are employed, and finally, of the unemployed. It is necessary to become more closely acquainted with the character of these particular strata, and thus to determine the role they have played so far in the socialist workers' movement, and to evaluate the influence they might have on the future shape of socialist politics. Only in this way is it possible to decide what changes in socialist tactics may be necessary in order to carry out the revolutionary task of the proletariat in accordance with its historical mission.

The danger posed by the inner economic differentiation of the proletariat is most easily comprehensible and conspicuous in the phenomenon of the so-called labour aristocracy. This comprises the workers in the better work situations, who are mainly but not entirely those in the highly skilled branches of labour; the stratum of the so-called 'high status' workers, and the office employees. This so-called labour aristocracy has gradually, and often without noticing it, separated itself profoundly from the rest of the proletariat in its mode of life and in its way of thinking and feeling. Its main characteristic is that its general outlook has changed from the social-revolutionary standpoint of the proletariat to a basically conservative mood. Admittedly, a large number of its members still deceive themselves by the traditional use of revolutionary class symbols and forms of expression, and as a result there is some diversity even within the labour aristocracy. One section, which has merely moved up into a more satisfying economic situation, simply displays a petty bourgeois character, while another section, the office workers, has also assumed the traits of bureaucracy, that is, the spirit of a caste which has acquired some petty power over others. Both strata have lost one essential feature of the proletariat; namely, the oppressive misery and the lack of prospects. The worker in a superior position is able to make small savings; the bureaucrat sees before him a certain possibility of advancement, and in any case has his pension.

In judging these conditions one should not be led astray by the fact that the prolonged economic crisis has not only worsened the situation of these strata but also threatens the very existence of such a labour aristocracy. The unprecedented growth of rationalization of factories erodes more and more the privileged position of the best-placed workers. Moreover, the insecurity of their employment has increased, and unemployment has made considerable advances in this sphere. In addition, rising prices and the greater cost of their children's education, because of their privileged situation, as well as the frequent impossibility nowadays of finding employment for their sons and daughters, has in many cases consumed the savings of this privileged stratum of workers. Those in official positions are also threatened by unemployment as a result of the rapid decline in party, trade union, and other dues. At present, the whole labour aristocracy is undoubtedly experiencing a serious decline. This fact alone is a crushing argument against the reformist orientation which was and is mainly represented by the labour aristocracy. But for our investigation of the causes and effects of the present divisions in the working class the issue is not the present condition of the labour aristocracy; what is crucial is those tendencies in the formation of this labour aristocracy which date back many years to the period of the active development of the socialist workers' movement. These tendencies have not only brought about the separation of a numerically large privileged stratum from the working class, but at the same time have allowed an ideology to develop which has disastrous consequences even in a period when the privileged strata are experiencing an economic and political decline.

It is worth noting that the danger of a 'labour aristocracy' was recognized very early in the modern labour movement. The second congress of the old Marxist International—the Congress of Lausanne (1867)—already discussed this question in detail. Evidently, it was the co-operatives, then in the forefront and overestimated as a result of the Lassallean movement, which caused the following topic to be placed before the congress for discussion: 'Will not an even more needy fifth estate result from the emancipation of the fourth estate through the co-operatives?' After a prolonged and passionate debate the Congress came to the conclusion that this would actually be the case; that the improvement of the workers' position by the co-operatives 'would leave a wholly impoverished fifth estate', if the co-operatives did not set as their main task the idea of a socialist transformation, and thus a *solidaristic* aim. Eccarius, Marx's spokesman, carried an amendment which based the hope of overcoming the labour aristocracy upon the development of modern large-scale industry, through which the significance of the co-operatives (especially the productive co-operatives) would be diminished in relation to the increasingly equal life situation and revolutionary aspirations of all workers. In this first discussion of an internal differentiation of the proletariat, we can see that the emphasis was placed upon revolutionary socialist ideology. It was the same task as confronts us today: that of preserving a revolutionary outlook and aspirations, preventing the emergence of divergent cultural orientations, and especially that which was characterized as the ideology of a fourth estate (in conflict with a fifth estate) whose main characteristic was that it had ceased to be proletarian. But it has actually developed, much more strongly than could have been seen or feared at that time.

This ideology is what has often been described, and was stigmatized by Engels in his letters of the 1880s and 1890s, as *embourgeoisement*, in the sense of petty bourgeois respectability and ideals. The proletarian class struggle, the phrases of which they retained for a long time but finally abandoned in favour of a struggle 'for human emancipation', has long since lost the revolutionary sense of a fundamental position of struggle against bourgeois society. Instead it has taken the form of a struggle for the continual improvement of its situation within existing society. One of its features is the aspiration of this stratum of workers to obtain higher education for their children. This is not from a consciousness that education is good in itself, and also a powerful weapon in the class struggle, but from a desire that the children should fare 'better' than their parents; that is, should leave the proletariat and if possible 'rise' into the bourgeoisie. The 'worker students' who in themselves represent a major step forward by the working class, and who could have produced an even greater revolutionary advantage for this class if they had made a point of infiltrating the bourgeois intellectual professions with proletarian-revolutionary elements, have become merely a breeding ground for the most sordid place hunting, and for an orientation which considers the role of party officials the most important element in the socialist movement. Thus for a large part of the proletariat, which expanded during periods of prosperity, the powerful idea of the liberation of the proletariat as a class took on a personal meaning. With an improved level of living, relative security through the progress of labour legislation, and an enhanced consciousness of their political worth as a result of the rise of social democracy in parliament, they saw only these 'achievements'. Admittedly, by comparison with the political and economic backwardness of an earlier generation of workers, and with the misery and persecution experienced in their own youth, this did signify an advance, which they conceived, however, as a realization of the emancipation of the proletariat. For them personally the great liberation struggle of the proletariat had, so to speak, already attained its goal. The extraordinary rise of some individual workers—for example, the career of Friedrich Ebert from saddlemaker to President of the Reich, or of Karl Severing from a simple metalworker to Minister of the Interior— was bound to become an impressive symbol for those who adopted this attitude, and a historical confirmation of its validity.

Inevitably, therefore, this brilliant spectacle (to which one's own modestly improved life-chances were felt to be related) completely overshadowed the gloomy and desolate picture of the working class in the background, although the latter showed increasing mass poverty and, in particular, the threat of growing unemployment. When this poverty eventually impinged upon the privileged stratum of workers, as was inevitably the case, they reacted to it as something already foreign to them, in the manner of the almsgiver to the beggar or the welfare official to the welfare recipient. They felt an obligation to help, but they regarded the misfortunes of others as being no longer typical of their own fate, and no longer a common class fate. It was this ideology that increasingly turned a part of the revolutionary proletariat into peaceful citizens. But they still lacked the world view of the bourgeoisie with its restless striving for power and expansion, and wanted to remain comfortably in their houses or on their allotments, or at most to attend the party meetings at which dues were paid.

The bureaucratic orientation, which was bound to emerge as a psychological necessity among the full-time officials in the party, trade unions, co-operatives, and the like, developed alongside this social-pacifist petty bourgeoisie. Above all there arose among this mass of employees a strongly developed consciousness of occupying a leading position in the labour movement, which was in itself justified inasmuch as it was based upon the functions they performed and the trust which was placed in them. But the development of highly professionalized activities, and the increasingly inaccessible specialized knowledge associated with them, was bound to produce a markedly one-sided interest, so that all these officials came to put the performance of their particular task (e.g. looking after trade union activities, or administering the sick fund) before the goals of the general revolutionary movement. Indeed, the latter was bound to appear ultimately as something unreal compared with their professional tasks. No wonder that the Marxist theory of revolution came to be regarded by them as 'impractical', 'outdated', and in any case disruptive.

Thus, this stratum gradually acquired for itself, and still more for the mass of workers, a legitimate and official character. The individual official behind his desk appeared to the simple proletarian facing him just like any other state official; all the more so as the proletariat infiltrated the state and municipal administration and began to occupy positions of authority in that sphere too. Frequently, the inquiry window was not just a physical barrier between the proletarian bureaucrat and his class comrades, but became a direct symbol of the cultural separation of the workers' stratum which had risen from its mass origin; a separation which also existed where— as in political life—no such real inquiry window was visible. In the end this stratum of office workers also came to feel, even more strongly than the workers in superior occupations, pride in what had been achieved. Through its activity in well-organized offices and factories, and in its own party and union offices; through its regular dealings with the authorities and with the official circles of bourgeois society, which often brought it into direct contact with ministers and with the higher circles of the state and municipal bureaucracy, as well as with similar circles among the entrepreneurs; through the need to work out clever diplomatic methods in representing the interests of the working-class struggle; through frequent journeys abroad to conferences and meetings of representative bodies—through such activities, personal ways of life were formed which were far removed from the social milieu and ways of thought of the proletariat. The simple proletarian sensed this immediately whenever he left the desolate oppressiveness of his life and went into that upper world. He was then bound to appear like the poor relation who is visiting his newly rich cousins. Here a propertied stratum had arisen in the proletariat; not property-owning in the individual sense, but as a class: the proletariat as owner of houses, factories, printing presses, places of business, banks, etc. This ownership had the same catastrophic effect as does all ownership;

it created anxiety in the owner about how to maintain and extend his property, and it also inevitably gave rise to a property-owning mentality. The proletariat now had something to defend and increase in present-day society. Hence this property ownership became a bond which chained the proletarian stratum of the labour aristocracy more strongly to the present time than to the future historical task of the proletariat.

The ultimate consequences of this attitude have been shown by the terrible developments in Germany, which indicate that the preoccupation with maintaining the possessions and conquests of the working class, falsely regarded as a desire to maintain the social-democratic labour movement, was in reality quite absurd as a means of attaining this goal. By eroding the revolutionary spirit of the leading strata and the labour aristocracy it produced the lifeless socialism and the intellectual disarmament of the party and trade unions, one obvious consequence of which was the neglect of any preparation for physical defence, thus leaving the German labour movement incapable of decision and action. We have even learned that the party and trade union leadership were ready to be incorporated into Hitler's Fascist system so that, in this way, they could 'sustain' what they regarded as the life of the socialist labour movement. But they were not successful, and all that they accomplished was to keep intact the accumulated and unused property of the proletariat for the benefit of the deadly enemy of the working class. There is no more terrible historical confirmation of Marx's remark that the working class is not on the proper road to its liberation until it knows that in bourgeois society it has nothing to lose but its chains.

It is unnecessary to explain in more detail how the labour aristocracy was, and is, the real champion of revisionism, of those policies that confuse parliamentarianism with proletarian democracy and instead of aspiring to the dictatorship of the proletariat—i.e. the seizure of political power—wanted only its rightful share of power. This reformism —as revisionism preferred to be called—this readiness for coalitions, which can be necessary at times, was not simply a matter of tactics, but a *mood*, a conviction of the proper, realistic road to socialism. Nothing is more characteristic of this outlook than

Ebert's words at one revolutionary moment: 'I hate revolution more than sin.' Similarly, a clear indication of this revisionist spirit of the leading strata is provided by one of the thinkers of the trade union movement, while it was still progressing after the war, in his characterization of the aim of socialist politics; that is, the aim of the working class. Karl Zwing writes in his *Sociology of the Trade Union Movement*:

One must not overlook the fact that the working class is part of the capitalist system. The decline of this system would also involve its own decline. Consequently, the working class has the great historical duty, through its integration into this system, to bring about the improvement of the whole condition of society, which is identical with its own social condition. (p. 161)

Obviously, revisionism had more profound causes than this orientation of the labour aristocracy. Anyone who failed to appreciate this would find himself on the quite un-Marxist path of 'Communist' demagogy, which dismisses all reformist phenomena purely and simply as betrayal by the leaders. Against this it must be pointed out that such 'betrayal' was itself the product of a great economic transformation in the capitalist process, which cannot be examined in detail here, but only briefly mentioned. For the differentiation in the upper levels of the proletariat is essentially the outcome of the transformation of capitalism into imperialism since the 1880s. This transformation did more than produce the vigorous mass development of the proletariat everywhere, which facilitated the growth of its political and trade union organization and hence necessarily created the party bureaucracy. From the beginning the development of imperialism was accompanied by frequent periods of great economic prosperity, which Sternberg quite rightly called the 'good old days' of the proletariat. The most outstanding of these periods lasted from about 1890 to the beginning of this century, but an equally notable, though shorter, phase of prosperity occurred in the period of stabilization and rationalization after the war. Both periods were especially fruitful for the revisionist tendencies in thought and outlook, which were influential far beyond the labour aristocracy, in the mass of the working class. These are the periods of what might be called the old classical revisionism of the Eduard Bernstein type, and of neo-revisionism, represented particularly by Rudolf Hilferding and Heinrich Cunow, and supported by the great mass of the workers. Reformism in the proletariat is not just a problem of leaders, but of the masses, and if only for this reason the phenomenon of the 'labour aristocracy' is one of great significance, since it is the surface manifestation of a current which is also present in the masses. It would be fundamentally misleading, therefore, to identify the labour aristocracy with the so-called 'bosses'. Just as not all leaders are bosses, so not all bosses and petty bosses are leaders. It is rather a mass mood and mass aspirations that we face here; the mood of parvenus, of those who have risen in the social hierarchy and those who would like to rise in the same way. This explains how the labour aristocracy even has a certain hold on the masses, namely among all those for whom they constitute an ideal. This whole phenomenon of the parvenus and their followers is at the same time the product of definite economic processes in capitalism, and an essential cause of the changes in the character of the proletariat.

We have seen that this influence operates, quite understandably, in such a way as to weaken the whole working class. But it is not so immediately obvious—indeed, on the contrary, it seems quite remarkable and unexpected—that a similar and even more harmful influence arises from that differentiation which has only appeared recently, in the lower strata of the working class, as a result of unemployment.

Before dealing with the unemployed, it is necessary to say something about the main body of the proletariat, the workers in town and country. One need only go once to a workers' mass meeting to have the immediate and depressing impression that despite all the democratic, social, and political achievements, the general image of the working class has remained just as Marx delineated it, and as it must be within the system of capitalist exploitation. Overworked and careworn individuals, many of the men and especially the women prematurely aged, all marked by the wretchedness of their life, which is revealed in their uncared-for appearance, their poor clothing, and their timid, mistrustful attitude toward anyone who is distinguished from them by a better appearance

or a more cultured way of speaking. What a difference
there is between this picture and that provided by the meetings of representatives of the proletariat at congresses and
party conferences! Here is the real manifestation of that class
whose most devastating feature, according to Marx, was that
they produce free time for others by transforming the whole
of their own lives into labour time. This is the class which in
present-day society can lead no life for itself, but must be
employed only for alien ends, for the economy, the state, and
the culture of the property owners. That is why even where
their consciousness has not yet attained full clarity, these men
have a kind of instinctive hatred of the whole system to which
they are sacrificed. A deep-rooted defiance, and a constant
readiness to express it, is ready to explode in all of them, if it
can be aroused. It is a consoling fact that the depression which
initially overwhelms everyone who attends such a workers'
meeting, as a non-proletarian but a socialist, soon changes to a
feeling of buoyant confidence as this passionate wave of
revolutionary determination rises, demonstrating that these
really are, and want to be, the men Marx called the pioneers
of a new society.

Of course, this revolutionary energy often remains dor-
mant. In the 'realistic' expositions of politics in lectures, and
especially in public meetings, which have all too often constituted a major part of party activity, the listeners are for the
most part respectfully attentive, and not seized with enthusiasm. Sometimes, especially in the case of older people, they
are even glad to hear about forms of struggle and possibilities
of victory which do not require the extreme efforts of the
class struggle. For the bitter phrase of Mephistopheles applies
to them as to other men: 'He soon becomes enamoured of un-
conditional peace.' Many people have been, and still are, too
easily persuaded that things are different and better since
Marx's time. But experience shows repeatedly how these proletarian meetings undergo a fundamental change when the
profound social truths and the powerful appeals of Marxist
theory reach them; how the most rapt attention prevails, the
silence which comes from apprehending truths that were only
dimly perceived, not clearly known; how the anxious faces
lighten, bodies become tense with readiness to do battle and

with revolutionary confidence, which works almost like a physical stimulant and rejuvenator. One senses that the social revolution is alive, not as a theoretical formula, but as a *need* of the masses for freedom and development. These masses, who are otherwise swept helplessly away, in the endless stream of renunciation, oppression, and humiliation of every kind, are only alive when the revolutionary proletarian mood grips them. But how is it that this basic revolutionary mood has so little effect upon the general character of the working-class movement, as has been shown most catastrophically by German social democracy, but also very often in the whole European social democratic movement, that it can be described as reformist-democratic rather than revolutionary socialist? Here we encounter a difficult problem that will be considered later from another aspect; namely, the development of an organization into a rigid apparatus. In this respect also, there becomes apparent the inescapable peculiarity of all social phenomena, which is their dialectical nature, producing inner contradictions that are closely related to their development.

So it is with organizations. They are born from the living recognition of the uniform life-situation of the proletariat and are sustained by the growing revolutionary class consciousness of their members, by their enthusiastic devotion to working for the great goal of liberation and socialism. Thus all the forms of working-class organization—political, trade union, and cultural—represent from the outset a living conviction and vigorous activity which expresses itself in love of the organization as the self-chosen form of unification, and in sacrificial loyalty to it even in difficult times, and above all in times of persecution. Thus the organization changes the nature and character of the worker in a remarkable way to his advantage, and the organized worker appears as quite a different man from the unorganized. In this case, unlike others, involvement with the masses does not diminish individuality or degrade the intellectual and moral level: on the contrary, it makes the worker aware of his own value and awakens the feeling of serving a historical cause. This association with the masses develops the personality of the worker, because the organization does not merely incorporate him in the mass, but also involves him in the idea which unites this mass. So the worker who was previously isolated, experiencing his misery and his lack of significance in a resigned and hopeless fashion, here becomes for the first time a proud, self-confident, future-oriented man who opposes his oppressors in the state and the economy with the considered view that 'Your world is not mine, which is the world of the future', and in consequence is detested by all his opponents who feel his resolve.

The significance of organization for cultural development cannot be valued too highly therefore, irrespective of its immediate usefulness for current trade union, political, and cultural struggles.... The larger it becomes and the more tasks it assumes, the more the organization, which originally depended upon the co-operation of all its members, has to assign important business to special agents who must also be given economic security, since they have to give up their other work. This is not only so that they can devote themselves entirely to the affairs of the organization, but also to make them independent of persecution by their capitalist providers. Hence, in every growing organization there must ultimately arise a growing stratum of salaried officials and representatives who, as direct employees of the organization, or as parliamentary representatives, are not only charged with looking after all aspects of the class leadership and representation of the proletariat but ultimately develop a particular technique, which increasingly becomes a kind of specialized knowledge and professional training. I have already outlined in the section on the labour aristocracy how this process tends to produce a harmful degeneration. But apart from this, the need for professional representation generally produces a fatal division of labour within the organization, whereby the great majority of members finds itself restricted, and ultimately restricts itself, merely to carrying out what the stratum of leaders and representatives decides. A whole multitude of circumstances, arising from the mechanism of an organization which has grown large, work in this direction, and are supported by what in themselves belong to the basic conditions, nay the virtues of every living organization, the trust and the discipline of the organization's members....

It has to be emphasized, above all, that the development of special committees within the organizations, together with the specialization of party and trade union work, has severely limited, and even made impossible, any initiative by the individual member. In the face of the continual appointment of the same type of official, initially on the basis of trust, but later increasingly in terms of tradition and piety, every attempt to bring new men, new energies, and even new ideas and directions into party work, seems an almost criminal rebellion. The usual objection is that it is essential to retain the expert knowledge of tried representatives. Leaving aside the fact that the representation of the working-class revolutionary struggle cannot be simply a problem for experts, it must be admitted that a certain amount of expert knowledge and experience is essential for representing the proletarian organizations. But then it is necessary to seek those forms of organization which will bring the leaders and representatives of party activities into such a strong, vital connection with the organized masses that the capacity of every member to become a representative is made possible by the general level of interest and information. The latter is most important, especially in times of crisis such as the present. But it was precisely the development of party committees and bureaus which had the evil consequence that such information was only available, in fact, at the higher levels, and only so much was transmitted 'downwards' as was considered to be necessary in 'the interests of the party'; and then only when the decisions themselves had already been taken in the small circle of leaders.

The idea of 'strict parliamentarianism' also contributed greatly to this evil, which developed at the same time as the párty bureaucracy and gradually, through the reformism of the labour aristocracy, came to be the dominant type of working-class politics. Generally it seemed to be enough that the parliamentary group knew what the issues were and had come to some decision about them. The well-informed parliamentary group and its view of policy was to replace the activity of the party as a whole, and the mass of party members needed only to be aware of what was decided there. To be sure, there were still great public meetings and occasional demonstrations, but always with the same style of communication from above to below. Moreover, any criticism of these tactics was always rejected as being 'disruptive' or an

'intrigue'; and a full discussion in the party press about important issues of policy was scarcely ever possible, since it usually
came too late, after the decisions had already been taken by
the leading party circles. It is a long-standing but fruitless
complaint in the party that the debates at the annual conference were hardly ever adequately prepared by a fundamental discussion in the press and in meetings. One aspect of
this preparation would be the prior publication of the main
reports in the party press. An effective contribution from the
party membership was thus extraordinarily difficult, even
without taking into account the bureaucratic organization of
the conference; and only in recent years has there been an
attempt to change this state of affairs by the German ·Left
Socialists who had their own party newspapers. It is well
known how pitifully this attempt to challenge the supremacy
of official party policies failed.

All this resulted in the great mass of the proletariat becoming accustomed to being led, and waiting for what 'they'
(the party executive, the parliamentary group) would decide.
Thus there was accomplished one of the most fatal changes
possible in a living party, its outcome being the weakening in
the mass membership of the readiness for action and responsibility. They were almost drilled to wait first for commands
from above, so that they did not have a view of their own; and
they regarded all those who formed their own judgements, or
were critical, as destroying or splitting the party. On the other
side, there developed a growing dissatisfaction and personal
embitterment among those party members who saw in the
party not just a mass to be set in motion where and when they
are needed in order to further the strategy of the high command, but a living revolutionary force, and who wanted to
make them effective.

Besides these elements which together helped to curb, and
even choke, the available revolutionary forces, there was
another factor; the adherence to the revolutionary terminology of Marxism, and the continued use of revolutionary symbols, as institutions of the masses, simulated a spirit which
seemed to correspond to these words and forms but which in
reality was lacking. A purely verbal Marxism did not only
confirm the all too numerous uncritical party members in

their belief that the party was really going where its revolutionary class instinct impelled it; at times it even reassured those for whom the Marxist phrases had not yet become purely traditional forms, because they still breathed life into them, the spirit of their own living Marxism. This is one factor in the decay and ultimate collapse of German social democracy which has still received too little attention. In fact, *the* party had not really existed there for a long time. From this point of view there had long existed, even after the Socialist Labour Party[6] had been expelled, *two* parties, one of which had already become completely bourgeois-democratic, while the other was revolutionary proletarian, though both of them bore the name of Social Democracy. In consequence, the former, which was dominant, could continually exploit the activism and enthusiasm of the latter (particularly its young members) for agitational purposes. While hiding behind the flags of the revolutionary youth they pursued their own cold *Realpolitik*. In the closing years of the German party, one could only be enraged to see how all Marxist party and youth education, which was looked at askance by the party authorities the more it was consistently Marxist, at the same time helped the official party leadership to maintain the semblance of a revolutionary class party, although for a long time they had had no vital connection with Marxism and were quite undeservedly detested by the anti-Marxists. In this way, the canonical demand for party unity became entirely vacuous, and only concealed by the use of a single party name the inner division. This unity then acted as a filter for all the revolutionary energies still present in the masses, only letting through the statesmanlike policies of the leading strata and leaving behind all revolutionary mass energies as an ineffectual sediment.

What happened in such a crude form in German social democracy was not only to be found there. It had, and still has, its counterpart (fortunately not yet so fully developed) in all the parties of the Zurich International, and not least in the International itself. The congresses of the International have always been afflicted even more than the conferences of the individual parties by being the preserve of the majorities

[6] The *Sozialistische Arbeiterpartei*, formed by a small radical group of Social Democratic M.P.s in October 1931. [Eds.]

and offering no scope for the minorities in the individual parties to present their views. The main aim was always to eliminate opposed opinions in the individual parties (so far as possible) by means of a resolution which all could accept, and which for precisely that reason is bound to say absolutely nothing. But by using a mainly Marxist analysis, the congresses of the International often gave support to an official Marxist phraseology which concealed from those who were really Marxist thinkers the fact that in reality nothing had happened.

These circumstances, and others which I cannot examine here—such as the persistent opposition between a purely trade-union outlook and revolutionary politics—account for the fact that the revolutionary orientation which might have grown spontaneously out of the main body of the working class (the workers in factory, mine, and countryside) has not only been impossible to establish but in many cases was weakened even in this part of the working class, and in any case was deprived of its agitational effect. Furthermore, in the most recent phase of the socialist workers' movement there has appeared the novel and extremely strong influence of the new differentiation in the lower strata of the working class, as a result of permanent unemployment. This had some unanticipated fatal consequences and we must now look more closely at its specific characteristics.

Present-day unemployment differs from that in the earlier stages of capitalist development in that it is not merely a consequence of an economic recession, but results increasingly from the structure of the capitalist process of production. This explains the horrifying phenomenon of *world* unemployment, which increases so rapidly that the statistical reports can scarcely keep pace with it. Only a short time ago it was twenty-five million; today, in the capitalist world, it is reckoned that there are thirty-five million unemployed. This figure, which needs to be multiplied by at least three to take account of family members, means that in so-called civilized and Christian society there are more than a hundred million men and women able to work, and children, and old people, who would literally starve if they were not miserably supported by the dole, handed out as unemployment benefit. This world unemployment is a new structural feature of capitalism, which is still not adequately grasped; namely, that the fabulous development of the productive forces and the modes of labour in modern capitalism no longer requires as many workers as are available. We have already entered the epoch that earlier enthusiasts and Utopians dreamed about, in which machines perform all the work almost unaided, so that less and less human work is necessary, and yet infinitely more is produced than the most extravagant fantasy could ever have imagined.

All this demonstrates that the present mode of production can no longer overcome unemployment, because it is a necessary consequence of the extraordinary development of technology. Even if there were a new upsurge of the economy, which it is Utopian to expect in any general or permanent form, only a part of the unemployed, surely the smaller part, could be employed again. The greater part, or at least half the unemployed, would still be excluded, and would find themselves subjectively in an even more terrible situation when they discovered that the economic improvement, anxiously awaited as a deliverance, did not produce any change in their condition. Mass unemployment has therefore become permanent. It is not simply a consequence of the business cycle, or the backwardness of capitalism, or some 'sickness' of capitalism; on the contrary, it results from the achievements of capitalism in technology, commerce, and the organization of labour. At the same time, what is novel in the present world crisis is that it prepares the final crisis of capitalism; not in the sense that capitalism will end tomorrow or the day after, but that it has entered a declining phase of its development, from which the economic system can only be rescued by the transition to socialism. This expression, the 'final phase of capitalism' is not merely a slogan for meetings, nor a subjective opinion produced by revolutionary impatience, but formulates the *objective* characteristic of a *fundamental change in the social function* of capitalism, which Marx foresaw long ago as the outcome of its development and which we are now experiencing for the first time. It is a change whereby capitalism, from being a champion of the development of the productive forces and hence of social progress, has become a fetter upon the forces of production and a cause of economic and political retrogression. Even this reactionary maintenance of the system is only possible by eliminating millions of workers from production and reducing the wages of the others; and this is a fatal measure which intensifies the crisis rather than overcoming it. In this way, there is produced a growing number of people who are no longer needed by capitalism, and who would not be needed even in a period of business expansion. They are still less necessary at a time when capitalism has to confine its activities to saving the only thing that concerns it; namely, profit and the power position of a small stratum of property owners.[7]

This increasing mass of superfluous workers now constitutes the permanent unemployment which has created quite a new type of proletariat. There are already today working men and women who have been uninterruptedly without work for four years or more. In addition, there is the vast number of these unemployed who already comprise half the membership in many trade union branches. Above all, there is the frightening fact that it is almost wholly impossible for young workers entering the labour force each year to get a job. Hence there arises a large and growing section of the proletariat for which the mode of thought of the employed factory worker, which it has never experienced, is quite alien.[8] Under such conditions it is vain to expect from these unemployed workers an appreciation of the social and political achievements of the workers' movement, or to appeal to them to uphold and defend them, since they do not experience, and have little prospect of ever enjoying, the benefits of these achievements. Unemployment benefit is the only thing that has a real interest for this stratum; and as this has to be reduced again and

[7] It may be asked what becomes of Marx's theory of surplus value when human labour power, from the exploitation of which surplus value arises, becomes superfluous in this way, and the process of production can be carried on with a steadily diminishing number of workers. Theoretically, surplus value should diminish, as indeed it does, relatively speaking, in accordance with the law of the declining rate of profit, although this is compensated by an absolute increase in the mass of surplus value. But this is only the case when the number of employed workers is increasing. When their numers decline profit is transformed more frequently into what it has always been in a disguised form; namely, a gain which is extracted by force. . . .

[8] This has particularly serious consequences for the political development of working class youth. . . .

again because of the economic crisis, while the socialist deputies are unable to prevent these reductions in the face of the
bourgeois majorities in parliament, so the whole complex of
democratic parliamentary institutions and the political
achievements of the working class have no particular attraction for the permanently unemployed.

Indeed it is in this sphere that the unemployed become the
quite uncritical victims of every kind of verbal radicalism.
After all, they are the ones who experience most brutally the
merely formal 'freedom' of a democracy and republic in which
the proletariat does not rule. Thus it seems to them quite unimportant what kind of state exists or what party rules. It
requires a good Marxist education to have a more critical
judgement on this point. But this political education cannot
reach the great mass of the unemployed at all, because the
effects of poverty and embitterment destroy the psychological
willingness to participate in such education. So it is understandable that the great majority of these workers regard the
failure of democracy as the specific cause of their condition.
They do not recognize that the nature of democracy in a class
state makes it all the more necessary to infuse its forms with a
proletarian content, and to convert it into a means for a revolutionary transition to the dictatorship of the proletariat. It is far
from being my intention to characterize Fascism and Communism in the same way as verbal radicalism, as is done not
only by the bourgeois opponents of Bolshevism, but also unfortunately by many of our party comrades. But in order to
understand the particular function of Bolshevism which may
allow it, under quite exceptional conditions, to become a successful movement of Marxist socialism, a critical socialist
education is necessary, and this is not to be found among the
great majority of the unemployed. The simple revolutionism
of such slogans as 'Away with democracy', 'Down with the
parliamentary talking shop', 'Down with the party system',
'Down with the bosses', etc. was bound to lead all those who
do not yet have a basic knowledge of Marxism to equate
Bolshevik and nationalist propaganda.

It is at this point that all the catastrophic influences resulting
from the domination of party policy by reformist tendencies
have their full effect. The more the official party pursued

a statesmanlike rather than a class policy, and the more the influence of the political and trade union labour aristocracy and bureaucracy became predominant in determining the party's image, all the more alienated from it were precisely these strata of the permanently unemployed. They could not help seeing that their existence was never taken into account as a permanent condition. There had been unemployment for years, while the official trade union policy still continued to refer to a merely temporary crisis, and regarded capitalism as having only a passing illness which they wanted to cure by sending it to bed. It is no wonder then that in Germany the unemployed were driven almost entirely into the ranks of the Communists, which only intensified the division in the proletariat. For now Social Democracy was, as it were, the party of those who were still employed, the satisfied workers, in opposition to the Communists as the party of the unemployed and the hungry. This was not only extraordinarily harmful for the formation of a revolutionary proletarian ideology, but also had a fateful significance for political practice, for the ever more urgent defensive struggle against Fascism. The division of the parties into a party of the employed and a party of the unemployed eventually acquired the political significance that the former still had the ability to engage in struggle and to carry out a revolutionary act, such as a general strike, but was led by those who thought they had to look after the 'property' of the party, and thus never succeeded; while the latter did appeal for a general strike, but since it was the party of the unemployed had no means of carrying it out.

The contrast between the 'hungry' and the 'well-fed' extends beyond this tragic political situation. It is the basic reason why the revolutionary power of the proletariat has not grown as its misery has increased, in the way that Marx thought it would. What is needed for the emergence of a resentment that grips and revolutionizes the whole class is the sense in all sections of the proletariat of class solidarity and a community of fate. Just this feeling of solidarity with those who are working is bound to be lacking today among the permanently unemployed; and this constitutes a major difference from earlier periods. In the earlier phases of development, the unemployed individual did not lose contact with the interests and outlook of his fellow workers, because his condition was still exceptional, and as a rule he would be employed again after a time. In this case, the unemployed worker returned to his work as an even more embittered and resolute fighter against the capitalist system, since he had become acquainted with its horrors in his own person. Thus, sporadic unemployment led, on the whole, to a considerable strengthening of socialist convictions among both employed and unemployed workers. But if unemployment lasts for years the whole manner of thought and feeling of its victims must necessarily change; they lose the sense of belonging to the working class and even see themselves as *déclassés*, and on the other side they are pitied and regarded with uneasiness by those who are employed. For in the latter case a change takes place which, although it is not always conscious, is often very clearly expressed. In spite of the serious problems which preoccupy the families of the workers who are still earning wages, there is to be found here the profound psychological distinctiveness of the social and mental attitude of someone who keeps himself, compared with the individual who lives from outside help.[9]

The unemployed themselves consider that they are receiving charity. As the help they get is hardly ever sufficient, and eventually ceases, they are always looking for an opportunity to earn some money wherever they can. It hardly needs to be said that under such conditions the trade union solidarity of the unemployed with those in work, especially during strikes, is seriously endangered.

The effects of permanent unemployment are to be found not only in this weakening of trade union activity, by enhancing the reformism of trade union policies, but even more in the field of political struggle. The hopelessness engendered by permanent unemployment produces in the unemployed and their families a feeling of resignation, which ultimately makes them indifferent to all political proposals. It is this mental attitude that the author of the study just referred to [footnote 9] characterizes as the attitude of 'exhaustion'. How

[9] Adler makes a reference here, and in the following paragraph, to some findings of the study of the unemployed in Marienthal. See the Introduction, p. 4, note 7 above. [Eds.]

widespread this mental condition is, can be seen from the survey of 100 unemployed families in Marienthal, where this kind of exhaustion was found in 84 per cent of the sample. Such political apathy does not necessarily mean that the unemployed cease to be members of the party; generally this is not the case. But their association with the party is more a matter of tradition, and it does not exclude the possibility that in critical situations it will yield to stronger political temptations, especially when these are linked with a direct economic improvement in the position of the unemployed, as for example through their recruitment into Fascist defence groups. Hence this apathy with respect to the party's policies is a terrible danger for the security and the progress of the socialist workers' movement, especially if the party no longer possesses any revolutionary force of attraction because of its domination by reformist thinking. What was originally just a mood of resignation eventually becomes indifference in the face of reaction, since many people think that the economic position of the unemployed can hardly get any worse, while the reactionary movement by enrolling the unemployed for its own ends at least relieves their oppressive situation for a short time.

It is very painful to have to assert these things. But in the first place it is useless, and quite un-Marxist, to shut our eyes to the facts. Secondly, these sad, unsolidaristic groupings are still today exceptional phenomena, which occur mainly among the indifferent and the forsaken. It is evident, on the other hand, that those unemployed workers who were already involved in social democratic organization and education have remained for the most part loyal to the party, even though their activity and readiness to participate have declined substantially.

Various circumstances, therefore, have contributed to forming within the proletariat a new and specific group, not to say a class. Initially it was, and still is, the economic conditions which make unemployment a permanent phenomenon. Subsequently, the general psychological transformation of this stratum leads it to be increasingly indifferent to social democracy, while the lack of understanding, jealousy, and mistrust of the leaders, which was never entirely absent in a considerable part of this stratum, has its effect; and last but not least, there is the influence of the moderate and cautious character of party policy, to some extent actually reformist, but in part imposed by specific political situations. Above all it is the mass character of this new section of the working class which was bound to change the whole character of the social democratic workers' movement. There are already very many districts where a third of all workers are unemployed, and many others where almost half the workers suffer this fate. It is clear that among the unemployed the idea of social revolution plays quite a different role from that which it has in the rest of the working class, who are not free of troubles, it is true, but whose elementary needs at least are satisfied. The unemployed cannot wait, and so the whole content of regular party work—the development of organizations, the improvement and defence of democratic rights and social policy, the diffusion of Marxist education and enlightenment—even where they recognize its importance, has no direct practical significance for them. All this becomes increasingly the concern of 'other people'. The unemployed, however, want to know how they can be helped, quickly and fundamentally, and they already feel more and more sharply that it is impossible except by a basic revolutionary change in the existing conditions. That is why one of the most widespread moods in this stratum is the desire to smash everything up—which is not simply a crude slogan—and even among those who are totally resigned the view prevails that it would be better if everything collapsed. For 'it can't get any worse' and 'perhaps something better will follow'. It is hardly necessary to explain how such moods create a fertile field of action for National Socialist or Fascist agitation, which presents itself to the masses as something new. It is clear, however, that those with more of a Marxist education have only *one* real interest which they want to speak and hear about, the interest that all workers should have, which has become an immediate necessity for development: the social revolution. . . .

What can be done about this calamitous differentiation in the proletariat? Above all it is evident that the problem of, and the demand for, the restoration of a united front of the proletariat has quite a different and more profound significance from the one that is usually considered; namely, the unification of the Second and Third Internationals. Indeed, it is clear that this more profound sense of re-establishing the working class itself as a united, harmonious community, capable of waging economic and ideological struggles, is the real precondition for that desired organizational united front. This problem of the unity of the working class is further complicated by the fact that we are no longer dealing just with the proletarian strata in the narrower sense of the term, but also with the growing strata of employees, officials, and proletarianized middle classes. Here, too, one must take into account the totally new economic situation which, although it corresponds exactly with the line of development predicted by Marx, is distinguished precisely by the degree of its development from the state of affairs that confronted Marx and Engels. At that time, and up to the beginning of the twentieth century, the proletariat alone formed the anti-bourgeois movement, and the attempt to abolish the dominant system was identical with the goal of proletarian socialism. Even though there were anti-capitalist tendencies in the various corporate, petty bourgeois, small peasant forms of the Christian Social movement, they never went beyond the bourgeois-capitalist system, and only sought reforms by combating what they called the 'excesses' of capitalism.

It was the rapid proletarianization of the middle strata in town and country after the war that first produced the vast army of the new proletariat, alongside the manual workers, though of course it is still ideologically remote and even hostile to the workers. Hence, we now confront a significant, and too little noticed, new economic structure, which means that the manual worker is no longer the sole representative of anti-capitalist interests, and what is particularly important, no longer constitutes a majority of the population, on which, after all, the social revolution must be based. On the other hand, the new and old proletariat together already constitute the overwhelming majority in every capitalist country, and this creates new conditions for the struggle of the socialist working class. This majority of those who are economically proletarianized must develop a corresponding class consciousness. . . .

KARL RENNER, *The Service Class*[10]

In addition to those changes already mentioned there is another which is no less important. In economic terms, the capitalist, *qua* capitalist, is an agent of circulation, and as such he makes use of paid assistants who, as we have explained, gradually take over his functions. These agents are not wage workers; they do not produce, but dispose of the values that have been produced. As long as a capitalist economy exists their services are also socially necessary.[11] The capitalist performs these services for profit, the manager for a salary, a fee, or a share in the profits (commission).

1. The Public Service The public service has served capital as a model for this arrangement. Historically the state has had a dual function: external and internal security (the military and police); and the creation and administration of law (the legislature and judiciary). In the feudal period, with its undeveloped money economy, the state officials were paid by investing them with the ownership of land and serfs, and priests were paid in a similar way by the church. It was the town burgesses and the bourgeois state which first began to pay salaries to their agents.

A salary differs fundamentally by its nature and in the way it is assessed from a wage. What the salaried person produces is not a commodity, not an 'economic' good, but law and order. His work is most effective when law and order are made so secure that he has very little to do. The best gendarme is the one who is effective merely by existing, like the judge whose established authority limits the number of disputed cases. The payment of a salary is not meant to provide food and shelter from week to week but to establish a life style and family situation which improves as the individual becomes older and terminates with an old age pension. The salary is used for consumption and procures commodities for the consumer without any economic counterpart, that is to say in exchange for money which is not acquired in the economic process, but is forcibly extracted from the latter by

---

[10] From *Wandlungen der modernen Gesellschaft* (1953), pp. 211–14. [Eds.]

[11] In a future social order they will become agents of distribution instead of agents of circulation, and as we have shown, distribution follows different laws from those which regulate circulation.

government taxes and duties. Thus salaries represent a
further diversion of the surplus value of society by means of
direct or indirect taxation.

The active capitalist pays his helpers in the same manner,
and in so far as he himself ceases to be active he pays substitutes as well as assistants, all those agents of management to
whom he refers quite properly not as workers but as officials
or employees.

2. *The Private Employee*   It is not only the state and economic enterprises, but also all the new associations developed
alongside the real economic process (especially in the sphere of
circulation), that create their executive agents in the same
manner. For the most part they establish this 'employee relationship' by means of a contract which does not create a
relationship of wage labour, although at first it is partly constructed on analogous lines (weekly or monthly payment,
agreements concerning length of service, conditions of dismissal). The more explicitly the service relationship becomes
one of trust, the more it tends to become firmly established.
The code of service as a more or less hierarchical norm replaces the labour contract. The position is officially confirmed
and dismissal is only possible in specific circumstances, for the
most part only by the decision of an arbitrator or judge.

A brief survey of the preceding development reveals the
remarkable extension of this kind of legal relationship and the
extraordinary numerical increase in the class of people whose
existence is regulated by it. The service class has emerged
alongside the working class in the strictly technical sense. The
expression 'service class' marks a fundamental distinction
from the traditional 'serving class', which performed real
labour, if only at a rudimentary technical level, and was for
the most part paid in kind. Three basic forms can be distinguished: economic service (managers, etc.), social service
(distributive agents of welfare services), and public service
(public, official agents).

3. *From a Caste to a Class*   Traditionally these new social
strata are at first both materially and intellectually opposed to
the working class. Since for the most part they are recruited
from the bourgeois middle class, and since their salary supple-

ments their own income from property, they could not be classified with the propertyless class. Initially they formed what might be called in sociological terms a caste (the priestly caste, the intellectuals, the officer caste, the caste of officials). These castes are separated from the general social milieu by particular qualifications, and set in opposition to society. It is a characteristic feature of these castes that they extend through all ranks and strata of society; from the Generalissimo down to the common soldier, from the cardinal to the village chaplain, from the head of the office down to the office boy, and so on. The same caste spirit imbues both high and low with the love of rank and of exclusiveness and sets them in opposition to the people as a whole. From this point of view, historical revolutions are very often the consequence of a struggle of the whole people against a ruling caste or of a struggle for supremacy between different castes (the secular bureaucracy against the ecclesiastical hierarchy, civil against military).

Before the Second World War, the service class was on the borderline between a caste and a class. Fascism was able to gain support not only from the bourgeoisie and the peasants but also from these castes, by flattering their caste pride and promising to maintain their position of superiority. According to different national conditions the totalitarian state supported itself in the first instance on the priestly caste (Spain, Dollfuss), on the military and bureaucratic caste (Germany), on the intellectuals (Italy), or on the new managers (Communism). Inflation, currency regulations, crises, war, and defeat have demolished these illusions.

This brief survey shows us that the stratum of those in service occupations has ceased to be merely a caste, and that in reality it has become a class—the service class just described —even if its caste spirit has not completely died out. The majority of its members have become in practice propertyless, since their inherited property is today either without value or at least socially insignificant. Thus the service class is closer to the rising working class in its life style, and at its boundary tends to merge with it. Nationalization and municipalization of powerful economic enterprises (railways, posts, water, light, and power supply) has established a bridge between the public services and private employment, between the situation of the worker, and that of the employee; and in crossing this bridge the caste spirit disappears. It is of the utmost importance for the eventual success of democratic socialism that these events should be closely studied and politically assessed.

On the other side, the trade union struggle has achieved for large sections of the working class a legal status which resembles that of officials; the trade union contract has become a kind of code of service. As a result of the technological revolution a great deal of work has come to involve the 'servicing' of machinery, and numerous occupational tasks increasingly require responsibility, as if they were positions in the public service.

Our analysis shows how superficially and carelessly many of those who claim to be Marxists approach the real study of class formation in society, and above all the continuous restructuring of the classes. It is abundantly clear that the factual substratum, the social basis, has been completely transformed in the past hundred years; that the working class as it appears (and scientifically was bound to appear) in Marx's *Capital* no longer exists. There remains only a narrow stratum of *déclassés* which is to serve the Communists as cannon-fodder in the struggle for power by the new caste which is to be presented to the world as its ruler; or as the dynamite to destroy a higher civilization which they do not understand and consequently hate—a civilization which will exclude all caste rule for ever, including that newly created by the Soviet bureaucracy and hierarchy.

VII. Ideology and Culture

M AX A DLER, *Ideology as Appearance*[1]

It is a very common opinion that Marxism not only starts from the duality of economic and ideological factors, but also devalues the latter by assigning all historical reality to the economic factor alone, while ideology, by contrast, is treated as a mere secondary phenomenon. It is in this way that the very widespread objection to Marxism, that it reduces ideology to a mere appearance, has arisen.

This view, which is held mainly by the opponents of Marxism, can only be sustained so obstinately because it appears to be based upon certain statements of Marx and Engels themselves, statements moreover that make a very strong impression upon the reader by their vivid terminology. I refer to the two well-known images which Marx and Engels used to elucidate the relation between economics and ideology: Marx's designation of economic phenomena as the basis or infrastructure of ideology, and Engels's occasional characterization of ideology as a reflection. The first image seems to illustrate especially the dependent character of ideology, the second above all its illusory nature.

But this view that Marxism regards ideology as unreal, or at least as less real than the economy, is so absurd that Engels's vehement rejection of it is quite understandable. In his letter to Mehring of 14 July 1893, in which he discusses problems of the materialist conception of history, he describes as an 'idiotic idea' that Marxism denies ideology any effectiveness in history. In fact, the frequently adduced claim that Marxism makes ideology a mere illusion, is only a further consequence of the introduction of materialist ideas and concepts into the sociological theory of Marxism. This can only reinforce our conviction that the linking of Marxism with materialism has had, and still has, disastrous effects upon the understanding

---

[1] From *Lehrbuch der materialistischen Geschichtsauffassung* (1930), Chapter 11. [Eds.]

of its fundamental conception. For it is only on the basis of materialism that the intellect can be regarded as having no independent significance, because it is only the product of physical processes and in principle a complete knowledge of physical processes would make all phenomena of conscious-ness merely epiphenomena.

But the similes that Marx and Engels employ in the pas-sages cited above cannot in any way be applied in such a materialist conception of the relation between ideology and economy, leaving aside the fact that, as we already know, eco-nomic phenomena themselves are never 'material' in the materialist sense, but have precisely a 'mental' character. On the contrary, the images used by Marx and Engels are meant to show precisely the inherent and specific reality of ideology, only pointing out that this does not signify an arbitrary inde-pendence. Let us then look rather more closely at these similes. If Marx initially describes the economy as the basis of society, this vivid image itself should suffice to exclude the view that ideology is less real or effective than the economy. For where is there a superstructure, however airy and delicate its construction, which is not just as real as the foundation? So far as effectiveness is concerned, the simile suggests far more a reversal of the vulgar opinion concerning the devalua-tion of the intellect by Marxism. For a foundation is not con-structed as an end in itself but only so that a superstructure can subsequently be erected upon it. Where does a person actually live, provided of course that he has not suffered the miserable fate of being a proletarian? The superstructure is therefore that part of the building in which its meaning and purpose are accomplished. In the same way the social superstructure is that part of society in which historical actions take shape; but in order to become effective they have to operate on the basis and within the limits and capacities of the foundation.

The simile, therefore, is really intended only to show this dependence of ideology for its historical effectiveness upon the economy. It means that just as a superstructure cannot stand in the air, but requires a base on which it can first be raised, so too ideas and views cannot arise and exist out of themselves but require a foundation in men's relations of work and exchange, upon which they constitute themselves and in relation to which they change, partly in correspondence, partly in contrast. In particular, when these economic relations in the course of historical development become differentiated into class distinctions and antagonisms, and so become, as it were, asymmetrical with the basis, so too does ideology show a similar diversity of class views and feelings, conditioned by the diverse locations in the social edifice, however much this fact may be concealed from human consciousness. The conception of ideology as a superstructure is mainly directed, therefore, against the spiritualist metaphysic which, above all in the case of the Hegelians, believed in a self-development of the idea; but it is subsequently directed against every kind of idealist or intellectualist conception of history which assumes an independent manifestation of ideas or believes in their pure spirituality free from any earthly taint.

The Marxist simile of basis and superstructure has however an even more profound significance than the mere rejection of the autonomy of ideology. In so far as this image makes clear that the superstructure is just as real as the base because both are parts of a real building, it provides further confirmation of what I have called the monism of the economic conception of history: economics and ideology are certainly different, but at the same time they are parts of a single social-cultural system of human life.

Engels's second simile also, according to which ideology is the reflex or reflection of economic conditions, does not mean what many people, oddly enough, have read into these words, namely, that ideology is thereby characterized as a mere inessential appearance. A reflex, just like a reflection, is not simply an appearance, but also a reality. The rebounding ball or reflected light can be intercepted, and the reflected image can even be deceptive, but only because it too is a reality. To repeat, this simile is meant only to emphasize the dependence of ideologies on the economy. At most the comparison has the further significance of stressing this dependence even more strongly than does the image of base and superstructure, because it is closer to the idea of the calculability, or determinability, of the reflected direction. But precisely for this reason, the reality of the reflex is even less brought into question.

Hence it cannot be said that ideology, in the Marxist sense, is something inessential and ineffective in historical development. This will become clearer when I come to discuss the significance of ideology in the constitution of social groups and in the formation of collective concepts. But ideology can be regarded as appearance in quite a different sense, which is also to be found in Marx and Engels. In this case, however, it is not an inessential appearance, but on the contrary one which, in all stages of historical development up to the present day, has had important consequences. This appearance occurs in two different forms. First, it appears as if ideologies had an independent existence and an autonomous development. Engels contested this view with great clarity in the letter to Mehring mentioned earlier:

Ideology is indeed a process which is carried on in the consciousness of the so-called thinker, but with a false consciousness. The real motive forces which impel him remain unknown to him, otherwise it would not be an ideological process. He therefore conjures up false or illusory motive forces. Because it is a thought process, he deduces both its content and its form from pure thought, either from his own or from that of his predecessors. He works with mere conceptual material which he accepts unexamined as created by thought, and does not look further for a more remote process independent of thought. Indeed this seems self-evident to him, because he regards all action, since it is mediated by thought, as being grounded ultimately in thought. The historical ideologist (the term historical here is simply a comprehensive expression for political, juridical, philosophical, theological; in brief, all those areas that concern society and not simply Nature) has therefore in every scientific field a material which has formed itself from the thought of earlier generations and in the brains of the succeeding generations has followed its own independent line of development. Of course external facts, which belong to its own or other fields, may have had a co-determining effect on this development, but according to the tacit assumption, these facts themselves are really only fruits of the thought process which has itself happily digested the most stubborn facts. It is this appearance of an autonomous history of political constitutions, systems of law, ideological conceptions in every sphere, which above all blinds most people.

In every case where a history of philosophy, of law, or of art is presented with the intention of showing that changes in scholarly views, conceptions of law, or artistic trends are simply deduced from the nature of these cultural formulations (as usually happens when Hegel's splendid model is followed), such a false appearance of the autonomy of ideology is being accepted. A deduction of this kind from the inner logic of the object (as it is customarily called) is admittedly not entirely incorrect because all these areas of intellectual creation ... rest upon a formal lawfulness of the mind which is self-confirming. But the particular contents which are produced by the lawfulness of the mind, and with them the concrete problematics, whether they are accepted or disputed, can only be understood, in the last resort, in terms of the stimulus that individual thinkers have received or been denied by the conditions and limitations of their life situation. Of course, the history of ideological creation from this standpoint has yet to be written.

Marx referred to ideology in a different and still broader sense when he observed that men for the most part imagine motives for their actions which are quite different from the real ones, and that in particular they do not acknowledge the economic motivation of their views, values, and actions, but believe that they are determined by some world view. Marx describes this state of affairs very clearly in the following passage:

Upon the diverse forms of property, upon the social conditions of existence, rises an entire superstructure of distinct and idiosyncratic sentiments, illusions, modes of thought, and views of life. The entire class creates and shapes them from its material foundations and from the corresponding social relations. The particular individual who acquires them through tradition and education may imagine that they form the real motivating forces and starting point of his actions.... And as in private life one distinguishes between what a man thinks and says of himself and what he really is and does, so even more, in historical struggles, must one distinguish the phrases and fancies of the parties, from their real nature and interests, their conceptions of themselves from their reality. (*The Eighteenth Brumaire of Louis Bonaparte.*)

The frequently quoted passage from the Preface to *A Contribution to the Critique of Political Economy* expresses the same idea, that in considering historical transformations '... The

distinction should always be made between the material transformation of the economic conditions of production, which
can be determined with the precision of natural science, and
the legal, political, religious, aesthetic, or philosophical—in
short, ideological—forms in which men become conscious of
this conflict and fight it out.'

The same notion is also to be found in *The German Ideology*,
where it is discussed in a particularly interesting context, for
here Marx attempts, in a manner to which he did not return,
to depict the social causes of ideology. He begins by stating
the familiar basic idea as follows: 'Whereas in everyday life
every shopkeeper knows very well how to distinguish between
what someone represents himself as being and what he really
is, our historiography has not yet attained this simple understanding. It takes every epoch at its word, what it says and
imagines about itself.' In this case, however, Marx does not
confine himself to stating the fact, but goes on to pose the
question of the origins of this appearance. He finds its source
in a fundamental differentiation within society, which
emerged already in very early times, that he terms a primary
form of the division of labour. In *The German Ideology* this
expression does not have its ordinary meaning of the division
of social labour into its various branches, such as agriculture,
industry, etc. or the division of each of these kinds of work
into specific, sub-divided tasks performed by specialized
workers, as in the division of labour in the factory. What is
meant here is rather the historical fact that already in early
times a rift occurred within the social body whereby all manual
labour was imposed upon one particular stratum while another stratum was liberated from all such labour. In this way
the latter group acquired leisure and freedom to develop and
satisfy its intellectual needs. The outcome is a division of
labour between purely manual and purely mental labour,
which involves, at the same time, the division of the social
body into two different classes. Thus a particular condition
of social life is attained in which the thoughts and views of the
mentally active class, which is at the same time the ruling
class, no longer reflect the whole reality of society, but only
that part which corresponds with the conscious, and still more
the unconscious, needs of this class itself. Nevertheless, this

part of reality assumes, in the consciousness of the ruling class, the significance of the whole and maintains the form of universal theoretical and moral ideas.

From the moment that labour is divided between material and mental labour, according to *The German Ideology*, 'consciousness really can imagine that it is something other than the consciousness of existing practice, can really conceive something, without conceiving anything real; from this moment, consciousness is able to emancipate itself from the world and proceed to the construction of "pure theory", theology, philosophy, morality, etc.' This separation of the contents of consciousness from their underlying social foundation, with which they have come into conflict, has become possible, '... because, with the division of labour, the possibility, indeed the reality, is created that mental and material activity, pleasure and work, production and consumption, devolve upon different individuals; and the possibility of avoiding the contradiction between them depends upon transcending once again the division of labour'.

From this starting point Marxism is able to show that the ideology of bourgeois society in particular is a false consciousness, because it presents itself as a universal social conception, so long as it is not yet in decline. Indeed, it is false in a double sense, in that its bearers are themselves deceived and use this ideology to deceive the mass of the people. *The German Ideology* continues:

... Further, with the division of labour, there arises a contradiction between the interest of the particular individual or family and the communal interest of all individuals who are involved in social intercourse; and this communal interest does not only exist in the representation of the 'universal', but initially in reality, as the mutual dependence of individuals among whom labour is divided. It is precisely out of this contradiction between particular and communal interests that the communal interest assumes an independent form as the state, distinct from the real interests of the individual and of the whole society, as an illusory community; but always on the real basis of the bonds of flesh and blood, language, the more extensive division of labour, and other interests which are present in every aggregate of family and tribe, and in particular (as I shall show later) on the basis of the classes already formed by the division of labour, which emerge in every such human group and of which one dominates all the others. It follows that all the conflicts within the state, the struggle between democracy, aristocracy and monarchy, the struggle for the suffrage, etc. are nothing but the illusory forms in which the real struggles among the various classes are carried on. . . . Precisely because individuals seek only their particular interest, which for them does not coincide with their communal interest, the latter is represented as being a distinct and specific 'universal' interest, which is 'alien' to them and 'independent' of them; or alternatively they must encounter each other in this situation of discord, as in democracy. On the other hand, this practical struggle also makes necessary a continual intervention and regulation of the special interests which oppose the real or illusory communal interests, by means of the illusory 'general' interest in the form of the state.

It will be necessary to return to this analysis of the illusory character of the ideology of a general interest within class society. At all events it is apparent already that this 'appearance' of an ideology of the general interest is by no means insignificant or unreal, but on the contrary, is one of the most powerful and fateful realities of history. In sum, it can be said that the characterization of ideologies as appearances or reflexes is not simply a way of dismissing them as superfluous or irrelevant, but is a critical challenge not to remain at the level of their superficial appearance, and especially of the conscious images that their bearers themselves have of them, but to advance to an analysis of the objective social relations from which they have emerged and in which their real meaning and their limitations are to be found.

Moreover, even according to Engels's own statements ideology is so little conceived as merely an insignificant appearance or reflex that he refers frequently to the reaction of ideology upon the economy and to their reciprocal action. In his letter of 21 September 1890 to a socialist academic (J. Bloch), he says:

The economic situation is the basis, but the various elements of the superstructure—political forms of the class struggle and its results, to wit: constitutions established by the victorious classes after a successful battle, etc. juridical forms, and even the reflexes of all these actual struggles in the brains of the participants, political, juridical, philosophical theories, religious views, and their further development into systems of dogma—also exercise their influence upon the course of the historical struggles and in many cases predominate in determining their form. There is an interaction of all these elements in which, amidst all the endless host of accidents ... the economic movement finally asserts itself as necessary.

Similarly, in a letter of 25 January 1894, to Heinz Starkenburg, Engels writes:

Political, juridical, philosophical, religious, literary, artistic, etc. development is based on economic development. But all these react upon one another and also upon the economic basis. It is not that the economic situation is *cause, solely active*, while everything else is only passive effect. There is, rather, interaction on the basis of economic necessity, which ultimately always asserts itself.... So it is not, as people try here and there conveniently to imagine, that the economic situation produces an automatic effect. No. Men make their history themselves, only they do so in a given environment, which conditions it, and on the basis of actual relations already existing, among which the economic relations, however much they may be influenced by the other, the political and ideological relations, are still ultimately the decisive ones, forming the thread which runs through them and alone leads to understanding.

Even though Engels sometimes expresses himself in an imprecise way in these passages from letters, as is the case in the first passage cited above where he does not include political phenomena (political forms, constitutions, etc.) among the ideological reflexes to which strictly speaking they belong, and refers on one occasion simply to the interaction of all social elements, and on another occasion to an interaction only upon the economic basis, nevertheless, the main idea is clearly formulated—that ideology is a substantial and essential element in the lawfulness of the social process.

MAX ADLER, *The Cultural Aims of Socialism*[2]

Socialism has already appeared in two forms to which the intellectuals are bound to feel attracted through a spiritual

[2] From *Der Sozialismus und die Intellektuellen* (1910), pp. 50–7. [Eds.]

affinity. One is the actual development of a society which would make real community life possible for the first time, which the intellectuals can neither exclude themselves from nor oppose. The other is an existing theory which they cannot ignore, even though they may oppose it. These two characteristics destroy the false appearance which previously made socialism seem to be purely a workers' movement, a bread-and-butter question. It is no longer paradoxical to assert that socialism is not fundamentally a workers' movement, but a cultural movement. The meaning of this cultural development is that socialism will attain a new culture through the working-class movement; that it will bring culture to the workers and will advance through their activities. The remarkable strength of socialism in implanting itself ineradicably in working-class consciousness is due precisely to the fact that it does not merely want to improve the condition of the worker, but to abolish his situation as nothing but a worker, that is, a man who must work simply in order to live.

The working-class movement signifies not only an emancipation of the proletariat from the forced labour of capitalism, but at the same time an emancipation of the spirit from the deplorable ideological pressure of an exclusively free-enterprise conception of work, in which it is seen not so much as the economic and organizational means by which society satisfies its needs, but only as the means by which the individual miserably 'earns his daily bread'. The idea, so familiar to us today, that one must work in order to live—Christianity even transformed the virtue of labour into a religious obligation, although the Bible had pronounced work to be a curse upon man—this real slave's view of work will one day be inconceivable in a healthy culture. Should we say that it is necessary to breathe in order to live? Let us not spend time discussing the obvious: work is a self-evident condition for the existence of society, the 'general condition of the exchange of material between man and nature, the eternal natural condition of human life',[3] which for this very reason must be planned by society and allocated among its members, once it has reached a level of economic development which makes this possible, as is now the case. We cannot possibly imagine the air not

[3] Marx, *Capital*, vol. i.

being a communal good, although in the strict sense it has not been so for a long time, since the overwhelming majority of our fellow citizens live in small, wretched dwellings, or are imprisoned in the foul air of their workplaces by excessive hours of work; and since so many who are ill or convalescent never succeed in enjoying the pure air of the sea or mountains, where a fortunate minority can while away their leisure for a whole year strolling about. And just as it is inconceivable that this essential minimum of fresh air could be withdrawn from anyone by law or society, so it will become inconceivable, and is already inconceivable to anyone who grasps the startlingly unnatural character of the present situation not just by external observation but by personal experience, that men should not know how they will live the following day, because they have no work which will allow them to 'earn' their livelihood.

The real meaning of socialism, understood as a working-class movement, is to eliminate this conception of work and this kind of worker from history, and this is a cultural meaning based upon a profound understanding and a dazzling breadth of vision. In this conception the final form of enslavement of the worker struggles for final liberation through the abolition of the economic basis 'on which rests the existence of classes and thus of class rule. Once labour is emancipated, every man becomes a worker, and productive labour ceases to be the characteristic of a particular class'.[4] Socialism is therefore only a class movement and a workers' movement in order to transcend both limitations, and in this spirit it brings about a self-transcendence in every worker who is genuinely inspired by it. From that moment he no longer feels himself to be merely a worker. His mind becomes filled with hopes which direct his attention to a better future, and all those other interests in a brighter more joyous existence and a richer content to life are awakened, far beyond what a merely working-class interest could provide. Indeed, although socialism does vigorously represent working-class interests, above all by means of trade union and political organizations, this is only the angry consciousness of a negative interest, as the poet says: 'We are the wrath of God, the proletariat.' [Freiligrath.]

[4] Marx, *The Civil War in France.*

Anyone who can distinguish between form and content will see clearly that while socialism in its form is a class movement, in its content it does not strive for anything which is merely a class interest, but is the first great example in history of a class movement which no longer formulates the general cultural interests of humanity simply as an ideological decoration of its own special interests. It can achieve its own class interests after the abolition of the enslavement of labour only if general cultural interests triumph. The mechanism of social laws is such that the progress of culture has always to be achieved by a struggle against a stratum of its privileged beneficiaries. Cultural interests are realized by appearing initially as the special interests of those who have to renounce the enjoyment of them. Just because a class is called upon to fight for certain goals as its own interests in this way, it does not follow that these goals have value only for that class, if they are of general cultural significance. And how could this not be the case with a class movement such as that of the proletariat, whose aim is to reconstruct society so that the economic differentiation of classes will be forever impossible and thus to establish the economic foundations of a truly universal culture. . . .

Hence the world in which socialism will be victorious can only be one in which the absolute common interest is established and safeguarded; in which, according to the famous phrase of the *Communist Manifesto*, 'the free development of each is the condition for the free development of all'. And if it is precisely the socialist workers' movement of our time which, although a class movement, claims the distinction of being the first to transcend its class character by its historical actions, it does not advance this claim in terms of the moral attainments of its followers (although it is true that there is nothing so effective as socialism in improving the workers morally), but because the particular nature of this class movement as I have described it is only possible at a level of technological and economic development which makes the achievement of a social organization of the common interest to safeguard our whole life urgent as well as feasible—and this level has been reached today. What Friedrich Engels wrote a generation ago in his *Anti-Dühring* has meanwhile become increasingly obvious: 'The possibility of securing by means of social production an existence for all members of society which is not only perfectly adequate in material terms and constantly improving, but which also guarantees them the completely free development and exercise of their physical and mental talents, now exists for the first time; but it does exist.'

This is, therefore, the historical and cultural character of socialism as a working-class movement. Once we have disposed of the misleading appearance which these concepts (of class and workers' movement) produced so long as nothing was known about the social regularities to which they refer, or about the developmental tendencies which they indicate, then socialism reveals a third, decisive significance for the intellectuals. For, so long as they were not understood, these concepts were bound to provide a motive for separation and indifference, if not opposition. The cultural interests of the intellectuals, and the mere interests of the working class, as a self-enclosed class, have little in common except the very general claim for a humanly decent existence. But once the historical function of this movement is recognized there is revealed a comprehensive and inspiring common goal. It has now become unmistakably clear that socialism itself is not the goal of the great mass movement of our time, is not an end that is desired for its own sake. What kind of ideal would that be—the socialization of production and the regulation of consumption? This is only a means for attaining a higher organization of society in all its material and intellectual aspects. Admittedly it is a means which, unlike the Utopian socialists of the past, we do not regard only as the most reasonable and appropriate, depending for its practical realization on the convictions of sincere and intelligent human beings; we recognize that its achievement is necessitated by the stage of development of economic forces, and that the historical process become conscious of itself must and will make use of this means.

The intellectual, who has such difficulty in liberating himself from his bourgeois ideas, may initially oppose this means (the abolition of the capitalist economy and thus of bourgeois society) out of timidity or even fear, but he cannot help but agree with the goal of procuring for all producers a genuine education, civilization, and enjoyment of life. Furthermore—

and this is the kernel which needs to be extracted from so many encrustations of artificially acquired interests—the intellectuals basically have an interest only in attaining this goal, not in how it is to be attained. This means that intellectuals as such, as people whose intellectual interests and activities have become a life-long vocation, and whose self-preservation requires not only the preservation of their physical existence, but also the necessary tranquillity and freedom for intellectual work, and the possibility of enjoying them to the full, can remain quite unconcerned if the means used by socialism threaten the existence of bourgeois society, provided that it secures their own cultural aims. That such aims are not achieved in bourgeois society is evident from the widespread and continually increasing misery of intellectual occupations; a misery which is even greater than that of the purely manual occupations, because it involves at the same time an atrophy, if not a prostitution, of the spiritual ego. Consequently, the intellectuals as such have no interest in preserving bourgeois society once they have come to regard it only a means to their universal cultural goal.

Let there be no misunderstanding. I am not speaking of those intellectuals who, as entrepreneurs or capitalists, are of course, even in terms of their intellectual interests, completely integrated into bourgeois society; nor of those who, as a result of their profession, regard themselves as defenders of the existing system, or least believe that they have the same interests, although in reality they are little more than the hired mercenaries of the bourgeois class; for example, government officials, judges, state prosecutors, and such like. Yet this whole group of intellectuals, which people like to adduce as a counter-instance of the possibility of a real, universal, inner relation of intellectuals to socialism, is only distinguished by its special social position, while in numbers and real intellectual influence it is disappearing into the mass of the liberal professions and middle-grade officials. These broad circles of the intelligentsia, as Kautsky once argued, may not perhaps be directly concerned with the class interests of the proletariat, but neither do they have a direct interest in capitalist exploitation. Hence they will 'be compelled neither by their possessions, nor by their profession, to support capitalist exploitation'.[5] Indeed, we can go further: as a result of their conditions of life—leaving aside the impulsion given by their material interests—they attain an unstable equilibrium between bourgeoisie and proletariat, and they are bound to incline toward the latter, as soon as they experience the impact of real cultural problems. Karl Renner has demonstrated this relationship very clearly and very well. He even includes in these circles, quite properly, those among the larger entrepreneurs who, having a commercial, technical, and economic education, are their own managers and could well regard one-half of their incomes as payment for their labour. Renner says of all those strata of intellectuals who are both owners and workers, but not at one extreme or the other, that they do not have any completely uniform economic class interest, except for 'a peaceful, persistent cultural development, regardless of where it eventually leads; whether to a regime of property, in which they would be property owners, or to a regime of labour, a society in which all labour is worth an honest wage and every highly skilled labourer also merits a skilled wage, in which they would in any case willingly co-operate'.[6]

KARL RENNER, *The Development of the Law*[7]

I maintain that Karl Marx deliberately set out to observe and describe each and every phenomenon of the capitalist epoch, correlating these to a continuous development of human society on the basis of an inherited legal system, rigid, retarded, and fossilized. Those who expect from his critique of political economy a guide for economic behaviour, or an analysis of subjective valuations, or something similar, are therefore bound to misunderstand him. Only if the great historical drama is approached as he approached it, only then is it revealed in a true light: a society of small commodity producers has overcome feudal restrictions by dint of hard struggle, and at last establishes a system wherein the producer

[5] *Neue Zeit*, xii. 2, p. 75.
[6] In *Deutsche Worte*, edited by Engelbert Pernerstorfer (1903), p. 321.
[7] From *Die Rechtsinstitute des Privatrechts und ihre soziale Funktion*. This excerpt is reprinted from the English translation of Renner's book, *The Institutions of Private Law and their Social Functions* (London: Routledge and Kegan Paul, 1949), pp. 292–300, by permission of the publishers. [Eds.]

freely disposes over his means of production. It is now declared that everyone shall own his means of production, that everyone shall be free to exchange the fruits of his labours for those of everyone else, it is ordained that everybody shall peacefully enjoy and keep his own as he has saved it from the ruins of the feudal system. The law leaves to every individual the use of his means of production, permitting him to work as he finds expedient. As the product of everybody's labours automatically becomes his property, the law may safely do so. The law also leaves it to every individual to provide for his descendants, and it may safely do so: for the father's property forms a fund of subsistence for the inheriting children. This plain and simple regulation of property merely attempts legally to stabilize[8] the existing living conditions of society.

But now we find the peaceful enjoyment of one's own property developing into the draconic control of alien labour-power, and giving rise to a new regulation of labour, more severe and in its initial stages more cruel than any regulation of feudal times or of the time of the Pharaohs—we need only mention child labour. Thus peaceful enjoyment of one's own object becomes constant appropriation of the proceeds of the labour of others; it becomes title to surplus value, distributing the whole of the social product as profit, interest, and rent among an idle class, and limiting the working class to the mere necessities of existence and procreation. In the end it reverses all its original functions. The owner has now no longer even detention of his property; it is deposited at some bank, and whether he is labourer or working capitalist, the owner cannot dispose of his own. He may not even be acquainted with the locality of the concern in which he has invested his property. Yet one function of capital is indestructibly linked up with his person, the function of appropriating the products of alien labour; and month by month the bank messenger delivers to the owner the revenue of his economic property.

This vast process of change, with all its accompanying

---

[8] The bourgeois revolution was so much easier because there was no necessity to form new social groups or to redistribute possessions, apart from the liberation of the peasants. Fundamentally it proclaimed only two commandments: a material one, that everyone should keep what he had, and a personal one, that everyone should mind his own business.

phenomena, is unfolded before the eyes of Karl
poses it as the problem of our time, as the vital q
whole of human society in our present era. His t
the whole of human society and at the same time
trate upon the inherent and most secret princip
tence; in his thoughts he is in advance of the c
majority of our generation.

He has made it clear to us that property in the capitalist
epoch fulfils functions quite different from those which it fulfilled in the era of simple commodity production, and partly
opposed to these. He has made it clear that property has become antisocial, intrinsically opposed to the real interests of
society. Yet all property is conferred by the law, by a conscious
exercise of the power of society. When society was in control
it endowed the individual with the power of disposal over
corporeal things; but now the corporeal object controls the
individuals, labour-power, even society itself—it regulates
the hierarchy of power and labour, the maintenance and procreation of society. Mankind has become tributary to its own
creation.

The norm is the result of free action on the part of a society
that has become conscious of its own existence. The society
of simple commodity producers attempts to stabilize its own
conditions of existence, the substratum of its existence, by
means of the norm. But in spite of the norm, the substratum
changes, yet this change of the substratum takes place within
the forms of the law; the legal institutions automatically
change their functions which turn into their very opposite,
yet this change is scarcely noticed and is not understood. In
view of all this the problem arises whether society is not
bound to change the norm as soon as it has become conscious
of the change in its functions.

An urgent demand for a human society that acts in freedom
and in full consciousness, that creates its norms in complete
independence: this is socialism. The very word expresses
this. The passing of man from the realm of necessity to the
realm of freedom cannot be conceived otherwise than as a
marshalling of the organized will of society against the paltry
presumptuousness of the individual, so that the object that
has become the master of man may again be subjected to the

ontrol of society. Common will can achieve this only by a direct, controlled, and well-aimed regulation of the relations among men and between man and nature, so that every person and every object may have its functions openly established and may fulfil them in a straightforward manner.

Utopians indulged in dreams and speculations as to how this could be achieved, fanatics of law and philosophy felt themselves obliged to preach fantastic remedies. It was thought that completely new legal institutions would have to be fashioned and the old ones abolished by decree, in order to bring about something that man had never known before. The socialists of this period, the Messianic era of socialism, failed to recognize that it is above all the way of experience which can lead to the new, that even the state of the future is conditioned by the past and that it cannot be otherwise. This era has long since passed away, nowadays we rely on empirical fact, and rightly so. But the socialists, and also unfortunately their leading group, the Marxists, disdain to apply this experience in the realm of the law and the state. They fail to comprehend and to investigate scientifically, how far it is true that the new society is already pre-formed in the womb of the old, even in the field of the law. May it not be true that here also new life is already completely developed in the mother's womb, waiting only for the liberating act of birth?

Some vista of the future, some answers to the questions which we have raised, must have occurred to anyone who has accompanied us on our journey through economics, who has joined in our study with critical regard to the sufferings of mankind. Every society requires a regulation of power and labour. Why do we not set out to create it directly? Why do we not appoint skilled teachers to be masters of our apprentices, why does society accept blindly everyone who takes over an enterprise by the chance of birth or inheritance, although he may be totally unfit to instruct? Why does not society select the best-qualified agriculturist to succeed to a farm that has become vacant, instead of the rich city man who buys it as a hobby, or instead of the fortuitous heir who may be no good? If hereditary appointments are now abolished as insufferable in the case of the most unimportant public office, why is it that the fortuitous heir may still succeed into an important economic enterprise which is responsible for the good or bad fortune of a thousand workers, and, maybe, for the adequate supply of certain goods the whole of society? Anyone can see that society is in immediate need of a regulation of appointments. Our expositions have shown that the real successor who serves the economic functions of a concern is appointed by contract of employment, so that the heir need only play the part of possessor of a title to surplus value without performing any function. We have seen that even today property is supplemented by complementary institutions which take over its real functions. Should we not come to the conclusion that the process of change toward a new legal order has already begun, that the complementary institutions already pre-shaped in the framework of the old order will become the principal institutions so that the institution which has previously played the principal part can be abolished, without any disturbance of the economic process, in so far as it no longer serves a useful social purpose?

Feasible as this idea seems, it nevertheless comes up against the most rampant prejudices. It would mean that the contract of employment would become the principal institution of the social regulation of labour, but this institution was during the last century denounced as the source of all social suffering. We are asked to revolutionize our conceptions completely. But we have already met two decisive reasons for changing this opinion. We have seen that the contract of employment, like all legal forms, is in itself neither good nor evil, that the value of the legal form is solely determined by the social function fulfilled by the legal institution. We have seen that it is not the legal form of the contract of employment but its connection with the institution of property which makes the former an instrument of exploitation. Secondly, experience has shown us that the contract of employment even today has developed into the established 'position' and has to a large extent become socialized and made secure by means of manifold social rights.

A second and probably even more important phenomenon becomes apparent and must be considered by the intelligent observer.

Property is a matter of private law. The whole body of our

legal doctrine is based upon this fact. We distinguish between private and public law as the two principal branches of our legal analysis, as we understand it. The normative content of our existing laws fully justifies this division and we cannot avoid making this distinction. Our observations, however, have led us to recognize that every legal order must grant to everybody a private sphere into which the common will does not intrude. After the victory of a liberalist philosophy with its concepts of natural rights, to which the victory of the bourgeoisie over the feudal system corresponded in practice, a theory of constitutional law was evolved which set limits to the powers of the state, affecting even the public law. Public law may not transgress these limits; within them the individual is free and not subject to the control of the state. Here he is no longer a citizen of the state but simply a human being who enjoys freedom of thought and religion, freedom of convictions which the state may not touch. We hold this freedom of the individual in high esteem. It is not a present of nature and it was gained as a precious good of civilization only after severe social and political struggle; and no thinking socialist would dream of surrendering it.[9] As far as we can judge looking into the future, material goods will also belong to this sphere, not only family portraits and other articles of sentimental value, but also the bulk of goods intended for consumption, household utensils, perhaps even the home itself. There will always be a private *suum*, a sphere of one's 'legal own', even with regard to rights *in rem*, no matter what social order men may give themselves.

But contemporary property, capital as the object of property, though *de jure* private, has in fact ceased altogether to be private. No longer does the owner make use of property in a technical way; the tenement house serves a number of strangers and the railway serves all and sundry. Property in its technical aspect has been completely estranged from the owner. The Roman civil lawyer believed that *dominus rei suae legem dicit*. As far as ownership of capital is concerned, this

---

[9] This has not prevented Bolshevism from again establishing the omnipotence of the state, from stringently curtailing human freedom in the spiritual sphere. I think this is a disastrous retrogression. It is not justifiable to surrender achievements of civilization even if they are branded as introductions of the enemy, the hated bourgeoisie.

pronouncement is no longer true: it is society that disposes of capital and prescribes the laws for its use. It may be maintained at least that the object has ceased to be private and is becoming social. An army of a thousand miners, an army with its own generals, commissioned and non-commissioned officers, all of them employees, have complete technical control of the mine; they search its depths and bring its treasures to light, securing not only its continuity but also its very existence; and they stake their own lives for this purpose. Evidently it is a mere provocative fiction that this army should be regarded as a disconnected crowd of strangers, and the shareholders, who may not even know where their property is situated, as the real owners. Language, indeed, revolts against such abuse.

What is it that makes this abuse nevertheless apparently tolerable? Public law has for a long time recognized that where the whole of society is in principle concerned with an object, it can no longer be treated as a matter that is merely private. So it comes about that private law is supplemented by rules of public law relating to the object; a process that was cautious and tentative in the beginning but soon became more decided and in the end was developed in full consciousness.

In the liberal epoch the state considered every interference with the economic system and therefore with private law as contrary to reason and natural law; accordingly it refrained from it completely and merely exercised the restricted functions of protection and administration of justice. But since the middle of the last century the state is no longer content merely to hold the mace and the scales, it begins to take an active part in administration. New norms are made year by year in increasing numbers in the form of statutes, orders, and instructions of the administrators of the state. Administrative law develops into a special branch of legal analysis, and economic administration soon becomes the most extensive part within this branch. Grievances arise out of the application of the law of property and the contract of employment to the factory, and therefore administrative law must step in. Regulations relating to the normal working day, factory inspection, and protection of women and children are institutions of public law which increasingly supplement these institutions of private law. Insurance against sickness, accident, and old age follow suit, public labour exchanges replace the private labour market, and so on. In the end the relations of labour are as to nine parts regulated by public law, and the field of influence of private law is restricted to the remaining tenth.

When we were dealing with the functions of capital, we nearly always had occasion to refer to complementary institutions of public law and to emphasize that these are new creations; in the main they were introduced or at least perfected only after the death of Karl Marx.

Thus we are led to surmise that a two-fold development is taking place: first, that the complementary institutions of private law have deprived the owners of their technical disposal over their property; and secondly, that the common will has subjected property to its direct control, at least from the point of view of the law. Elements of a new order have been developed within the framework of an old society. So it may not be necessary to clamour for prophets whose predictions of the future will flow from esoteric qualities of the soul. It may well be that there is no need to proclaim premiums for those who would draft the new legal constitution of a reasonable social order: perhaps the truth is that we can simply deduce the law of the future from the data supplied by our experience of today and yesterday.

Should this be so, and we have good reason to believe it, our only problem would be to burst the shell which still obstructs the new development; to set free the complementary and supplementary institutions and to use them straightforwardly in accordance with their present and real functions, freed from restriction: to elevate them, the previous handmaidens of property, into the principal institutions: and to liberate them from the fetters of traditional property, which has lost its functions and has itself become a restrictive force.

Our observations have shown, however, that this cannot be the automatic result of a change of functions, that new norms are required to achieve it. For there can be no doubt that only a norm can break another norm. The norm, however, is a conscious act of will performed by society.

If society has become conscious of the changes in the functions of property and its contradictory effects, the question arises whether it must not change the norm. If it has surrounded property with so many barriers that these have gained the specific and paramount importance of a legal construction *sui generis*, should it not set free this new construction from the obstructions caused by its origin? Or has it surrendered so much of its autonomy that it can no longer perform this last step or dare not do so? Does society still enjoy freedom of will, the power to create new norms?[10] Even if it disposes of the instruments of legislation, if its legal title to free legislation is beyond dispute, the question still remains: is society still able to control technically the forces of development which have been set free? Society is sovereign as the legislator, but is it equally sovereign in practice? Or can it achieve in practical life only what it must? We have already become acquainted with the external limits which restrict the efficacy of the norm. If the law changes its functions, does this enforce a change of norms as well? Why do the norms not change equally automatically? If a change in functions is always also the cause of a change in norms, why is it that this cause cannot equally take effect in the quiet way of facts? How is the law determined by economics?

We have seen that the economic substratum dislocates the functions of the norm, that it reverses them; but the norm itself remains indestructible. The capital function also remains indestructible, and all development serves only its perfection. Therefore it may seem as if the crudest change of function does not react on this nebulous creation, this immaterial formula, those imperatives which apparently have no existence or only modestly vegetate in the documents of the statutes. Does it mean that the norms are indestructible, eternal, changeless, or at least determined by no other power than their own?

Given that, like all else under the sun, norms have their

---

[10] The law relating to labour and the law relating to economics are, as branches of legal analysis, today overshadowed by the law of obligations on the one hand and the law of administration on the other: these latter belong to a sphere where public law and private law merge into one another. The trend of development indicates, however, that these two latter branches will eventually be the basis of a new regulation of labour and of society.

causes, wherein do these lie? Given that they enjoy a real existence, what are its characteristics, what is the mode of their existence, and how do they change? Given that their origin lies in the conditions of life of the human race, that they are nothing more than a means of preserving human society, what part do they actually play in the existence and development of our own generation?

These are open questions of jurisprudence. The time has come to engage in an attempt at their solution.

WILHELM HAUSENSTEIN, *The Social and Political Context of Art*[11]

From what previous historical conditions has the present socio-economic condition of painting developed? In the early Middle Ages the need for art, like the needs for farming and trade, was satisfied by the household, the so-called closed household economy. Since painting at that time was mainly religious, the domestic practice of art took place chiefly in religious communities, in monasteries, parsonages, chapters, and bishops' courts. At first the practitioners themselves belonged to the clerical estate, but according to Drey[12] it has been shown that there were already lay artists in the ninth and tenth centuries.

The essential feature of the domestic economy is that the production and consumption of one and the same article take place within one and the same household community, and the extent of production is determined by the needs of consumption. An *economy of surplus* is quite distinct from the domestic economy. In this case production exceeds the requirements of the household, and the surplus enters into exchange. Historically, this process is connected, at an early stage, with the specialization of production and occupations. The first stage of painting in the surplus economy was the illustration of books in the monasteries.

Painting in the surplus economy at first took the form of

---

[11] From 'Zur Sozialpolitik der Kunst', *Der Kampf*, iv (1910–11), pp. 586–92. Hausenstein was not, in the strict sense, a member of the Austro-Marxist School, but he was a regular contributor of articles on art to *Der Kampf*. He also published an introduction to the sociology of art, *Bild und Gemeinschaft* (1920). [Eds.]

[12] Paul Drey, *Die wirtschaftlichen Grundlagen der Malkunst* (1910).

occasional surplus creation. Its first disciplined professional form was painting as wage work. The wage-working painter produces for commerce, that is to say as a specialist and for pay. But he only produces to order, and quite often, for the duration of the work, he still participates in the household community of the customer. He is paid partly by time, partly by piece work; thus his wages belong partly to a natural economy, partly to a money economy. A phenomenon which throws light on the period of a weakly developed money economy is that the customer always paid for the most expensive colours—gold and ultramarine blue—at a specially fixed rate. A second feature is still more important: the painter had to travel in the exercise of his profession. Abbots, bishops, princes, knights, and town councils summoned the painter from afar to his workplace. No longer did the painter live permanently as a member of the household community. The painter Giotto lived in this way as a wandering artist. There were three reasons for this situation. First, communications were not favourable for the transport of works of art. Second, artistic activity in general, in harmony with the character of a predominantly feudal and immobile economy, was directed to the decoration of specific places in a particular locality, such as cathedrals, castles, town halls. The third reason, namely the technique of painting, was historically the result of the preceding two causes; the technique used was that of the fresco, which involved painting the colours on a lime base, which was firm only in places, but generally damp and not easily moved.

There was a strange interaction: so long as painting, the thing, the picture, was immobile, the artist was mobile and so to speak nomadic. When painting became mobile, an article of furniture, a movable commodity, the artist became stationary. Toward the end of the Middle Ages, the first stages of a *commodity economy* developed, an economy which produces without special orders, at risk, for an indeterminate market. The causes of this phenomenon are to be found in general economic history and thus lie outside our present theme. We need only note the outcome: namely, that the principle of commodity production was carried over into painting. Dürer worked to a large extent without paying any particular attention to public demand and this was even more true of Rembrandt a hundred years later. The technical possibilities for art as a movable object in a commodity economy were provided by the board and canvas, by tempera and oil colours.

In the late Middle Ages the painter, who was still half wage-worker, but already half commodity-producer, did not remain entirely self-sufficient. He used the means of the age to provide security for himself: organization in guilds and corporations. According to Drey, the oldest of these were the Lukas guild in Venice (founded in 1290) and the Florentine guild (founded in 1339), both of which adopted the same patron—the patron saint of painters. The first German painters' guild, according to Drey, was that established in Prague in 1348. In the house of a guild painter the apprentice had a thorough training, after which he did journeyman work, and then went on his travels, mainly to Flanders and Italy, which were economically as well as artistically the most developed countries. Finally he produced his masterwork and was then recognized as a master. If the number of master painters was restricted he had to wait many years, and unless he was the son or son-in-law of a master, he could not easily enter the world of the masters. The guild offered its members the usual advantages: a protected market, that is, the allocation of a specific selling area closed to competition from other guilds; life insurance providing benefits for his dependents; a regulated, co-operatively organized supply of materials; and similar benefits. During its best periods the guild also gave him the guarantee of a skilled artistic tradition.

From the beginning of the modern period the guilds were both economically and artistically dead. But they survived into the eighteenth century and persecuted non-members whenever they could. So, for example, it was made impossible for the brilliant Swiss portrait painter Anton Graff to work in Augsburg because he had not spent the requisite number of years as a journeyman. Graff went to the court of Dresden. It was the courts above all which dissolved the guild system. Already in the fourteenth century court painters are to be found. Jan van Eyck was court painter to a prince in Burgundy; though his title was *valet de chambre*, or room servant. The younger Holbein was a portrait painter at the English court. Lukas Cranach was the court artist in Wittenberg and was ennobled. On the other side, the capitalistically developed towns began to eliminate the guilds. In 1640 the town council of Genoa ordered that the guild system should operate only for lesser painters with open shops, and in the same year the town council of Nymwegen declared painting a free art. For the countries of absolute monarchy the French development is typical: in 1648 Mazarin organized the Paris artists into an official court society, the Royal Academy; and in 1666 this was joined by the French Academy in Rome, founded by Colbert. Court academies were established in Berlin (1694), Vienna (1704) where in 1773 Maria Theresa formally abolished compulsory guild membership for painters, St. Petersburg (1724), Copenhagen (1754), London (1769), and Munich (1770). The academies, too, were societies that provided security for their members, but they represented a courtly-aristocratic rather than a bourgeois-craftsman form. Moreover, the academies, like the guilds, handed down a definite style, and secured an assured market for the painters. The academician found ample work at the court and among the nobility. Furthermore, in France for example, he received an allowance from the king and after a certain number of years of service might expect to be granted a grace and favour atelier in the Louvre. On the whole, the academicians were much better provided for than the guild masters had been. While Dürer only received at most 700 francs for a picture, the French academician Rigaud—who was greatly inferior to Dürer—obtained a record price of 40,000 francs for one picture, and on average had an income of about 30,000 francs in good years.

The favour of the Court created social differentiation among painters. The higher a small minority rose in socio-economic terms, the lower the majority sank. A proletariat of artists, which was really pauperized, both artistically and socially, developed for the first time in the age of absolutism, which coincided historically with the early period of capitalism. Outside the court academies the essential features of capitalism developed in the sphere of art, even producing real atrocities. Around 1700 there existed in Paris a great number of art factories in which commodities were produced by the dozen. In his youth, the great Watteau was a journeyman with an unscrupulous bourgeois artist who subjected his men to an ingenious division of labour; one painted heaven, the second trees, the third figures. Watteau had the privilege of being allowed to paint whole pictures several dozen times. His weekly wage was three francs. Between this proletariat and the academicians, whose works were regularly exhibited in the Louvre, there was a middle stratum of painters who relied upon art dealers and private patrons.

How do things stand today? First, the academic organizations of artists no longer have either the economic or the aesthetic significance which they had in 1750. They do not now provide any important element of security, either stylistically or economically. For the rest, the present economic conditions of art still bear quite a strong resemblance to those of the past century. The official culture has not in principle gone beyond the individualism that was let loose at that time. We have a number of artists who make great fortunes from their work, and a larger number who make a tolerable living from art. There is also an art proletariat which is much larger than in earlier periods, from which occasionally great revolutionary figures emerge, as the case of Van Gogh shows. Drey suggests that in France the highest annual income is between 200,000 and 300,000 francs. It is difficult to get exact information on this subject. In Germany, Konrad Lange estimates the price for an average picture of an established master (that is to say, more or less an elite price) at 6,000–10,000 marks, while Rosenberg sets it less definitely at 3,000–15,000 marks. These prices are in many cases greatly exceeded, but much more often they are not attained. We are in an area of uncertainty: artists seldom display their accounts, and when they do, they do not show all their cards. According to Drey, somewhat more reliable information can be gained from the development of art dealers' profits. Drey suggests that when a dealer buys a new picture he would pay about 60 per cent of the price he expects to get when he sells it, while if he buys on commission a discount of 10–15 per cent is customary. But the value of a picture to a connoisseur, and the growing fame of an artist, very often bring the dealer many times the purchase price. The history of Millet's 'Angelus' is well known. The artist sold it for a few hundred francs, but in a short time it was the object of a million-franc transaction.

Just as the specialized art trade has progressed for a hundred or a hundred and fifty years, so has the satisfaction of even the most minor fashions by means of art factories, naturally, in a capitalistic way. Clearly, it is difficult to obtain exact information in this domain, since factories of this kind shun public attention.... Finally, we should mention in this context the petty trade in art which produces its most noteworthy characters in the hotel porters and barbers who deal in semi-professional or amateur art commodities.

Apart from the specialized art trade, the most important issue is the supply of pictures by societies of artists through the well-known annual exhibitions which are held in every large town. A thorough survey of the societies of artists and their activities would take us too far afield, and it will suffice to note Drey's conclusions. These are essentially two: first that the organizations essentially serve the struggles of artistic tendencies, and so far, in spite of good intentions, socio-political tasks have received only limited attention; and second, that the principal activity of the artists' associations, the exhibitions, have relatively little importance as economic institutions and at all events are not commercially profitable.

It remains to consider the expenditure on paintings by public bodies. This is, unfortunately, the most wretched chapter in the art policies of our age, as Drey indicates in an alarming statistical appendix to his book. Bavaria, which is so to speak a country of art, had in its budget for the year 1908–9, a special item of 90,000 marks for the purchase of modern paintings and sculptures. At the present time this sum would buy three or four worthwhile pictures. The corresponding amount for Prussia is 60,000 marks, and for the Reich (but including money for the purchase of older works) 100,000 marks. This is quite shocking when a single municipality, such as Leipzig, in the year 1909, provided 60,000 marks for new acquisitions out of a total sum of 165,326 marks for artistic purposes. But we must put alongside Leipzig the wealthiest German town, Charlottenburg, which spent a total of 300 marks on art. In the period from 1884 to 1901, Munich spent 1,270,951 marks, or an annual expenditure of around 70,000 marks.

We can measure the economic significance of the production of pictures in two ways: by the foreign trade figures and by the statistics of occupations. According to Drey, the German foreign trade in pictures in 1908 amounted to 16·8 million marks for imports and 11·1 million marks for exports. The number of persons economically active in the Reich as artists, according to the occupational statistics for 1907, was 14,610; in 1895 it was 9,337. This leaves aside both the indirect economic benefits of art, and its ideal value. We are concerned therefore, with a factor of considerable economic importance, and also with a large number of fellow citizens.

What can be done to improve the socio-economic situation of painting? Drey considers the following possibilities: (1) the artistic education of the people could be raised to a higher level by elementary schools, further education, middle and high schools, especially through specialized art teaching; (2) the techniques of museums need to be adapted to popular artistic education, taking into account, in particular, the working hours and the lack of means of working people; (3) public bodies should recognize their obligation to indulge in collective extravagance in matters of art; (4) appropriate measures should be taken to increase the export of art, which is hampered, for example, by the American tariff on art and harmed by the official policies with regard to international exhibitions; (5) the rights of the artist in his picture should be given more effective and more precise legal protection than is provided by the existing national and international copyright arrangements; (6) every contract of sale for a painting should contain a profit-sharing clause, which obliges any future seller to pay a proportion of the unearned increase in value to the artist or his legal heirs; (7) artistic training should be completely transformed in a reformed academy; (8) artists should be more strongly organized, in particular for the purpose of marketing pictures, control and production of painting materials, obtaining loans, insurance, and so forth.

It will be useful to mention here four proposals that have been made by von Bülow:[13] (1) national art production should

<hr>

[13] Joachim von Bülow, *Künstlerelend und-proletariat* (1911).

be increased by imposing tariffs; (2) a value-added tax on the profits on resale should be introduced; (3) a part of the admission charges to exhibitions should be paid to the exhibitors, including those who do not sell any of their works; (4) one objective should be the establishment of a state valuation office to determine price norms. It must be said that the first of these proposals is both paltry and highly questionable from an economic point of view, while the third makes little sense in many cases because of the small profits from exhibitions. The fourth proposal is worth discussing, although it is a very delicate question. What about the second proposal? Drey substitutes for the idea of a value-added tax that of a profit-sharing clause, and he rejects completely the notion that the state should function as a collection agent for painters or receive taxes for individuals. He regards as more plausible a value-added tax the proceeds of which would be applied to general objectives of a social policy for art. Of course, it is conceivable that an official policy for art would be administered in a reactionary way. And on the other hand it is not altogether obvious why a profit-sharing clause in a private contract should benefit distant, or even immediate, legal heirs. There are problems here which need further discussion.

As for Drey's own proposals, the first of them overlooks the alpha and omega of any artistic education of workers, or of the mass of the people, its most elementary precondition, which cannot be too strongly emphasized; namely the housing question. From an economic and aesthetic point of view mass education can only be carried out in conjunction with a reform of housing. The second proposal demonstrates once again the social and pedagogic necessity for a reduction of working hours, while the third and fourth proposals reveal the need for an artistically oriented political opposition and more generally for a lively association between art and politics.

The seventh and eighth proposals require a more thorough examination. The reformed academy that Drey advocates would have three stages. First, there would be an obligatory primary course in handicrafts, which would make the separate existence of handicraft schools superfluous and would relate the somewhat abstract pursuit of art by the academies to

handicrafts and industry. This would be followed by an intermediate course for the specialized training of painters, sculp-
tors, and those working in the applied arts, in which there
would be instruction in the technology of materials, in economics, and also general education. Finally, there would be
a master class for those of exceptional talent. If I understand
him correctly, Drey conceives the further course of events in
the following manner. Those who complete the intermediate
stage satisfy, as good average artists of the period, the conventional (in the good sense) needs of their time. In the future,
as at present, this good average artist, whose economic situation is quite favourable, will have to be left to his own devices
and the public. By contrast, those who complete the higher
stage, the 'evolutionary' and 'revolutionary' geniuses, who
usually have little economic success, need to be given security
by society through the provision of a collectivist economic
basis, and to be constituted as a collectivist fraternity.

What can one say about this project? It is not the strong
point of the book. It bears, very notably, the stamp of a pre-
Marxist Utopia. The idea of combining handicraft and free
art is splendid, but a collectivity of aristocrats of art is more
than problematic. It seems to be the rather naïve expedient
of an economist who sees the socialist trends of our time, and
draws from them individualist-aristocratic conclusions. His
policy is one of partial collectivism. But that can never be.
Does Drey really believe that a society in which the great
majority of people pay the average price in a private enterprise economy will provide genius—which as Drey himself
says, they do not recognize at all—with the means to establish
a special collectivist economy? Out of pure, abstract idealism?

No—collectivism will embrace the whole society. And it is
precisely that which provides the assurance that even the
rarest genius will be understood and made economically
secure. Drey does not believe in artists working together
stylistically; he believes only in individual great achievements
of revolutionary and evolutionary artists. Here, what Drey
lacks is precisely sociological insight into style. Van Gogh,
whose work he knows well, could have taught him that a great
genius does not shrink from working with others stylistically;
he says so in one of his letters. We can also learn something

from the great Gothic artists. Even the greatest of them—Jan van Eyck, Goes, Memling—conform to a conventional style, which is intelligible to the masses, and their personal contribution is not manifested in unsocial subjectivist excesses, incomprehensible to the people, but in fine nuances, in the most significant choice of individual elements.

Rather than the higher stage of the reformed academy, it is the points of view formulated or sketched in the eighth proposal that will provide a starting point for debate about a policy for art: such matters as the supply of materials through a co-operative wholesale society to which all artistic schools would belong, and perhaps before long the independent production of such materials; public management of the sale of pictures with salaried sales personnel; compulsory insurance of artists through a self-managed company; reduction of the often absurdly high price of some pictures, and increase of the unjustifiably low price of others, to conform with appropriate maxima and minima, which could be established by a statistical office of the artists' organization; and finally, a major issue which Drey usefully brings to our attention, the guarantee of credit by the organization which, as has already been said, would have to bring together all artistic parties for purely economic and professional goals. The matter of credit should probably be dealt with in such a way that the views of the special organization concerned with questions of style and taste affecting the mortgage value of the picture would be binding on the central body of the purely economic organization. But enough. It is one of the great tasks of the present time to think more profoundly about this problem. Social democracy would gain prestige if it were as great a driving force in elaborating a future policy for art, as it is already in the social and political action of the industrial proletariat.

Biographical Notes on the Principal Austro-Marxists[1]

ADLER, Friedrich.   Born 9 July 1879, Vienna; died 2 January
   1960, Zurich.
Son of Viktor Adler (q.v.), the founder of the Austrian Social
Democratic Party. Studied physics and mathematics at the University of Vienna and the University of Zurich, where he became
interested in the doctrines of Ernst Mach, on which he later published several studies. For a time he taught physics at the University of Zurich, but then accepted a post as one of the secretaries of
the Austrian Social Democratic Party, and in 1913 also became an
editor of *Der Kampf*. He was a vigorous opponent of the First
World War, and in October 1916, in protest against the war and
the state of emergency, he assassinated the Prime Minister, Count
Stürgkh; he was condemned to death, but in view of popular
feeling the sentence was commuted to eighteen years' imprison-
ment and he was released in 1918 after the collapse of the monarchy. Founded and became secretary of the '2½ International',
which he hoped would promote a reunification of the international
working-class movement. From 1923 to 1939 he was secretary of
the Socialist International. During the Second World War he
lived in the U.S.A., and on his return to Europe in 1947 established
himself in Zurich, where he devoted himself to literary activity,
and in particular to the publication of his father's correspondence
with Bebel and Kautsky.

ADLER, Max.   Born 15 January 1873, Vienna; died 28 June
   1937, Vienna.
Not related to Viktor and Friedrich Adler. After studying jurisprudence at the University of Vienna he became a lawyer, but
devoted most of his time to theoretical studies in philosophy and
sociology and to his activities in the Austrian Social Democratic
Party. Founded the *Marx-Studien* with Rudolf Hilferding (q.v.)
in 1904. He was also particularly interested in popular education
and established, with Karl Renner (q.v.) and Hilferding a workers'
school, 'Zukunft', in Vienna in 1903. During the First World War

[1] For their major publications, and biographical sources, see the Selected Bibliography.

he associated himself with Friedrich Adler and others on the left of the party, and after the war became a strong partisan of the workers' councils movement. He was sympathetic to the Russian Revolution, but did not regard it as a model to be followed everywhere; he took a position close to that of Rosa Luxemburg, with whom he had an extensive correspondence (that part of it in his own possession unfortunately destroyed after his death). After the insurrection of 1934 he was imprisoned for a short time, but was then allowed to resume his university teaching.

ADLER, Viktor. Born 24 June 1852, Prague; died 11 November 1918, Vienna.

Studied chemistry and medicine at the University of Vienna and practised as a doctor. In 1882 he made the acquaintance of Karl Kautsky and published his first article in *Neue Zeit* (on the occupational illnesses of workers). He worked steadily to reunify the Austrian Social Democratic Party and succeeded at the Hainfeld Congress of 1888. From that time he was the acknowledged leader of the party, founded the *Arbeiter-Zeitung* (1891), organized the campaign for universal suffrage (from 1893 until its success in 1906), and became a deputy in the Reichsrat (Imperial Council) in 1905. In the First World War he supported the Austro-Hungarian monarchy, largely out of fear of the consequences of a victory for Tsarist Russia, and influenced most of the Social Democratic Party to adopt a similar attitude, but a minority of the party, led by his son Friedrich, vigorously opposed the war. Viktor Adler was a political leader rather than a contributor to the theory of Austro-Marxism; his principal writings were on current political issues, such as universal suffrage, or on questions of public health.

BAUER, Otto. Born 5 September 1881, Vienna; died 4 July 1938, Paris.

Became interested in Marxism and the revisionist controversy while still in high school. Studied philosophy, law, and political economy at the University of Vienna. In 1904 he sent to Karl Kautsky an article on the Marxist theory of economic crises, and became a regular contributor to *Neue Zeit*. He was asked by Viktor Adler to write a Marxist study of the problems of nationalities, which was published in 1907. Became parliamentary secretary of the Social Democratic Party in 1907, and in the same year founded, with Adolf Braun and Karl Renner, the monthly theoretical journal *Der Kampf*, of which he was the principal editor and a frequent contributor. Mobilized in the First World War he became a prisoner of war in Russia from 1914 to 1917 and learned Russian.

After the collapse of the Austro-Hungarian Empire he was, for a short period in 1918–19, Secretary of State for Foreign Affairs, but resigned when his proposals for the unification of Germany and German Austria (which he considered too small and economically weak to be viable as an independent nation) were rejected by the Allied Powers. In 1919 he strongly opposed, as did Friedrich Adler, the idea of a Bolshevik type revolution (on the Hungarian model) in Austria, arguing that it had no chance of success. In the following years he elaborated his ideas of the 'slow revolution' and 'defensive violence' (the latter adopted as party policy at the Linz Congress in 1926). The victory of Austro-Fascism in 1934 was attributed by some critics to Bauer's policies, though it could also be argued that it resulted from events in Europe that were quite beyond the control of the Austrian socialists. On the other hand, the social and educational achievements of 'Red Vienna' demonstrated, to many observers, the effectiveness of the 'slow revolution' when the socialists had power (see Charles A. Gulick, *Austria from Habsburg to Hitler*, vol. i. After the defeat of 1934 Bauer had to leave Austria, and lived first in Brno (Czechoslovakia), and then in Paris.

BRAUN, Adolf.   Born 20 March 1862, Laag (Austria); died 13 May 1929, Berlin.
Studied philosophy, history, and political economy at the universities of Basle and Fribourg. A close collaborator of Viktor Adler's at the Hainfeld Congress. His principal interest was in trade union affairs, on which he wrote extensively in the *Arbeiter-Zeitung* and *Der Kampf* (of which he was co-editor). In 1913 he settled in Germany, sought to preserve the unity of the German Social Democratic Party during the war while belonging to its left wing, became a German citizen, and was elected in 1919 to the National Constituent Assembly in Weimar.

DANNEBERG, Robert.   Born 23 July 1885, Vienna; died 12 December 1942 in the concentration camp at Auschwitz.
Studied law at the University of Vienna, and became responsible in 1908 for the educational and cultural work of the Social Democratic Party. Edited *Die Bildungsarbeit* from 1909, and contributed frequently to *Der Kampf* on cultural questions. He was largely responsible, as president of the regional assembly of Vienna, for the programme of working-class housing there. After 1934 he continued his political activities in contact with the clandestine socialist movement until he was arrested by the Gestapo in 1938.

DEUTSCH, Julius. Born 2 February 1884, Stegersbach (Burgenland); died 17 January 1968, Vienna.

Worked as a compositor and studied in evening courses. Became acquainted with Marxist literature through the Association for Workers' Education. Took his doctorate of philosophy at the University of Zurich in 1907. Among his major interests were the situation of young workers and the development of the trade union movement. During the First World War he created a clandestine military organization from which the soldiers' councils later emerged; he then created the *Schutzbund* (workers' militia) which he led until 1934. During the civil war in Spain he was a military adviser to the Republican Government, then took refuge in France, and went to the U.S.A. in 1940. On his return to Austria in 1946 he became director of the foreign affairs section of the socialist party, and also directed the party press and publishing house. In the early 1950s he retired from active politics after disagreements with the party leaders.

ECKSTEIN, Gustav. Born 19 February 1875, Vienna; died 26 July 1916.

Studied law at the University of Vienna. Published in *Neue Zeit* one of the first critical essays on the Austrian marginalist school of economics. He was more attracted by the doctrines of Mach than by neo-Kantianism, studied the natural sciences, and wrote on the biological theory of evolution. His ill-health frequently interrupted his intellectual work, but he was regarded as one of the most able of the Austro-Marxist thinkers.

HILFERDING, Rudolf. Born 10 August 1877, Vienna; died February 1941, Paris.

Studied medicine in Vienna, but devoted most of his time to problems of political economy, and became known for the studies which he published in *Neue Zeit*, and for his critical examination of the ideas of Böhm-Bawerk. In 1904 he founded, with Max Adler, the *Marx-Studien*, and the two thinkers outlined in their preface to the first volume the ideas of the emerging Austro-Marxist school. In 1906 he moved to Berlin, to lecture in the party school, and then became foreign editor of *Vorwärts*. At the beginning of the First World War he opposed voting for war credits; he was mobilized as a doctor in the Austrian army, and after the war returned to Berlin as editor of *Freiheit*, the journal of the U.S.P.D. (Independent Social Democratic Party of Germany). He opposed joining the Third International, and participated in the '2½ International'. Became a German citizen in 1920, and was Minister of Finance in Stresemann's government 1923. Elected a member of the Reichstag 1924. During this period he directed the journal *Die Gesellschaft*. In 1928–9 he was again Minister of Finance in the government of Hermann Müller. After Hitler's seizure of power he moved first to Denmark and then to Switzerland. In 1938 he joined his friend Breitscheid in Paris and after the defeat of France moved to Arles in the unoccupied zone. In 1941, after several demands from the German authorities, the Vichy Government handed Hilferding and Breitscheid over to the Gestapo; they were taken to Paris where Hilferding was murdered or committed suicide after being tortured.

RENNER, Karl.   Born 14 December 1870, Unter-Tannowitz (Moravia); died 31 December 1950.

After completing his secondary education Renner joined the army in order to support himself until he could continue his studies, and later studied law at the University of Vienna. One consequence of his military service was that he became acquainted with the great variety of nationalities in the Austro-Hungarian Empire and developed a strong interest in the problems of nationality, on which he wrote some of his earliest works and which remained one of his principal concerns. In his legal studies Renner became interested primarily in the theory and sociology of law, and his major work (first published in the *Marx-Studien* in 1904) on the social functions of law was a pioneering contribution to Marxist analysis of the relations between the economic structure of society and one important element in the political and ideological system. During the First World War Renner adopted a patriotic standpoint and came to be regarded as the leader of the right wing of the Austrian S.D.P. In 1918 he became the first Chancellor of the Austrian Republic, but when the S.D.P. entered into opposition it was Otto Bauer who acquired the dominant influence in the party while Renner represented the more reformist minority. During the interwar period his writings were mainly concerned with the need to revise the Marxist theory of classes and of the state to take into account changes in the organization of the capitalist economic system, in the situation of the working class, and in the character of political power. In 1945 he became President of the Second Austrian Republic.

SCHLESINGER, Thérèse.   Born 6 June 1863, Vienna; died 5 June 1940, Blois (France).

She was an early participant in the feminist movement in Austria, and collaborated in an investigation in 1896 of the condition of women workers in Vienna. From this time she became active in the socialist movement, and founded in 1902 the Association of

Social Democratic Women and Girls. During the First World War she aligned herself with the left wing of the party in opposition to the war. Her articles, contributed to *Neue Zeit* and *Der Kampf*, and her books, were concerned mainly with the economic and political situation of women, and the development of the women's movement.

Selected Bibliography

A. PRINCIPAL WRITINGS OF THE AUSTRO-MARXISTS

See also for a selection of Austro-Marxist writings, *Austro-marxismus*, edited and introduced by Hans-Jörg Sandkühler and Rafael de la Vega. Vienna: Europa Verlag, 1970.

Max Adler

For a complete bibliography see Hans Schroth and Herbert Exenberger, *Max Adler: Eine Bibliographie.* Vienna: Europa Verlag, 1974.

Kausalität und Teleologie im Streite um die Wissenschaft. Vienna: Wiener Volksbuchhandlung Ignaz Brand, 1904. (*Marx-Studien*, vol. i.)

Der Sozialismus und die Intellektuellen. Vienna: Wiener Volksbuchhandlung Ignaz Brand, 1910.

Marxistische Probleme. Beiträge zur Theorie der materialistischen Geschichtsauffassung und Dialektik. Stuttgart: J. H. W. Dietz, 1913.

Der soziologische Sinn der Lehre von Karl Marx. Leipzig: C. L. Hirschfeld, 1914. Reprint published separately from *Archiv für die Geschichte des Sozialismus und der Arbeiterbewegung*, vol. iv, Pt. 1, 1914.

Die Staatsauffassung des Marxismus. Ein Beitrag zur Unterscheidung von soziologischer und juristischer Methode. Vienna: Wiener Volksbuchhandlung, 1922. (*Marx-Studien*, vol. iv, Pt. 2.) New impression, Darmstadt: Wissenschaftliche Buchgesellschaft, 1964.

Kant und der Marxismus. Berlin: E. Laub'sche Verlagsbuchhandlung, 1925.

Politische oder soziale Demokratie. Ein Beitrag zur sozialistischen Erziehung. Berlin: E. Laub'sche Verlagsbuchhandlung, 1926.

Lehrbuch der materialistischen Geschichtsauffassung. 2 vols. Berlin: E. Laub'sche Verlagsbuchhandlung, 1930, 1932. Republished, with the omission of some philosophical chapters from the first volume and the addition of a previously unpublished third volume, under the general title *Soziologie des Marxismus.* 3 vols. Vienna: Europa Verlag, 1964. (i. *Grundlegung der materialistischen Geschichtsauffassung*; ii. *Natur und Gesellschaft*; iii. *Die solidarische Gesellschaft.*)

Das Rätsel der Gesellschaft. Zur erkenntnis-kritischen Grundlegung der Sozialwissenschaft. Vienna: Saturn-Verlag, 1936.

'Mach und Marx, Ein Beitrag zur Kritik des modernen Positivismus', *Archiv für Sozialwissenschaft und Sozialpolitik*, xxxiii (1911), 348–400.

'Zur Ideologie des Weltkrieges', *Der Kampf*, viii (1915), 115–29.

'Zur Geschichte des soziologischen Denkens', *Der Kampf*, xvii (1924), 472–86.

'Zur Kritik der Soziologie Othmar Spanns', *Der Kampf*, xx (1927), 265–70.

'Zur Soziologie der Revolution', *Der Kampf*, xxi (1928), 570–6.

'Wandlung der Arbeiterklasse?', *Der Kampf*, xxvi (1933), 367–82, 406–14.

Otto Bauer

Die Nationalitätenfrage und die Sozialdemokratie. Vienna: Wiener Volksbuchhandlung, 1907. (*Marx-Studien*, vol. ii.) Second enlarged edition with a new Preface, Vienna: Wiener Volksbuchhandlung, 1924.

Der Weg zum Sozialismus. Vienna: Wiener Volksbuchhandlung, 1919.

Bolschewismus oder Sozialdemokratie? Vienna: Wiener Volksbuchhandlung, 1920.

Die Österreichische Revolution. Vienna: Wiener Volksbuchhandlung, 1923. New edition, with a preface by Ernst Winkler, Vienna, 1965. An abridged English version, translated by H. J. Stenning, was published New York: Burt Franklin, 1925 (reprinted 1970).

Das Weltbild des Kapitalismus. Jena, 1924. New impression, Frankfurt/Main: Makol Verlag, 1971.

Kapitalismus und Sozialismus nach dem Weltkrieg, vol. i, *Rationalisierung oder Fehlrationalisierung?* Vienna: Wiener Volksbuchhandlung, 1931.

Zwischen zwei Weltkriegen? Bratislava: Eugen Prager Verlag, 1936.

'Marx' Theorie der Wirtschaftskrisen', *Die Neue Zeit*, xxiii (1904–1905), 133–8, 164–70.

'Marxismus und Ethik', *Die Neue Zeit*, xxiv (1905–6), 485–99.

'Was ist Austro-Marxismus?', *Arbeiter-Zeitung* (Vienna), 3 November 1927, 1–2.

'Max Adler. Ein Beitrag zur Geschichte des Austromarxismus', *Der Kampf* (New Series), iv (1937), 297–302.

'Der Faschismus', *Der Sozialistische Kampf* (Paris), 16 July 1938,

75–83. Reprinted in *Die Zukunft* (Vienna), February 1948, 33–41. Also reprinted in Wolfgang Abendroth (ed.), *Faschismus und Kapitalismus: Theorien über die sozialen Ursprünge und die Funktion des Faschismus.* Frankfurt/Main: Suhrkamp Verlag, 1967, 143–67.

Rudolf Hilferding

For a more comprehensive bibliography, see Wilfried Gottschalch, *Strukturveränderungen der Gesellschaft und politisches Handeln in der Lehre von Rudolf Hilferding.* Berlin: Duncker und Humblot, 1962, 268–73.

Böhm-Bawerk's Marx-Kritik. Vienna: Wiener Volksbuchhandlung, 1904. (*Marx-Studien*, vol. i.) An English translation by Eden and Cedar Paul was first published about 1920 and is reprinted in the volume edited and introduced by Paul Sweezy, *Böhm-Bawerk: Karl Marx and the Close of his System.* New York: Augustus M. Kelley, 1949.

Das Finanzkapital. Eine Studie über die jüngste Entwicklung des Kapitalismus. Vienna: Wiener Volksbuchhandlung, 1910. (*Marx-Studien*, vol. iii.) New editions of the work were published in 1920, 1923, 1927, 1947, 1955; and in 1968 in Vienna with a preface by Eduard März.

'State Capitalism or Totalitarian State Economy', *Socialist Courier* (New York), 1940. Reprinted in *Modern Review* (New York), vol. i (1947).

'Das historische Problem.' From a manuscript on which Hilferding was working in his last years, edited and introduced by Benedikt Kautsky, *Zeitschrift für Politik* (New Series), vol. i (1954).

Karl Renner

For a complete bibliography, see Hans Schroth, *Karl Renner: Eine Bibliographie.* Vienna: Europa Verlag, 1970.

Der Kampf der Österreichischen Nationen um der Staat. Leipzig and Vienna: Franz Deuticke, 1902.
Die Soziale Funktion der Rechtsinstitute, besonders des Eigentums. (Published under the pseudonym J. Karner.) Vienna: Wiener Volksbuchhandlung, 1904. (*Marx-Studien*, vol. i.) Revised edition under the title *Die Rechtsinstitute des Privatrechts und ihre soziale Funktion. Ein Beitrag zur Kritik des bürgerlichen Rechts.* Tübingen: J. C. B. Mohr, 1929. English translation by Agnes Schwarzschild, edited with an introduction and notes by Otto Kahn-Freund, *The Institutions of Private Law and their Social*

Functions. London: Routledge and Kegan Paul, 1949. Reprinted 1976.

Marxismus, Krieg und Internationale. Stuttgart: J. H. W. Dietz, 1917.

Mensch und Gesellschaft. Grundriss einer Soziologie. (*Nachgelassene Werke,* vol. i.) Vienna: Wiener Volksbuchhandlung, 1952.

Wandlungen der Modernen Gesellschaft. Zwei Abhandlungen über die Probleme der Nachkriegszeit. (*Nachgelassene Werke,* vol. iii.) Vienna: Wiener Volksbuchhandlung, 1953.

An der Wende zweier Zeiten. Lebenserinnerungen. [Memoirs.] Vienna: Danubia-Verlag, 1946. Second impression, 1950.

'Der Krieg und die Internationale', *Der Kampf,* viii (1915), 49–62.

'Probleme des Marxismus', *Der Kampf,* ix (1916), 154–61, 185–93, 229–39, 275–81, 312–21, 354–9, 383–6, 417–21.

'Demokratie und Rätesystem', *Der Kampf,* xiv (1921), 54–67.

B. PERIODICALS

Die Arbeiter-Zeitung (Vienna). The newspaper of the Austrian S.D.P. Founded by Viktor Adler in 1891 it became a daily in 1895, edited by Friedrich Austerlitz (1862–1931) until his death, and subsequently by Oscar Pollack (1893–1963).

Marx-Studien. Blätter zur Theorie und Politik des wissenschaftlichen Sozialismus (Vienna). Founded 1904, and edited, by Max Adler and Rudolf Hilferding, it appeared at irregular intervals until 1923. Vol. i (1904). Preface by the editors. Rudolf Hilferding, 'Böhm-Bawerks Marx-Kritik', pp. 1–61. Joseph Karner (Karl Renner), 'Die soziale Funktion der Rechtsinstitute', pp. 65–192. Max Adler, 'Kausalität und Teleologie im Streite um die Wissenschaft', pp. 195–433.

Vol. ii (1907). Otto Bauer, 'Die Nationalitätenfrage und die Sozial-demokratie', pp. v–vi, 1–576.

Vol. iii (1910). Rudolf Hilferding, 'Das Finanzkapital', pp. xii–xi, 1–477. Tatiana Grigorovici, 'Die Wertlehre bei Marx und Lassalle', pp. 483–575.

Vol. iv, Pt. 1 (1918). Max Adler, 'Die sozialistische Idee der Befreiung bei Karl Marx', pp. vii–xxiv. Gustav Eckstein, 'Der Marxismus in der Praxis', pp. 3–119. Karl Kautsky, 'Kriegs-marxismus', pp. 123–206.

Vol. iv, Pt. 2 (1922). Max Adler, 'Die Staatsauffassung des Marxis-mus', pp. 7–316.

Vol. v, Pt. 1 (1923). Otto Leichter, 'Die Wirtschaftsrechnung in der sozialistischen Gesellschaft', pp. 7–109.

Der Kampf. Sozialdemokratische Monatsschrift (Vienna, vols. i–
xxvii; New Series, Prague, vols. i–vii). Founded 1907, and
edited, by Otto Bauer, Adolf Braun, and Karl Renner. Subsequently Friedrich Adler became an editor, and he was the
principal editor from 1924. The leading Austro-Marxists wrote
frequently in *Der Kampf*, and other contributors, at various
times, included Kautsky, Trotsky, Riazanov, Julius Braunthal,
Otto Neurath, Alfred Adler, Ernst Fischer, Paul Lazarsfeld,
Adolf Sturmthal, Hendrick de Man. From 1934 a new series
of *Der Kampf* was edited by Otto Bauer from his exile in
Czechoslovakia.

Der Klassenkampf (Berlin). A journal published from 1927 to 1931
by a left wing group in the German Social Democratic Party.
Max Adler was one of the editors and contributed some thirty
articles to it.

C. LITERATURE ON AUSTRO-MARXISM

General

LESER, NORBERT. *Zwischen Reformismus und Bolschewismus. Der
Austromarxismus als Theorie und Praxis.* Vienna: Europa
Verlag, 1968.
NENNING, GÜNTHER. 'Biographie C. Grünberg', in *Indexband zu
Archiv für die Geschichte des Sozialismus und der Arbeiter-
bewegung (C. Grünberg).* Graz: Akademische Druck- u. Verlags-
antalt, 1973. Pp. 1–224.

See also the relevant biographies and the concluding historical
essay in *Dictionnaire biographique du mouvement ouvrier international. I. Autriche.* Paris: Les Éditions Ouvrières, 1971.

Max Adler

BOURDET, YVON. Introduction to *Max Adler: Democratie et con-
seils ouvriers.* Paris: François Maspero, 1967. Pp. 11–44.
HEINTEL, PETER. *System und Ideologie. Der Austromarxismus im
Spiegel der Philosophie Max Adlers.* Munich: Verlag R. Olden-
bourg, 1967.
LESER, NORBERT. 'Max Adlers geistesgeschichtliche Bedeutung.'
Post-script to Max Adler, *Die solidarische Gesellschaft* (vol. iii
of *Soziologie des Marxismus*). Vienna: Europa Verlag, 1964.
Pp. 163–92.

Otto Bauer

BOURDET, YVON. Introduction to *Otto Bauer et la révolution.*
Paris: Études et Documentation Internationales, 1968.

BRAUNTHAL, JULIUS. 'Otto Bauer: Ein Lebensbild', in *Otto Bauer: Eine Auswahl aus seinem Lebenswerk*. Vienna: Weiner Volksbuchhandlung, 1961. Pp. 9–101.

LEICHTER, OTTO. *Otto Bauer: Tragödie oder Triumph?* Vienna: Europa Verlag, 1970.

WANDRUSZKA, ADAM. 'Otto Bauer und der "Austromarxismus"', in Heinrich Benedikt (ed.), *Geschichte der Republik Österreich*. Vienna: Verlag für Geschichte und Politik, 1954. Pp. 443–52.

CROAN, MELVIN. 'Prospects for the Soviet Dictatorship: Otto Bauer', in Leopold Labedz (ed.), *Revisionism: Essays on the History of Marxist Ideas*. London: Allen and Unwin, 1962. Pp. 281–96.

BOTZ, GERHARD, 'Genesis und Inhalt der Faschismustheorien Otto Bauers', *International Review of Social History*, xix (1974), 28–53.

Rudolf Hilferding

BOURDET, YVON. Introduction to the French translation of *Finanzkapital: Le Capitalisme financier*. Paris: Editions de Minuit, 1970. Pp. 1–52.

GOTTSCHALCH, WILFRIED. *Strukturveränderungen der Gesellschaft und politisches Handeln in der Lehre von Rudolf Hilferding*. Berlin: Duncker and Humblot, 1962.

Karl Renner

HANNAK, JACQUES. *Karl Renner und seine Zeit*. Vienna: Europa Verlag, 1965.

KAHN-FREUND, OTTO. Introduction to the English translation of *Die Rechtsinstitute des Privatrechts und ihre soziale Funktion: The Institutions of Private Law and their Social Functions*. London: Routledge and Kegan Paul, new impression 1976. Pp. 1–43.

D. LITERATURE ON THE AUSTRIAN LABOUR MOVEMENT

For a comprehensive bibliography see Herbert Steiner, *Bibliographie zur Geschichte der österreichischen Arbeiterbewegung*. Vienna: Europa Verlag, 3 vols. 1962–70.

BENEDIKT, HEINRICH (ed.). *Geschichte der Republik Österreich*. Vienna: Verlag für Geschichte und Politik, 1954. Section on 'Das sozialistische Lager' by Adam Wandruszka.

BRAUNTHAL, JULIUS. *Viktor und Friedrich Adler. Zwei Generationen Arbeiterbewegung*. Vienna: Wiener Volksbuchhandlung, 1965.

DEUTSCH, JULIUS. *Geschichte der österreichischen Arbeiterbewegung.*
Vienna: Wiener Volksbuchhandlung, 1947.
KAUTSKY, BENEDIKT. *Geistige Strömungen im österreichischen
Sozialismus.* Vienna: Wiener Volksbuchhandlung, 1953.
LEICHTER, OTTO. *Zwischen zwei Diktaturen. Österreichs Revolutionäre Sozialisten 1934–1938.* Vienna: Europa Verlag, 1968.
SHELL, KURT L. *The Transformation of Austrian Socialism.* New
York: State University of New York, 1962.
WINKLER, ERNST. *Die österreichische Sozialdemokratie im Spiegel
ihrer Programme.* Vienna: Wiener Volksbuchhandlung, 1971.

See also *Archiv: Mitteilungsblatt des Vereins für Geschichte der
Arbeiterbewegung* (Vienna). Published quarterly since 1961.

E.   OTHER WORKS CITED IN THE TEXT

ADLER, FRIEDRICH. *Ernst Mach's Überwindung des mechanischen
Materialismus.* Vienna: Wiener Volksbuchhandlung, 1918.
BOUDIN, LOUIS. *The Theoretical System of Karl Marx.* Chicago:
1907; reprinted New York, Monthly Review Press, 1967.
BRAUNTHAL, JULIUS. *History of the International,* vol. i, *1864–1914,*
vol. ii, *1914–1943.* London: Nelson, 1966, 1967.
DEUTSCH, JULIUS. *Putsch oder Revolution?* Karlsbad, 1934.
FISCHER, ERNST. *Erinnerungen und Reflexionen.* Reinbek bei Hamburg: Rowohlt Verlag, 1969. English trans. *An Opposing Man.*
London: Allen Lane, 1974.
FISCHER, KUNO. *Kants Leben und die Grundlage seiner Lehre.*
Mannheim, 1860.
FLEMING, DONALD and MAILYN, BERNARD (eds.). *The Intellectual
Migration: Europe and America 1930–1960.* Cambridge, Mass.:
Harvard University Press, 1969.
GRÜNBERG, CARL. *Festrede.* Frankfurt, 1924.
—— *Festschrift für Carl Grünberg zum 70 Geburtstag.* Leipzig,
1932.
GULICK, CHARLES A. *Austria from Habsburg to Hitler.* 2 vols.
Berkeley and Los Angeles: University of California Press, 1948.
HICKS, J. and WEBER, W. (eds.). *Carl Menger and the Austrian
School of Economics.* Oxford: Oxford University Press, 1973.
HOBSON, J. A. *Imperialism: A Study.* 1902. Third rev. edn. London: Allen and Unwin, 1938.
HUGHES, H. STUART. *Consciousness and Society.* London: MacGibbon and Kee, 1958.
JAHODA, MARIE, LAZARSFELD, PAUL F. and ZEISEL, HANS. *Die
Arbeitslosen von Marienthal.* Leipzig: S. Hirzel, 1933. English

trans. *Marienthal: The Sociography of an Unemployed Community*. London: Tavistock Publications, 1972.

JANIK, ALLEN and TOULMIN, STEPHEN. *Wittgenstein's Vienna*. New York: Simon and Schuster, 1973.

JAY, MARTIN. *The Dialectical Imagination: The Frankfurt Institute of Social Research, 1923–1950*. Boston: Little, Brown & Co., 1973.

KANN, ROBERT A. *The Multinational Empire: Nationalism and National Reform in the Habsburg Monarchy*. 2 vols. 1950. Reprinted New York: Octagon Books, 1964.

KELSEN, HANS. *Hauptprobleme der Staatsrechtslehre*. Tübingen: J. C. B. Mohr, 1911.

KOLAKOWSKI, LESZEK. *Positivist Philosophy*. Harmondsworth: Penguin Books, 1972.

KORSCH, KARL. *Marxism and Philosophy*. 1923. English trans. London: New Left Books, 1970.

LABEDZ, L. *Revisionism: Essays on the History of Marxist Ideas*. London: Allen and Unwin, 1962.

LAZARSFELD, PAUL F. *Jugend und Beruf*. Jena: Gustav Fischer, 1931.

LENIN, V. I. *Imperialism, the Highest Stage of Capitalism* (1916), in *Collected Works*, vol. xix. London: Lawrence and Wishart, 1942.

LIEBMANN, OTTO. *Kant und die Epigonen*. Stuttgart, 1865.

LUKÁCS, GYORGY. *History and Class Consciousness*. 1923. English trans. London: The Merlin Press, 1971.

MICHEL, BERNARD. *Banques et banquiers en Autriche au début du XXe. siècle*. Paris: Presses de la Fondation Nationale des Sciences Politiques, 1976.

NEURATH, OTTO. *Empiricism and Sociology*. Dordrecht: D. Reidel Publishing Co., 1973.

SCHILPP, P. A. (ed.). *The Philosophy of Rudolf Carnap*. La Salle, Illinois: Open Court Publishing Co., 1963.

SCHUMPETER, J. A. 'Zur Soziologie der Imperialismen', *Archiv für Sozialwissenschaft und Sozialpolitik*, xlvi (1919), pp. 1–39, 275–310. English trans. in *Imperialism and Social Classes*, ed. with an introduction by Paul M. Sweezy. New York: Augustus M. Kelley, 1951.

—— *Business Cycles: A Theoretical, Historical and Statistical Analysis of the Capitalist Process*. 2 vols. New York: McGraw-Hill, 1939.

—— *Capitalism, Socialism, and Democracy*. 1942. Third enlarged edn. London: Allen and Unwin, 1950.

SWEEZY, PAUL M. (ed.). *Karl Marx and the Close of his System by Eugen von Böhm-Bawerk and Böhm-Bawerk's Criticism of Marx by Rudolf Hilferding.* New York: Augustus M. Kelley, 1949.
TROTSKY, LEON. *My Life.* London: Thornton Butterworth, 1930.
VEBLEN, THORSTEIN. *Imperial Germany and the Industrial Revolution.* 1915. New edn. New York: The Viking Press, 1939.
VORLÄNDER, KARL. *Kant und der Sozialismus.* Berlin: Reuther und Reichard, 1900.
WINSLOW, E. M. *The Pattern of Imperialism: A Study in the Theories of Power.* New York: Columbia University Press, 1948.
WOLFF, KURT H. (ed.). *Georg Simmel, 1858–1918.* Columbus: Ohio State University Press, 1959.

Index

Index